CW01613473

Volume 2 Number 2 2001

Visual Culture in Britain

General Editor: Ysanne Holt

Reviews Editor: Paul Barlow

ASHGATE

northern arts
PROMOTING THE ARTS IN THE NORTH

Published by Ashgate Publishing Limited
Gower House, Croft Road
Aldershot, Hants GU11 3HR, England

Ashgate Publishing Company
131 Main Street, Burlington
Vermont 05401-5600, USA

Visual Culture in Britain is published with the assistance of the University of Northumbria.

ISBN 0 7546 0312 1

JACKET ILLUSTRATION
Antony Gormley, *Angel of the North*. Photograph by Jim McAdam, February 1998.

Visual Culture in Britain
Vol.2 No.2
1. Art – Great Britain – History – Periodicals 2. Performing arts – Great Britain – History – Periodicals 3. Art and society – Great Britain – Periodicals 4. Performing arts – Social aspects – Great Britain – Periodicals I. Holt, Ysanne
700.9'41'05

Printed and bound by MPG Books Ltd, Bodmin, Cornwall, UK.

Contents

This new twice-yearly journal encourages original material and introduces innovative work with the aim of placing visual culture – painting and sculpture, architecture and design, print, film, photography and the performing arts – in relation to the wider culture historically and geographically from the eighteenth century to the present. The journal addresses a range of contemporary debates involving constructions of racial, ethnic and gender identities, nationality and internationalism, colonialism, high and low culture, the role of institutions and cultural groupings, and models of production and consumption. Each issue strikes a balance between those articles engaged primarily with theoretical and interpretive issues and those concerned with empirical research in relation to cultural production and representation. Material which will stimulate discussion and demonstrate connections across relevant disciplines is particularly welcome.

Information for Subscribers

Visual Culture in Britain is published twice a year, and the subscription period runs from January to December.

Subscription rates: £60 to institutions, £30 to individuals

Available from: Subscription Department, Ashgate Publishing Ltd., Gower House, Croft Road, Aldershot, Hampshire GU11 3HR, UK.
Telephone: (0) 1252 351804. Fax: (0) 1252 351839.
Email: nstaszkiewicz@gowerpub.com Website: http://www.ashgate.com

ISSN 1471 4787

Editor's Note

The articles in this issue were first delivered as papers at *Visual Culture in a Changing Society: Britain 1940–2000*, a conference held in July 2000 at the University of Northumbria with support from the Paul Mellon Foundation, which coincided with the publication of the first issue of this journal. Participants in this event considered the historical transformations within cultural identities and the practices and consumption of visual culture throughout the period. Particular sessions explored the extent to which post-war experiences such as the end of Empire, multiculturalism and globalization have impacted upon shifting formations of identity at regional, national, institutional and personal levels. Debate focused on how we go about examining the effects of change on issues of representation and on the diversity of visual culture.

Thanks are due to the convenors of the six strands – Paul Barlow, Rosemary Betterton, Simon Faulkner, Steven Gartside, Joanne Morra, Neil Mulholland, Marq Smith and Andrew Stephenson, to the two plenary speakers – Jonathan Harris and Stephen Bann, and to all the speakers, chairs and delegates.

As a result of the lively and stimulating discussion generated, another post-war visual culture conference is being planned for 20–21 September, 2002 at Tate Britain. Sessions will engage with the four themes of 'Visual Culture: North and South', 'Americanization', 'Visual Culture and Class' and 'Whiteness'.

A conference on eighteenth-century visual culture is being planned in association with the Paul Mellon Foundation for September 2003.

We are grateful to Northern Arts for their generous financial support of this issue.

Fran Lloyd

Arab Women Artists: Issues of Representation and Gender in Contemporary British Visual Culture

> This double consciousness affords you a particular space when you are negotiating your place in relation to others. It's a space which is often referred to as 'in-between'. I don't like to see it as a negative place; rather I see it as an active site of exploration that speaks of different histories and locates identity to a place which is endlessly remade through our negotiation of boundaries – this obviously presents challenges to those who are and who are not familiar with this sense of perspective.[1]

Until recently, one of the most invisible and little-recorded areas in contemporary visual culture – and indeed within British society in general – has been the presence of an Arab diaspora and the related issue of the imaging of Arab identities. This article considers that absence.

In 1998, my involvement with an exhibition project on contemporary Arab women's art presented the challenge of researching Arab artists working in Britain.[2] This proved to be remarkably difficult. Although there are over 130,000 Arabs in Britain – a small number when compared to Asian or Afro-Caribbean communities, but still a significant one – there is relatively little material of any kind on this diverse community, and even less on visual culture, particularly in relation to contemporary art practice.

This is surprising given the presence of such major practitioners as Mona Hatoum – a Palestinian born in exile in Lebanon; the Libyan-born painter Ali Omar Ermes; Zaha Hadid – the Iraqi architect; and the Tunisian-born fashion designer, Azzedine Alaia. In fact, as further research showed, there are a large number of artists of different generations who would see themselves as part of an Arab diaspora in Britain and, significantly, the greater number are women.[3] One could include, for example, Houria Niati, the Algerian-born painter who showed in the first black women's art exhibition in Britain, 'Five African Artists', held at the Africa Centre, Covent Garden, London in 1983, and in 'Black Women's Time Now', of the same year at Battersea Arts Centre, London; the installation artist Saddeh George, born in Iraq and brought up in Lebanon; the Lebanese-born writer and installation artist, Mai Ghoussoub, and the Iraqi-born Jananne Al-Ani, who works in video installation and photography. All of these trained in Britain in the 1980s and the early 1990s and continue to work in London (Figure 1).

Equally, there are a large number of Arab women artists who, having trained abroad, are now resident here. These include the Iraqi artists Suad Al Attar, Maysaloun Faraj and Batool Al-Fekaiki, who trained in Baghdad before moving to London, and the Lebanese artists Leslie Hakim-Dowek and Ida Alamuddin.[4]

Given this presence, immediate questions are raised about why Anglo-Arab

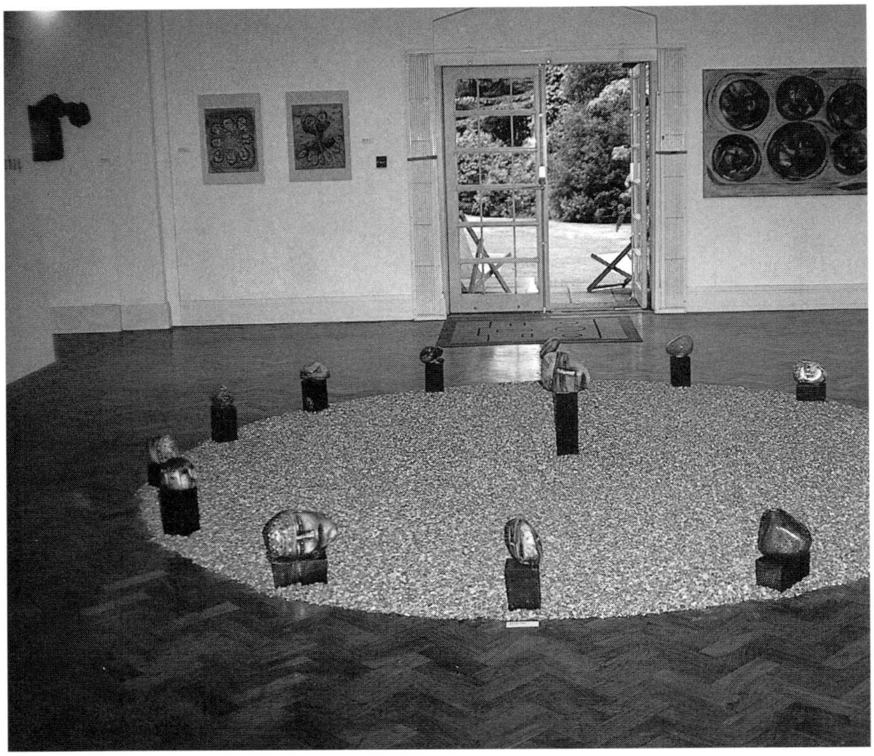

Figure 1. 'Dialogue of the Present: Site and Performance', Pitshanger Manor and Gallery, London, July–August 1999, curated by Siumee Helen Keelan. View of exhibition including work of Batool al-Fekaiki, *Children of the Future*, 1999. Installation of painted stones and gravel. Photocredit: Fran Lloyd.

art has remained relatively invisible in Britain in spite of the 1980s' interest in multiculturalism and the more recent concerns of cultural diversity. How might this invisibility be accounted for within the complex nexus of specific historical conditions of Britain, definitions of race and ethnicity and issues surrounding representation? Given the recent concern with the concepts of diaspora in Britain and the need for more inclusive definitions of British culture, it may be timely to begin to think about Arab diasporic spaces existing alongside and intersecting with the accepted diasporas of the Jewish, the African and the Caribbean.

Before beginning to address these questions, it is important to emphasize that my major concern here is to highlight an area of contemporary art practice that has been little recorded or researched, in order to contribute to the rethinking and broadening of what constitutes contemporary visual culture in Britain. Starting from the position that there is no one homogeneous group and no pre-given fixed identity, the intention is not to produce a new so-called 'minority' group to join the many 'others' outside of the mainstream of British culture or to ghettoize the work. Rather, it is a strategic intervention to foreground the pressing need to recognize and acknowledge cultural diversity in all its complex, hybrid and often contradictory forms within British post-Second World War culture. For, as Stuart Hall eloquently stated in his opening address to the 'Re-inventing Britain' conference in 1997: 'Cultural diversity is not something that is coming in from the outside; it is also something that is going on, inside, in relation to Britishness itself. After cultural diversity, Britishness cannot be what it was before.'[5]

With these concerns in mind, I want to focus on the work of Zineb Sedira, an Algerian-French artist, who engages directly with these issues of visibility, of diaspora, hybridity, representation and gender, as an Arab artist based in Britain. Questions of cultural identity are always complex and this is particularly the case when we consider Arab identities which cannot be ascribed to a 'sacred homeland', a particular territory, or tied to one nation. Historically, the Arab world is made up of multiple and disparate geographies and peoples extending over the three continents of Europe (Andalusian Spain), Africa and Asia, linked primarily by language and culture, rather than 'race' or nation. However, links of language are further complicated by differing dialects and the effects of colonization where whole generations in some parts of Morocco or Algeria, for example, may not have written or spoken Arabic.[6] Thus Arab ethnicities, like all ethnicities, are a way of locating the self through the variable and often contradictory factors of history, language and culture.[7]

To be Arab therefore predominately involves the recognition of a cultural identity which co-exists alongside geographical markers such as, for example, being British or being Algerian and African. It is a sense of cultural belonging that is continuously created and recreated against, and through, the specificities of differing colonial and postcolonial geographies, histories and politics. Moreover, like all other forms of identity, Arab identities are always multiple and differently constituted by religion, gender, sexuality, class, generation and so forth. Contrary to popular perceptions, 'Arab' is not synonymous with 'Muslim', for although Muslims are in a majority there are, for example, Christian Arabs and Jewish Arabs. Conversely, 'Muslim' is not synonymous with 'Arab', as the large communities of South East Asian and Iranian Muslims show.

Historically, Britain has long been the site of an Arab diaspora, most evident in the nineteenth century with the presence of Arab traders from Lebanon, and Yemeni and Somalian seamen centred around Cardiff and South Shields.[8] This history, however, has tended to be forgotten because there was never the large-scale post-Second World War immigration of the 1950s and 1960s associated with the British Empire in the Indian sub-continent and the Caribbean.

The British, of course, ruled over many Arab countries, including the Sudan, Egypt, Iraq, Kuwait and Jordan, but there was no significant British settlement in these countries, which were officially still part of the Ottoman Empire until the end of the First World War. Furthermore, the newly independent Arab countries once ruled by Britain did not join the Commonwealth and thus the number of immigrants to Britain from these places was always small. Until recently, therefore, Arabs were not recognized as a cultural presence or 'racialized grouping' and, although they existed, they were to all intents and purposes 'invisible'.[9]

This invisibility is directly interlinked with the way in which ethnicity and racial difference were (and to an extent still are) constructed in post-Second World War Britain. As several writers have shown, the dominant British Empire model abroad was to provide the basis for divisions at home where racial difference was constructed within a black/white paradigm.[10] Hence, within Britain, race was primarily a matter of different skin colour which, in the context of the multiple geographies of Arab immigrants, resulted in the continual difficulties of classification from, alternatively, white or black or in-between.

The impact of such an unstable and, at times, ambivalent classificatory system is the subject of a rare essay, published in 1999 by the sociologists Max Silverman and Nira Yuval-Davis, which focuses on Arab identity and questions of race in Britain. This essay demonstrates how race was defined in post-war Britain through a study of race-relations legislation designed to combat racism.[11] Centring on the Race Relations Acts of 1965, 1968 and 1976, the authors point out that the minority groups identified were those that were members of the NCWP (the New Commonwealth countries and Pakistan), with no reference to other groups, including Jews or Arabs, and that subsequent theorization on race in Britain almost exclusively concentrated on these same NCWP groupings. (Interestingly, Jews in Britain, like Arabs, were excluded from these acts because they could not be defined solely by race.)

Furthermore, Silverman and Yuval-Davis argue that the replacement in the 1980s of the category of NCWP by the term 'Black' to cover Britain's post-colonial immigrants, and its subsequent subdivision into 'Black' and 'Asian', not only divided immigrants by the colour of their skin, but also 'did not embrace all the racialised minorities in Britain'.[12] One consequence of this theorization of race is the scarcity of material on Arab communities in Britain. As the authors note, this is particularly marked in sociological work on racism, which has continued to focus on the communities formerly covered by NCWP and, in the case of racism against Muslims, on the Asian communities exclusively, thereby rendering Arab Muslims invisible.[13]

The same theorization continues to underpin government methods of gathering statistics on ethnic groupings, whether through census forms, immigration forms or demographic surveys. For example, the 1998 *Estimates of the Population by Ethnic Grouping* produced by the Office for National Statistics uses the categories 'Black – Caribbean', 'Black – African', 'Black – Other', 'Indian', 'Pakistani', 'Bangladeshi', 'Chinese', 'Other – Asian (non-mixed)', 'Other' and 'White', which leaves little space for several groups, including Arabs.[14]

While such invisibility may be useful in a system designed to separate and mark out through difference, and certainly demonstrates the instability of constructions of race, it also denies agency and representation. However, as Silverman and Yuval-Davies observe, this different history to other 'coloured aliens' in Britain is particularly marked given that in other ways the imaging of Arabs has been a highly visible part of British history and collective memory.[15] Arabs have been the traditional enemies of Europe from the Crusades to the First World War as part of the Muslim empires and then the Ottoman Empire.[16] Equally, running alongside this has been a strong romantic tradition evidenced by *The Arabian Nights*, personified by Lawrence of Arabia and, in part, embodied in harem literature and in Orientalist imagery of the nineteenth and twentieth centuries.

Certainly, until recently, the dominant and most pervasive imaging of Arab identities has been that articulated through Orientalist literature, painting and photographs which foreground cultural difference *vis-à-vis* Britain and the East. Edward Said, in his polemical book on Orientalism, for example, not only sees the Orient as 'one of its deepest and most reoccurring images of the Other'[17] for the west but goes as far as to argue that 'because of Orientalism the Orient was not (and is not) a free subject of thought or action'.[18]

As much subsequent literature on Orientalism has shown, the Arab woman's body is central to Orientalist imagery as the site of this extreme difference or otherness: of eroticism combined with passivity and anonymity, and as a sign of the unknown to be conquered.[19] Such images of gendered, sexualized and racially determined bodies are evident not only in the paintings of such nineteenth-century artists as Jean-Léon Gérome and John Frederick Lewis but also in widely circulated colonial postcards. Examples of this imagery have been reproduced by Malik Alloula in his book on French colonial postcards (published in 1986) although, as Rey Chow argues, such reproductions, in spite of the author's intentions, may sustain rather than deconstruct the imperialist gaze in their re-presentation.[20]

Recent events in the Middle East and North Africa have both resurrected these stereotypes and created others. The 1973 oil crisis in the Middle East produced a popular male-gendered construction of Arabs as rich, cruel, anti-westerners, while the subsequent events of the 1978 Iranian Revolution, the 1979 Islamic Revolution led by Ayatollah Khomeini and the rise of Islamic Fundamentalism have tended in Britain to reinforce the stereotype of the Arab male as aggressor and fanatic, despite the elision of the Persian and the Arab in the public imaginary. Meanwhile, stereotypical images of the anonymous, passive bodies of Arab women continued to dominate the media in the 1980s. As Mona Hatoum observed in 1988, in relation to the Lebanese War: 'whenever I watched news reports about the Lebanon, I was struck by how the Arabs were always shown en masse with mostly hysterical females crying over dead bodies. We rarely heard about the personal feelings of those who lost their relatives.'[21] In part, Hatoum's video installation, *Measures of Distance,* was a response to these stereotypical images and, through text, image and sound, Hatoum presents a different imaging of Arab women based on her various communications with her Lebanon-based mother.[22]

Predictably, perhaps, the same stereotypes continued to dominate the imaging of the 1991 Gulf War in Britain. However, significant changes had occurred in relation to Islam and Britain, which, together with the broader issue of national identity, had a critical bearing on the diverse Arab communities in Britain. First, as Yuval-Davis observes, the rise of religious fundamentalism had led to what she terms the 'increasing racialization of religion' which reached a peak after the 'Rushdie Affair' in 1989. Hence, 'groups previously known by national or regional origin ... are now all seen as part of a single Muslim community. This categorization of minority communities in primarily religious terms assumes them to be internally unified, homogeneous unities with no class or gender differences or conflicts'.[23] Secondly, as Charles Husband, among others, noted in 1994: 'It is difficult to exaggerate the extent to which "race" and nation have been fused in the last decade of British politics. New Right political discourse has presented ethnic-minority communities in Britain as an "enemy within".'[24] Within these dominant framings, the images and stereotypes that circulated located Arabs (now exclusively read as Muslims) and Islam as 'alien to British life and culture'. [25]

Culturally, these recent events have clearly played an important part both in making Arab visual culture more visible in Britain and in creating new Arab identities through the contestation and negotiation of images in the media. It is within these shifting constructs of Arabs as the alien other, the Arab as the fundamentalist and, in particular, the Arab woman as anonymous, passive, oppressed and an object of erotic fantasy, that I want to look at the recent photographic and video work of Zineb Sedira. Acutely aware of the dangers of foregrounding the primacy of ethnic difference against other points of identification across groupings, and of ignoring difference within diverse Arab communities, Sedira's work uses the Arab female body to negotiate, contest, transgress or unfix dominant stereotypes, while simultaneously producing new modes of representation.

Born in 1963, Sedira was brought up in the Parisian suburb of Gennevilliers (in the Algerian diaspora in France) in the aftermath of the Algerian war where 'intense political and racial animosity towards the Algerian community' was evident.[26] Coming from an Algerian Arab and French-speaking family and educated in French Catholic schools, Sedira was conscious of being perceived as a 'beurette' (the colloquial expression for a female born of North African immigrant parents) which signified 'difference, a particular history and context, and a sign of cultural ambiguity'.[27] Sedira moved to London in 1986 and, in common with many *émigrés*, the move to another place provided the conditions for reflection and another space from which to explore and negotiate locatedness and questions of belonging and unbelonging. She subsequently trained in fine art at Central St Martin's School of Art (1992–95) and at The Slade School of Art (1995–97).

Since the mid-1990s Sedira's work has centred on issues surrounding the veil, which has come to be one of the most visible and much-debated external signs of difference, social positioning, gender, desire and exclusion/inclusion. The veil is a complex symbol that carries a multiplicity of frequently shifting and often contradictory meanings in differing postcolonial geographies. Associated with both freedom and oppression, it is particularly significant in the context of Algerian history where the French enforced the public unveiling of Algerian women, and where subsequently, during the Algerian War of Independence, the veil simultaneously acted as a marker of tradition and an aid to revolution.[28]

Born in the diaspora, Sedira never actually wore the veil but her work returns frequently to the motif and to the less visible effects of veiling which she describes as 'the concept of veiling the mind . . . a metaphor for censorship and self-censorship'.[29] While fully aware of external cultural pressures, both within and outside Arab communities, Sedira's concept also alludes to the complex internal processes whereby one is made to experience one's self as 'Other', described so powerfully by Fanon. [30]

In the large black and white photographic work, *Silent Witness*, of 1995 (Figure 2), it is the eyes of the artist, confined or framed by the slit-like open-

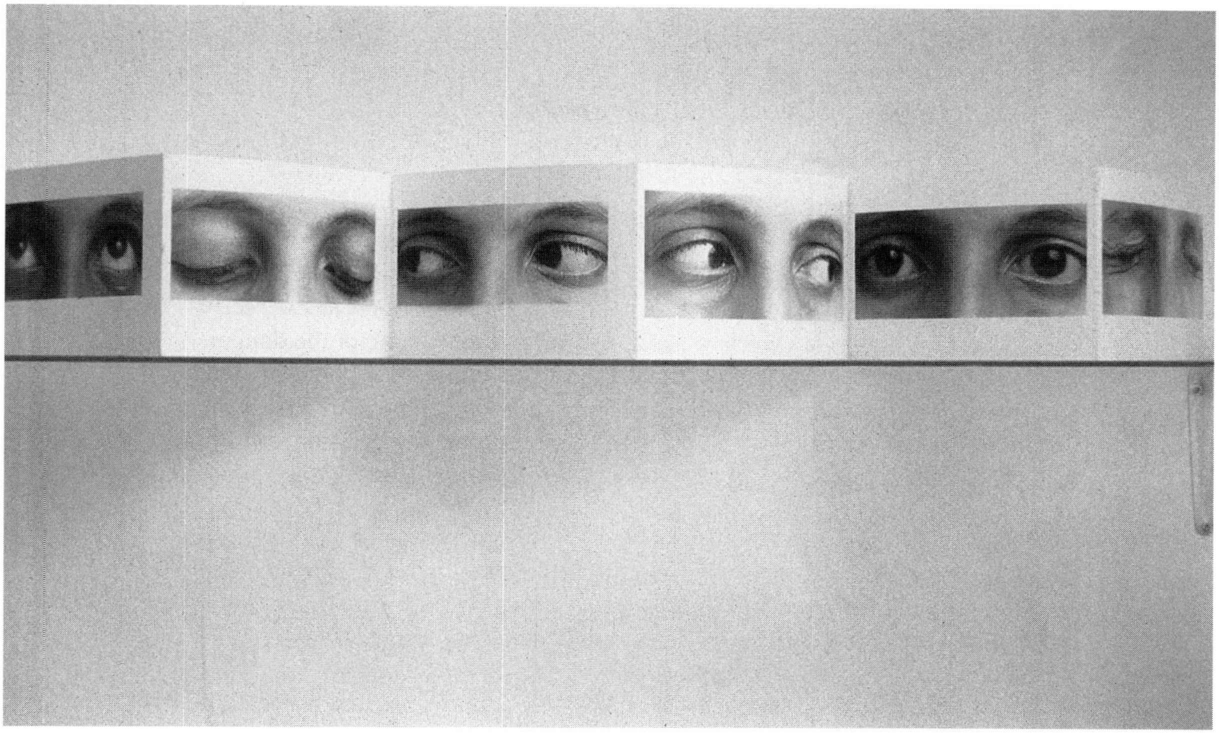

Figure 2. Zineb Sedira, *Silent Witness*, 1995. Black and white photographs stitched together, 40 × 180 cm. Reproduced courtesy of the artist.

ing, which evoke an invisible veil, dramatically confronting the spectator. The public scale of the work and its directness are challenging. On one level it suggests the different ways in which Muslim and/or Arab women are usually framed by western audiences as anonymous, veiled women, as submissive objects or as objects of fantasy. The title, *Silent Witness*, and the disembodied eyes emphasize this positioning.

However, the concentration on the eyes (eyes are ever-moving and therefore active) foregrounds the specificities of the female Arab gaze, as opposed to the male gaze which has dominated western cultural discourse until recently, particularly in writing on the Orient.[31] It also points to the importance of the concept of the gaze within Islamic thought, where sight is associated with the arousing of sexual desire. Although the *Qur'an* does not specifically refer to veiling, it instructs both male and female believers 'to lower their gaze and be modest', while later commentaries emphasize the dangers of 'the fornication of the eye'.[32]

Thus, in effect, Sedira's image carries multiple and contradictory meanings for different audiences: a decentred image of disembodiment, of restriction, of woman as object, and an image of active resistance where the object becomes subject of, rather than subjected to, the gaze. Furthermore, in the context of the gallery, a space designed for looking at objects, *Silent Witness* directly references the performative act of looking and being seen, and the accompanying, contradictory play of who is the subject and who is the object.

Sedira explores the contradictions of multiple positionings and viewpoints further in *Don't Do To Her What You Did To Me, No. 2*, of 1996 (Figure 3). She

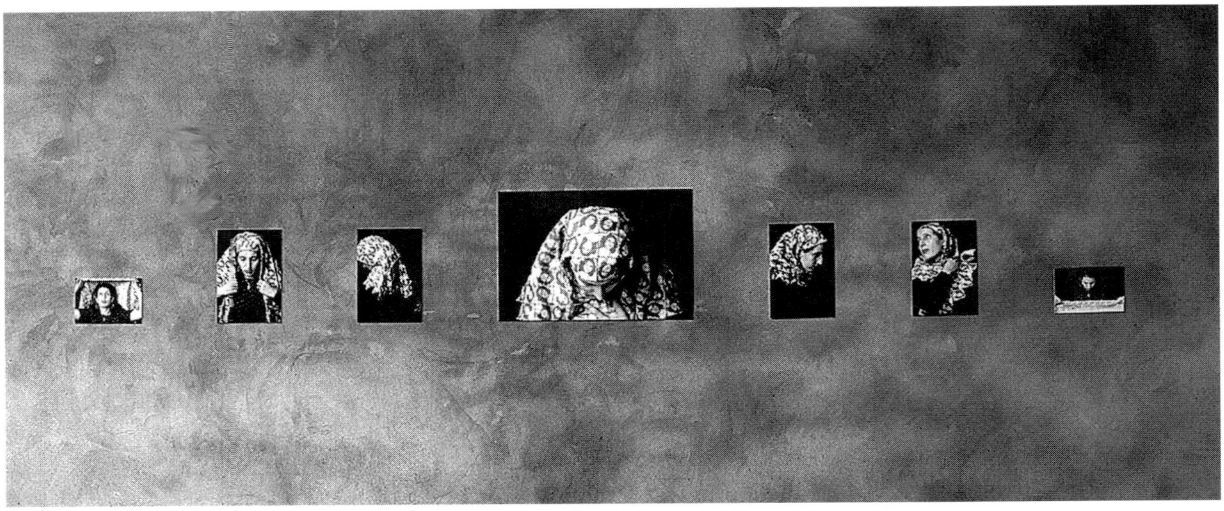

Figure 3. Zineb Sedira, *Don't Do To Her What You Did To Me, No. 2*, (detail) 1996. Installation of colour photographs, scarf made and worn by the artist. The Gallery of Modern Art, Glasgow. Reproduced courtesy of the artist.

again is both subject and object, while the powerful adversarial title addresses and positions the spectator more directly through the use of the first and second person. The over-life-size installation, made up of a series of colour photographs set against a gold background, present the artist veiling and unveiling herself with a *hijab* or scarf. The averted gaze of the artist and the veil suggest an image of subjugation, but on looking closer it reveals that the scarf (which was made by Sedira) is a patchwork of photographs of an unveiled female with her hair down (the artist's sister) (Figure 4).

Effectively and economically, the installation encapsulates and problematizes the continual negotiation of the boundaries between being veiled/unveiled, of subject/object and of art/craft that have so preoccupied the west. Simultaneously, by the insertion of the image of the female artist within the architectural gold surrounding which evokes both an older tradition of Arab culture and the medieval icons of veiled Madonnas, the artist is made part of both histories as they interact and intermingle in the present.

Such a simple and direct act of performativity carries significant weight in a Muslim culture in which eyes 'become subject to regulation for men and women', where the representation of the body itself has been subject to discontinuities and heated debate, and where women artists have been little acknowledged as part of a central artistic tradition.[33] Moreover, the process of veiling and unveiling foregrounds the complexities of how veiling is perceived by different cultural audiences. Meyda Yeğenoğlu argues in her recent book that

> veiling is a specific practice of situating the body within the prevailing exigencies of power; so is unveiling . . . Not-to-veil is also another way of turning flesh into a particular type of body. However, the body that is not veiled is taken as the norm for specifying a general, cross-culturally valid notion of what a feminine body is and must be.[34]

At once seductive and distancing, the work may disrupt stereotypical views of Muslim women, but it also clearly demonstrates through the physical enactment of veiling and unveiling the uncomfortable awareness that the female

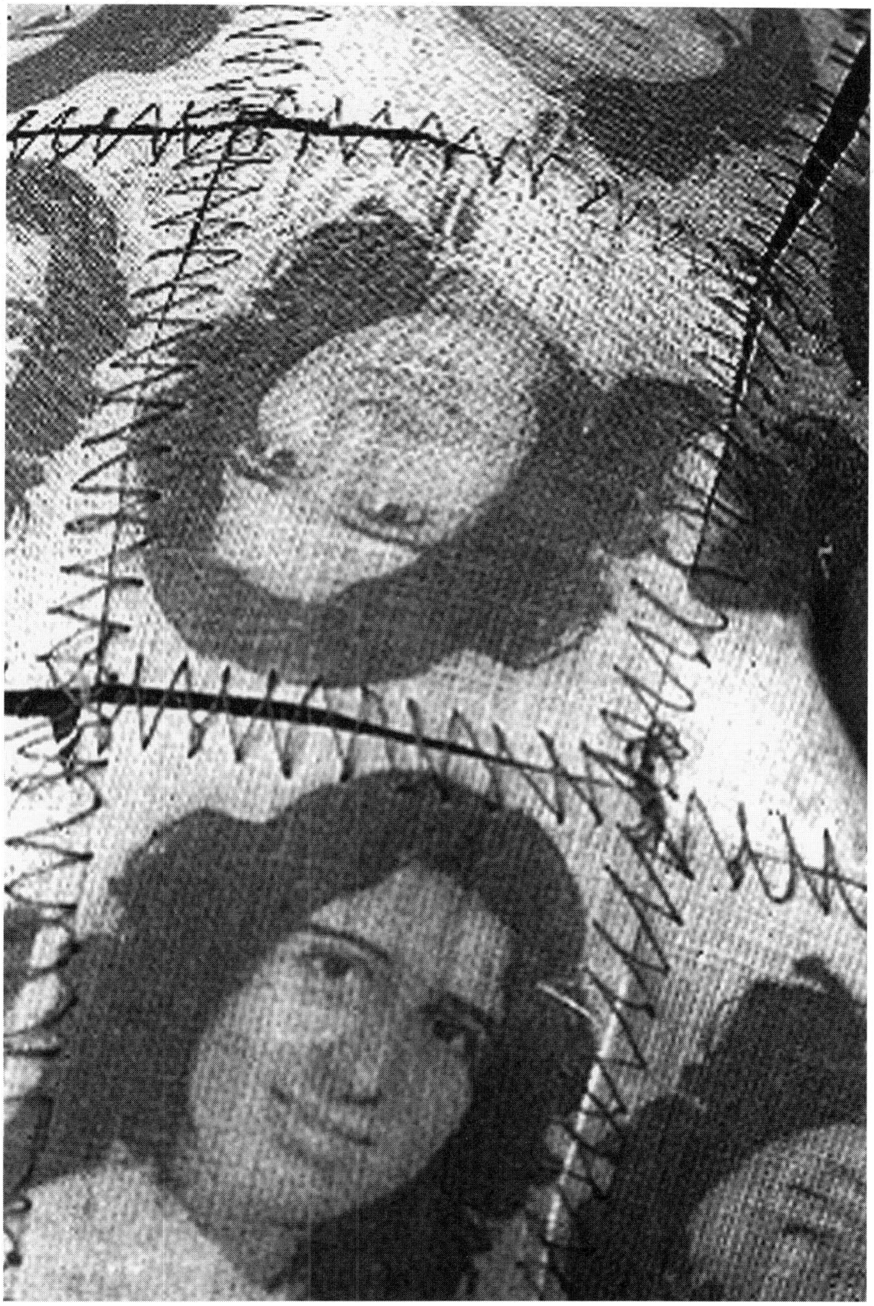

Figure 4. Zineb Sedira, *My Sister's Scarf*, 1996, scarf made by the artist. Reproduced courtesy of the artist.

subject has been 'veiled' or made invisible culturally both within and outside Britain, and as spectators we are located as the 'you' and 'put on the spot'. Made aware of the 'politics of location', the spectator is less able to claim a space free of gender or power considerations.

Sedira returns to the question of the veil in her recent *Self-Portrait* (1999) (Figure 5) where, unusually, she presents three colour photographs of herself wearing a full-length white veil. Set against a white background and back-lit,

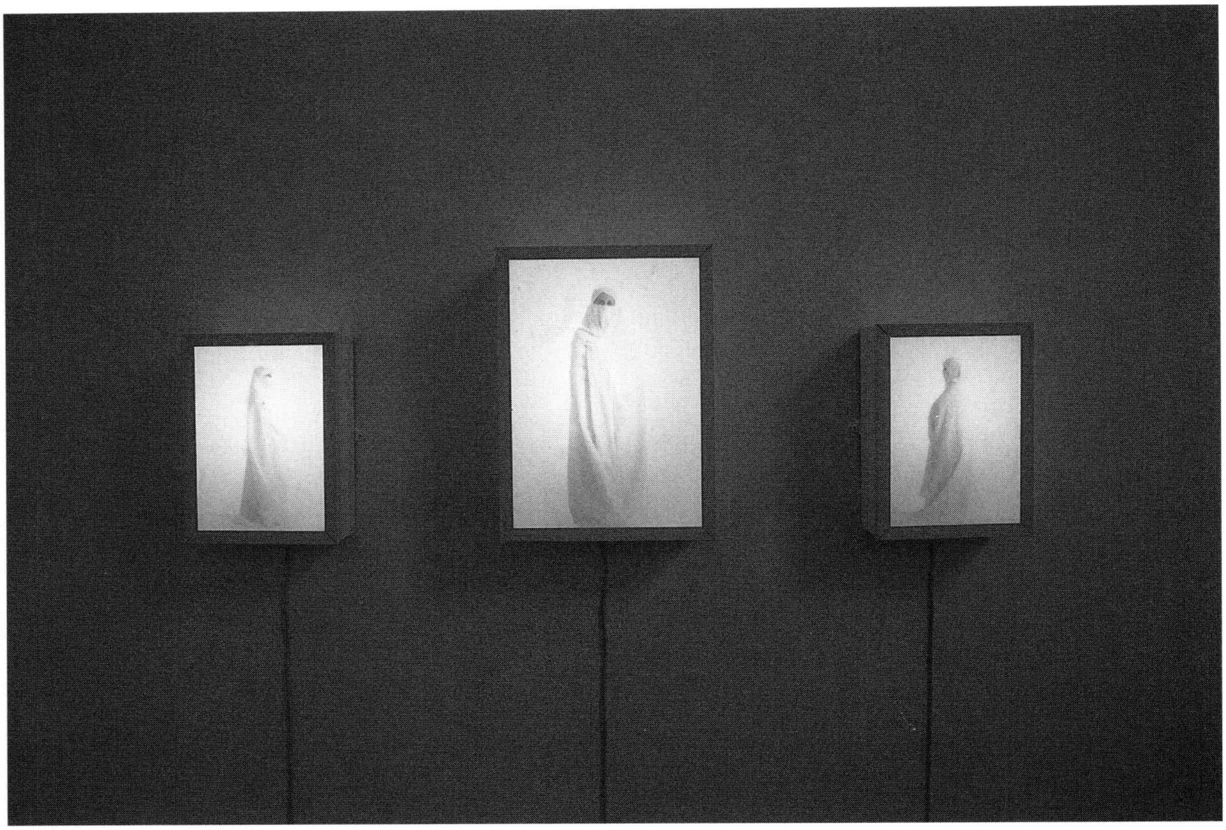

Figure 5. Zineb Sedira, *Silent Sight (Self Portrait)*, 1999. Three computer-generated photographic images, back-lit 100 × 45 cm overall. Reproduced courtesy of the artist.

the images appear shroud-like, almost as dematerialized forms where all colour has been drained except for the eyes, which stare out defiantly. The work is deeply embedded in personal and collective memory. The Muslim veil and 'voilette' (the small white covering for the bottom of the face) belonged to the artist's mother who, now living in Algeria, is no longer required to wear it because of her age (see Figure 6). The use of the triptych form (usually associated with Christianity) and the veiling (which is simultaneously reminiscent of the Virgin Mary and a nun's habit) recalls the in-between *beurette* culture of Sedira's youth where the icons and rituals of French Catholicism co-existed with those of Islam and an Algerian history. In the context of Britain, I would suggest that the dress, the triptych format and the gendered Arab body work as destabilizing and disruptive signs. They throw into question markers of ethnic and cultural difference by evoking icons and symbols that link cultures rather than separate them. In doing so, Sedira's work suggests not only points of historical connections long ignored, but also the hybridity of diasporic spaces which are part of the culture of contemporary Britain.

Furthermore, the self-portrait can be seen to focus on the complex relationships between age, power and visibility, the ways in which women's bodies are always subject to cultural coding and are regulated across and within different geographies, whether in the name of religion, nation, revolution or tradition.[35] Here the continuous effects of history, culture and power on the

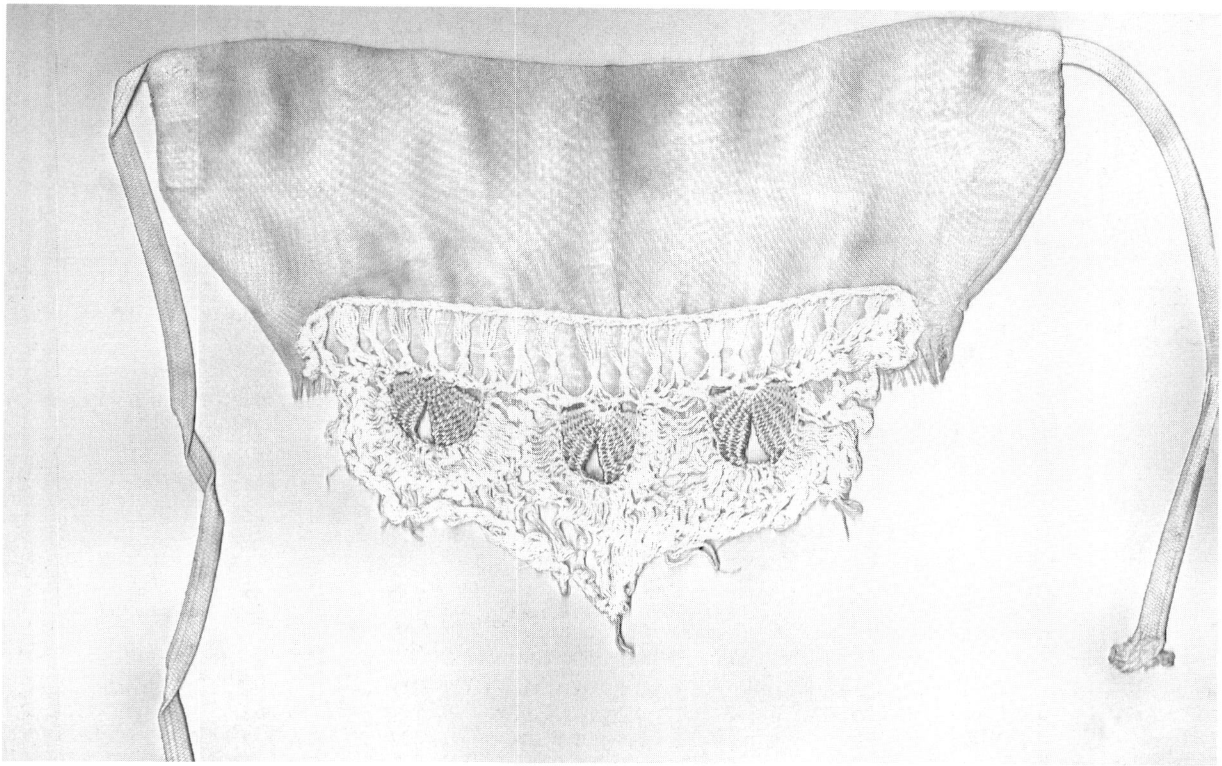

Figure 6. Zineb Sedira, *Mum's Veil*, 1999. Reproduced courtesy of the artist.

body are deftly echoed in the presentational mode of the light boxes in which the images are set and framed. The materials and processes of making become a powerful metaphor for the diverse ways in which the female figure can be absent and present, veiled and unveiled through the act of spectatorship and, by extension, the cultural forces that mediate visibility, including curatorial practices and policies.

Part of a postconceptual generation, Sedira's use of computer-generated photographic and video images places her work firmly within the frame of contemporary visual culture in Britain. Strategically it resists the curatorial tendency to categorize work of cultural minorities as 'ethnic art' while also signalling that Sedira, as an Arab artist, is part of contemporary visual culture rather than locked in a tradition of the past or relegated to an unchanging ahistorical space as in most histories of Islamic art.[36]

The artist's use of time-based media which explicitly connote the process of change or becoming is therefore significant as an artistic strategy both within a history of contemporary Arab art and within contemporary British visual culture. While referring to past stereotypes and conditions, Sedira uses the media frequently associated with forms of documentation to locate her work firmly in the present. For example, in the video work *Don't Do To Her What You Did To Me* (1998) (Figure 7) the specificities of time and place are used to recall her past in Paris as a comment on 'often invisible' racism. Memories are powerfully evoked by the black and white format where the materialities of the photographic images slip in and out of view. Using the initial framing or veil-

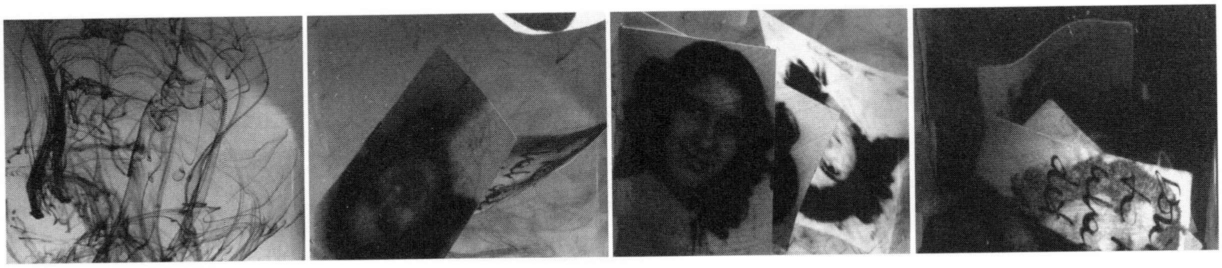

Figure 7. Zineb Sedira, *Don't Do To Her What You Did To Me*, 1998. Video stills. Reproduced courtesy of the artist.

ing device of a glass being filled with water, the viewer is presented with the imagery and sound of running water and the film of a hand writing. Black ink drops into still, clear water: unfurling, veil-like and staining. This is followed by photographs of a young Arab woman and glimpses of hand-written text which fall through the water and are slowly mixed together and then spun until they dissolve into a pulp. Evoking the senses and the materialities of photographs as a 'class of objects formed specifically to remember',[37] the images are powerful reminders of loss, absence and death. Sedira explains the particularities of the work in the following way:

> The talisman subverted in the video is one I remember I was forced to drink, in order to become a good girl, a good Muslim. A taleb, a priest, would write verses of the *Qur'an* on a piece of paper that would subsequently be carried or swallowed by whomever needed the help of God. The piece is a homage to a girl who died through the conflicts of her mixed identity, when I was sixteen. I used the girl's last words in the talisman to exorcise the sacrifice of the deceased woman, to release her from the racism and pressure of French culture.[38]

The experience of the diaspora is central to this work through the interweaving of form and content. In confronting the complex and tragic consequences of the specific intersections of race, gender, sexuality and religion both within and outside of the Arab diaspora, the artist is actively re-negotiating identity through and against these memories, feelings and events. The work is therefore a dual site of enquiry. It is both the site of what Stuart Hall concisely calls 'the production of identity' through a negotiation of the past in the present through memory and locatedness,[39] and simultaneously an act of discovery and articulation in which a new awareness of identities and their consequences is formed in the context of contemporary Britain.

Significantly, in her most recent computer-generated photographs such as *Work in Progress* (2000) (Figure 8), Sedira represents a range of female Arab bodies which inhabit an anonymous, indeterminate space. Dressed in western clothes, the frontal figures are presented as if part of an identity parade, but, disturbingly, the heads of the individuals are missing, visible only in the ominous shadow cast. Placeless and without identity, the images carry several meanings. At the most obvious level they can be seen to continue the theme of invisibility where, although adopting the dominant cultural norms of dress, the Anglo-Arab female is still not recognized as an individual within contemporary Britain. However, in the context of recent traumatic events in Algeria where women were decapitated on the spot for being unveiled, the images evoke the horrific effects of the regulation of women's bodies in the name of nation and/or religion.[40]

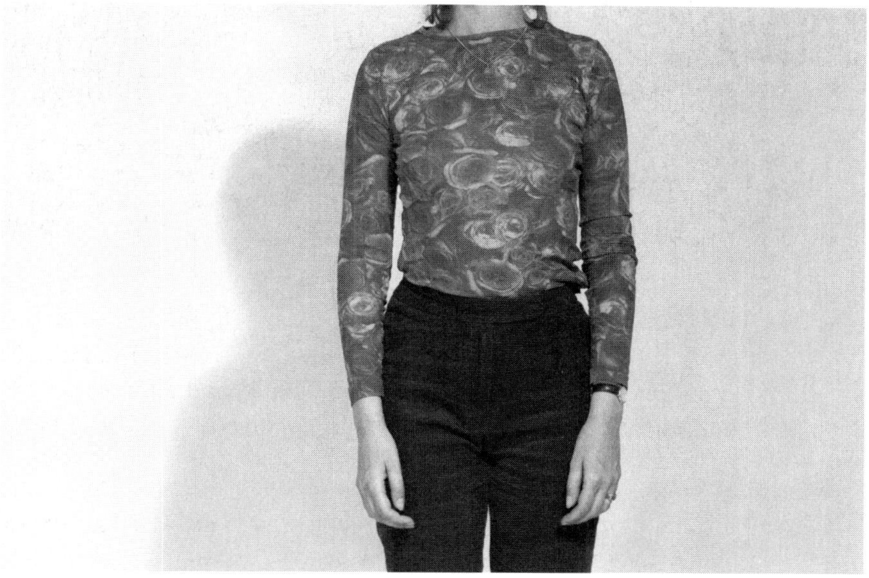

Figure 8. Zineb Sedira, *Work in Progress*, 2000. Computer generated photographic image. Reproduced courtesy of the artist.

To summarize briefly, I have argued that within the current historical and political context of Britain, Sedira's work is important for a number of reasons. It foregrounds the continual performing of multiple diasporic identities through an autobiographical mode which destabilizes, disrupts and negotiates dominant views that have become further entrenched in recent years in terms of the binaries of veiled/unveiled, Islam/Christian, and the xenophobic fear of 'Britain as a foreign land'.[41] Moreover, the range of her veiled imagery, from her sister's scarf to her mother's redundant veil and *voilette*, foregrounds the generational and geographical differences which undo the fixity of the monolithic veil and suggest the material traces of the invisible matrilineal histories within contemporary visual culture.[42]

Finally, Sedira's work also examines the identity of an Arab diaspora in Britain. In terms of visual culture one of the most evident shifts is the renewed interest in the diaspora, the movement of a nation or a group of people from one homeland to another. In Britain, the writings of Stuart Hall and subsequently Paul Gilroy have been of immense importance in dismantling the concept of a singular, unified national identity and of establishing the concept of a diaspora as a site of transformation and difference where cultural identities are continually remade both through and against past andpresent conditions.[43]

Building upon this work, Nicholas Mirzoeff's recent writing on African and Jewish diasporas argues that the diaspora can no longer be seen in the singular or predominantly along a trajectory of the homeland and the place of displacement. For many in the twenty-first century, it has become more frequently a new home from which return may not be envisaged or indeed possible and, as Mirzoeff observes, 'the hybridity generated by diaspora is not just with the "host" nation but among diasporas themselves'.[44] This awareness of the historical and continuing interactions between different diasporas, the increasing frequency with which individuals may inhabit various successive diasporas in the course of a single lifetime as multiple immigrants, and the further complexities of what Irit Rogoff calls the 'diaspora's diaspora', point to the numerous and often contradictory intersecting points of cultural identification that we are just beginning to envisage in Britain.[45]

Thus, Sedira's use of the female body contests gendered stereotypes which – in parallel with many other women artists working in the diasporic spaces of Britain, such as Sutapa Biswas or Zarina Bhimji – focuses on what Gilane Tawadros refers to as 'the ambivalence of identity and a redundancy of exclusive absolutes ... predicated on resistance and change'.[46] In other words, aware of historical and social conditions, her work both deconstructs and resists dominant stereotypical images while also negotiating, opening up and locating new points of identification and difference within the heterogeneity of a postcolonial and multicultural Britain.

I would like to thank Zineb Sedira for permission to reproduce her work.

Notes

1 Zineb Sedira, unpublished interview with the artist by Edith Marie Pasquier, 1997.

2 'Dialogue of the Present: the Work of 18 Arab Women Artists', curated by Siumee Helen Keelan, toured Britain, 1998–2000. See Fran Lloyd, ed., *Contemporary Arab Women's Art: Dialogues of the Present*, London: Women's Art Library and I. B. Tauris, 1999.

3 See Fran Lloyd, 'Re-making Ourselves: Art, Memories and Materialities', in Fran Lloyd, ed., *Displacement and Difference: Contemporary Arab Visual Culture in the Diaspora*, London: Saffron, 2000, pp.81–155; see also Wijdan Ali, *Contemporary Art from the Islamic World*, London: Scorpion Publications Ltd, and Amman: The Royal Society of Fine Arts, 1989.

4 See Salwa Mikdadi Nashashibi, *Forces of Change, Artists of the Arab World*, Lafayette, California: International Council for Women in the Arts, 1994; for Hakim-Dowek see Rosemary Betterton, *An Intimate Distance: Women. Artists and the Body*, London and New York: Routledge, 1996, pp.183–7.

5 Stuart Hall, 'About Re-inventing Britain', opening address at the 'Re-inventing Britain' conference, 21 March 1997, School of Oriental and African Studies, London University, British Council, 2000: see http://www.britcoun.org/studies/reinventing_Britain/index2.htm.

6 See Margot Badran and Miriam Cooke, eds, 'Introduction', in *Opening the Gates: A Century of Arab Feminist Writing*, Bloomington and Indianapolis: Indiana University Press, 1990, pp.xxv–vi.

7 See Stuart Hall, 'New Ethnicities,' in James Donald and Ali Rattansi, eds, *'Race', Culture & Difference*, London, California, and New Delhi: Sage Publications in association with The Open University, 1992, pp.252–9; and Avtar Brah, *Cartographies of Diaspora, Contesting Identities*, New York and London: Routledge, 1996, pp.234–41.

8 See Fred Halliday, *Arabs in Exile: Yemeni Migrants in Urban Britain*, London: I. B. Tauris, 1992, and Richard I. Lawless, *From Ta'izz to Tyneside*, Exeter: University of Exeter Press, 1995.

9 Halliday, *Arabs in Exile*, p.131.

10 See Avtar Brah, Mary J. Hickman and Máirtín Mac an Ghaill, eds, *Thinking Identities: Ethnicity, Racism & Culture*, London: Macmillan Press Ltd, 1999, chapter 1, pp.1–21.

11 Max Silverman and Nira Yuval-Davis, 'Jews, Arabs and the Theorisation of Racism in Britain and France', in Brah, Hickman and Mac an Ghaill, eds, *Thinking Identities*, pp.25–48.

12 Ibid., p.28.

13 Ibid., pp.34–5.

14 *Labour Force Survey: Estimates of the Population by Ethnic Group and Area of Residence, 1998, Great Britain*, London: Office for National Statistics (ONS), 1999.

15 Silverman and Yuval-Davis, 'Jews, Arabs', p.3.

16 Ibid., p.3.

17 Edward W. Said, *Orientalism, Western Concepts of the Orient*, London: Routledge & Kegan Paul Ltd., 1978, p.1.

18 Ibid., p.3.

19 See Linda Nochlin, 'The Imaginary Orient', in *The Politics of Vision*, London: Thames and Hudson, 1991; Çeylan Tawadros, 'Foreign Bodies: Art History and the Discourse of 19th Century Orientalist Art', *Third Text*, No. 3/4, Spring/Summer, 1988.

20 Malik Alloula, *The Colonial Harem*, trans. Myrna Godzich and Wlad Godzich, Minneapolis and London: University of Minnesota Press, 1986. For argument see Rey Chow, *Writing Diaspora, Tactics of Intervention in Contemporary Cultural Studies*, Bloomington and Indianapolis: Indiana University Press, 1993, pp.39–41.

21 Michael Archer et al., eds, *Mona Hatoum*, London: Phaidon Press, 1997, pp.139–40.

22 For an incisive analysis of *Measures of Distance* see chapter 8, 'Esthetics of Resistance', in Ella Shohat and Robert Stam, *Unthinking Eurocentrism: Multiculturalism and the Media*, London and New York: Routledge, 1994, pp.318–21.

23 Nira Yuval-Davis, 'Fundamentalism, Multiculturalism and Women in Britain', in Donald and Rattansi, eds, *'Race', Culture & Difference*, p.284.

24 Charles Husband, 'The Political Context of Muslim Communities' Participation in British Society', in Bernard Lewis and Dominique Schnapper, eds, *Muslims in Europe*, Social Change in Western Europe Series, London & New York: Pinter Publishers, 1994, p.80.

25 Ibid., p.83.

26 Edith Marie Pasquier, 'The Oblique Gaze', in Lloyd, ed., *Contemporary Arab Women's Art*, p.215.

27 Ibid., p.216.

28 Marie-Aimée Hélie-Lucas, 'Women, Nationalism and Religion in the Algerian Liberation Struggle', in Badran and Cooke, eds, *Opening the Gates*, pp.108–13. See also Frantz Fanon, 'Algeria Unveiled', in *A Dying Colonialism*, trans. Haakon Chevalier, New York: Grove Press, 1965, published originally in French in 1959.

29 Unpublished interview with the artist by Edith Marie Pasquier, 1997.

30 Frantz Fanon, *Black Skins, White Masks*, London: Pluto Press, 1986.

31 See Reina Lewis, *Gendering Orientalism, Race, Femininity and Representation*, London and New York: Routledge, 1996.

32 *Qur'an* 24: 31; for discussion of the eye as an erogenous zone see Fatima Mernissi, *Beyond the Veil*, Cambridge, Mass., New York and London: Schenkman, 1975.

33 Pasquirer, 'The Oblique Gaze', p.218.

34 Meyda Yeğenğolu, *Colonial Fantasies: Towards a Feminist Reading of Orientalism*, Cambridge: Cambridge University Press, 1998, p.115.

35 For the linking of women and nation see Deniz Kandiyoti, 'Identity and its Discontents: Women and the Nation' , in *Millennium: Journal of International Studies*, vol.20, no.3, 1991, pp.429–43.

36 Subsumed under Islamic art, the majority of exhibitions and publications which encompass Arab art focus predominantly on earlier historical moments or traditional art forms, ignoring contemporary developments.

37 Elizabeth Edwards, 'Photographs as Objects of Memory', in Marius Kwint, Christopher Breward and Jeremy Aynsley, eds, *Material Memories: Design and Evocation*, Oxford and New York: Berg, 1999, p.222.

38 Unpublished interview with the artist by Edith Marie Pasquier, 1997.

39 Stuart Hall, 'Cultural Identity and Diaspora', in P. Williams and L. Chrisman, eds, *Colonial Discourse and Post-Colonial Theory*, A Reader, Cambridge: Harvester/Wheatsheaf, 1993, p.393.

40 Declared originally to be the act of Islamic Fundamentalists, such decapitations may have been committed by Algerian government forces.

41 William Hague's recent speech (February 2001) is part of a continuing political anxiety about national purity echoed previously in the speeches of Enoch Powell in the 1960s and by Margaret Thatcher in the 1980s.

42 For a contemporary view on veiling in Egypt, for example, see Soroya Duval, 'New Veils and New Voices: Islamist Women's Groups in Egypt', in Karin Ask and Marit Tjomsland, eds, *Women and Islamization, Contemporary Dimensions of Discourse on Gender Relations*, New York and Oxford: Berg, 1998, pp.45–72.

43 See the Hall texts cited above and Paul Gilroy, *The Black Atlantic, Modernity and Double Consciousness*, London and New York: Verso, 1993.

44 Nicholas Mirzoeff, ed., *Diaspora and Visual Culture: Representing Africans and Jews*, New York and London: Routledge, 1999, pp.3–4.

45 See Irit Rogoff, 'Daughters of Sunshine – Diasporic Impulses and Gendered Identities', in Lisa Bloom, ed., *With Other Eyes: Looking at Race and Gender in Visual Culture*, Minneapolis and London: University of Minnesota Press, 1999, p.163.

46 Gilane Tawadros, 'Beyond the Boundary: The Work of Three Black Women Artists in Britain', in Houston A. Baker, Jr., Manthia Diawara and Ruth H. Lindeborg, eds, *Black British Cultural Studies, A Reader*, Chicago and London: University of Chicago Press, 1996, p.274.

Adele Patrick

A Taste for Femininity: Subordinated Pleasures in Fashioning 'Feminine Excess'

This article is part of a research project that started in 1996 when I began to reflect critically upon the socialization and construction of my own (history of) self-fashioning. Recent feminist auto/biographical work on British visual culture offers models for interrogating social constructions of 'self'.[1] In her work *Family Secrets*, Annette Kuhn draws on Frigga Haug et al.'s innovative methodology 'memory work', which enables the empirical (but not empiricist) use of memory for research, where 'anything remembered constitutes a relevant trace – precisely because it is remembered – for the formation of identity'.[2] In Haug's ground-breaking work, memories or 'stories' written by participants were analysed as texts indicative of an individual's relationship to shifting social and cultural contexts, 'as written signs of the relations within which identity is formed'.[3] Using memory work methodology, I generated a corpus of stories/memories in the third person using banal 'triggers' associated with female fashioning, femininity and glamour. Perhaps unsurprisingly given the memory work findings of Haug, Crawford, Kuhn, Spence and others, many of the texts I generated construct the notion of a female (body) subordinated by or embattled in social and cultural contexts, which might be interpreted as patriarchally determined spaces and places: at school (a humiliating, 'unjust' confrontation with a headmaster over 'inappropriate', or what Noliwe Rooks has called 'dissident' hair),[4] family occasions (she 'fails' as a bridesmaid due to inadequate, 'small' hair) and so on. Perhaps less predictably, other texts that record a failure to perform appropriate fashioning are stories of subordination experienced within the context of 'feminist' or 'women-centred' spaces (women's groups, conferences, reading groups and so on). Significantly, memories/stories of failure to enact appropriate forms of normative, patriarchally endorsed femininity (and contingent 'success') were matched in number by failures in affecting an appropriate 'feminist' fashioning, experienced through specific encounters and the routinized 'policing' of desired but 'repressive' forms of fashioning (femininity).[5]

Female relatives and childhood friends figured in these texts as fashioned in forms broadly indicative of the femininity disparaged by 'high culture'. Was my own nostalgia for fashioning forms of femininity (notwithstanding these memories of later feminist sanctions) distorting the apparent ongoing political case against it? How could the (diverse/uniform) tastes of feminists' self-fashioning be analysed? Does the genealogy of feminism reveal enough of the paradoxically individual and social forms of female self-fashioning? These initial questions and a review of relevant literature pointed up the inadequacy of terms such as 'femininity', 'camp' or 'kitsch' to describe or define the array of forms of female self-fashioning, even within the range of constructions of myself reflected in family photographs or in the memory-work texts.

In the process of examining the social and cultural meanings of femininity, and in particular hairdressing and other cosmetic acts, I began by aligning myself with feminist research on 'subjugated knowledges'. Jane Ribbens and Rosalind Edwards suggest that this Foucauldian notion has been useful in feminist efforts to elaborate more fully 'knowledges that have been disqualified as inadequate to their task'.[6] Hairdressing and cosmetic acts are rarely considered to be important to high culture or feminist theory, but persist in being of enormous interest to millions of women and audiences of popular culture, fashion and 'star systems'. Can feminists be satisfied with a continued bracketing of such a spectrum of enthusiasms and desires as 'false consciousness' and do feminist politics and theory take full account of the (historical and contemporary) fashioned 'tastes' of feminists? My efforts to chart significant historical and cultural definitions of femininity exposed what Katherine Stern has interpreted as mainstream and feminist neglect: 'There is no comprehensive account of the aesthetic category, no analysis of the details that characterise femininity'.[7] Rather, Stern discovers historical consistency in objections to artifice that are a paradigm for both patriarchal and feminist rhetoric against the 'cosmetic acts'.[8] Revisiting myself some influential feminist texts (consumed at intervals in my developing self-identification as 'feminist'), the powerfully prescriptive anti-'fashioning to excess' rhetoric evoked just such comparisons with 'malestream' historical models. In *Femininity*, Susan Brownmiller states,

> To care about feminine fashion and to do it well is to be obsessively involved in inconsequential details on a serious basis. The desperate wounding absorption in the drive for a perfect appearance – call it female vanity – *is the ultimate restriction on freedom of mind*.[9]

For Sandra Lee Bartky, 'Repressive narcissistic satisfactions stand in the way of the emergence of an authentic delight in the body'.[10] Bartky concludes that 'Narcissistic satisfaction is to some degree conditional upon a sense of successful adaptation to standards of feminine bodily presence generated by the enemies of women'.[11] The emphases in these texts, prescriptive rather than descriptive, concur with dominant second-wave feminist knowledge in providing philosophical rather than empirical or ethnographic accounts of fashioning femininity.[12]

Although Stern's project questions the notion of femininity's absolute synonymy with false consciousness, her perspective suggests that there can be no real claims for the importance of femininity disengaged from the 'twinned' form of effeminacy.[13] In an earlier research endeavour, I had unsuccessfully attempted to examine femininity from the perspective of camp.[14] Not only did I conclude that it is currently irretrievably over-determined as a gay male trope, I began to consider female performances of feminine excess, particularly those exemplified by specific working-class communities of women, including those of women of colour, as misinterpreted and marginalized by three specific methods: appropriation by/for gay male culture, the historical excision or subordination of specific forms of femininity in feminist theory and politics, and the dominant Modernist refutation and degradation of the decorative – the 'low' taste of the masses – governed by women.[15] In her project to define the positive effects of 'feminist camp', Pamela Robertson stated that it 'tends to speak from and to a working-class sensibility'.[16] However, her commitment to the project of recuperating *camp* from the domain of men rather obscures the fact that fashioning *feminine excess* in the post-Second World War period, insofar as British visual culture is concerned, has unquestionably been principally the work of women.

The fact that the fashioning of a spectrum of forms of feminine excess, performed routinely by a significant number of women, should have been collapsed into a gay male cultural prerogative in the post-war period suggests that an expansion of empirically grounded feminist knowledge in this field is required, as is the interrogation of what femininity means and has meant *to women*, particularly where feminine excess persists in being associated pejoratively with working-class women's taste. Through gay male appropriation and, as Stern argues, 'feminist neglect', along with the totalizing effect of Modernist taste in Britain in the period, (female) forms of femininity have been 'discounted unthinkingly'.[17]

The corpus of my memory-work yielded descriptions of women remembered as embodying feminine excess but who also defied the mainstream and/or feminist notions of signifying passivity or false consciousness. Here, femininity was not indexically linked to lack of agency, capitulation to masculine value systems or convergence with popular fashions. Such memories of encrusted femininity were both biographically and *autobiographically* remembered. The women remembered were not 'othered', but were interpreted as sharing forms of embodied knowledge. In contrast, Haug et al. report in *Female Sexualisation* that they found it 'easy' to differentiate themselves from women who dressed to (feminine) excess:

> In our group the question of the ways in which women constitute themselves as slave girls was discussed initially in a seminar in Hamburg. At this stage we were still contemplating the process of subjection simply in terms of women's display of their bodies, in other words, in terms of what seemed to us to constitute unambiguous sexual invitations – the wearing of short skirts, or see-through blouses for example, it seemed relatively easy to place ourselves at a distance from such things; we ourselves dress differently in any case – in jeans and jumpers for the most part.[18]

On the basis of this dissonance between dominant feminist (and mainstream) assumptions concerning women who self-fashion to excess and my own auto/biographical accounts of what the spectacle of fashioned female bodies could entail, I began to develop a multi-valenced research project that sought to describe the neglected aspects of the *something that femininity displays*. Following recent feminist research that has texts and/or 'forms of looking' as the focus for theorizing forms of femininity and pleasures, my broader concern, introduced here, is the aim to provide specific historically, culturally and socially grounded accounts of women's constructed relationships to 'feminine forms'. Have feminist theories been insensitive to the medium of the cosmetic acts, as Stern suggests? And what parts do 'class', 'ethnicity' and 'taste' have to play in women's historically determined experiences of self-fashioning femininity and, perhaps more controversially, in feminism? How can feminist academics with histories of and *embodied* knowledges of 'excessively feminine' or 'working-class' forms of fashioning begin to expand feminist knowledge of the meanings of such practices for women beyond their historical and contemporary reading as 'low' and unworthy of research?

In addition to the illuminating accounts of acquiring (and performing) femininity in work by memory-work collectives, models for empirical research with women in this field can be found in a number of studies. In Jackie Stacey's ground-breaking *Stargazing: Hollywood Cinema and Female Spectatorship*, which has as its focus British female spectators of Hollywood movies of the 1940s and 1950s, an expansive account is made of the specific (dis)pleasures, identifications and uses white female viewers made of nostalgically remembered representations of femininity embodied by specific stars.[19] Stacey's interrogation of identifications and intimacies between femininities suggested the fertile ground upon which further 'unofficial discourses' could be examined. Although her focus is principally on the audience/star relationship, more ethnographic work on women's self-fashioning by researchers such as Frida Kerner Furman has recently been developed. Furman's evocative exploration of the socio-moral significance for a group of elderly Jewish female regulars in their American beauty-shop experiences interprets the salon as a 'safe space', where women can resist the sexism and ageism that oppresses them:

> Resistance to socio-cultural oppressions is embedded in the way that older women treat one another – with respect, affection and attentiveness; in conversations and gestures that affirm and hence make visible older women's pride in and attention to their bodies, and that acknowledge the pain, suffering and loss that accompany embodiment; in discussions of their work of caring as work that is valuable, necessary and demanding.[20]

Significant work on fashioning hair can also be found in scholarship that examines the multiple meanings to be derived from the stylings of black hair.[21] In 'Black Hair/Style Politics', Kobena Mercer calls for the depsychologizing of the question of hair-straightening in favour of recognizing hair-styling 'for what it is, a specifically cultural activity and practice'.[22] Mercer contests that the processing of hair socializes it, 'making it the medium of significant statements about self and society and the codes of value that bind them or do not'.[23] He defines two logics of black hair-stylization, 'one emphasising natural looks, the other involving straightening to emphasise artifice'. This binary opposition, where artifice occupies the degraded or negative instance, can be rhetorically linked to the paradigmatic definition of Modernist taste (versus popular/feminine taste) and the analysis of (good) 'feminist taste' versus (bad) feminine artifice to be found in second-wave feminist politics. My own work benefited from this expanded conceptualization of (women's) self-fashioning practices as *meaningful*. In an effort to reconsider the 'crimes' of artifice and expand the scope for considering women's engagement in 'cosmetic acts' as more than self-deception, I developed a programme of research with women.

In order to begin to determine how women construct and articulate femininity, I employed feminist qualitative research methods. Such methods require that the researcher aims towards a continual process of reflexivity in efforts to contribute to academic discourse, directly addressing and incorporating 'other' knowledge forms, including those remembered in our own histories, rather than relinquishing them.[24]

In a series of semi-structured interviews with individual participants and clusters of women in Glasgow, and drawing on 'triggers' developed through memory work, accounts of self-fashioning, femininity and feminism were generated in conversations about an array of past experiences and present routines involving cosmetic acts and forms of adornment such as jewellery, footwear, hair-styling, make-up, garments and dress-making and private and collective beauty regimes. In addition, and following Stacey, interview participants were asked to relate their memories of music, film or TV stars, interpreted as 'iconic' or 'narrative'.[25] Participants also volunteered many accounts of memorable, and/or influential (self-)fashionings performed by 'non-stars'. In tandem, I undertook an analysis of post-war forms of femininity found in specific popular and feminist literature aimed at women to map the shifting construction of forms of un/acceptable femininity (found in abundance within these texts), much of which illuminated the genealogy (insights and limitations) of feminist knowledge of femininity.[26]

Interviews with predominantly white, female participants aged between 17 and 83 took place in their domestic spaces and my own, in salons and at a beauty-therapy course at a Glasgow college. The resulting spectrum of accounts of self-fashioning forms of femininity constitute knowledge/s relevant to, but as yet under-theorized in, feminism and generally lacking representation within the groups and texts of academia and feminism. There is scope here to summarize three 'nodes' that have surfaced in female participants' accounts of their current and past constructions of themselves as feminine and/or fashioned.[27]

'Intimacies between femininities': unofficial accounts of cosmetic acts

In her analysis of sociological and psychoanalytic interpretations, Stacey concludes that

> Identification [between women] itself has been seen as a cultural process complicit with the reproduction of dominant culture by reinforcing patriarchal forms of identity ... Identification of any kind is ... criticised for reproducing sameness, fixity and the confirmation of existing identities.[28]

However, the identifications within and between visual cultures produced in the fashioning of female identifications between women and stars exceed the monolithic interpretations of psychoanalytic theory and early second-wave feminist constructions of passivity and narcissism, as Stacey demonstrates. My research extends this claim in its inclusion of accounts of identification between 'non-stars': female relatives, female friends, women who are strangers, across ages, classes, ethnicities as well as those between 'real' women and representations of women in popular cultural and feminist texts.

Frequently, identifications between women consisted of pleasurable encounters that can be interpreted as forms of *intimacies between femininities*.[29] Describing her work with customers at Glasgow hair and beauty salons, 'Joni' states that:

> Getting hands-on care, you know, for someone to touch you and care about you and that's done in a nice way, a sort of nurturing thing, you know, and I do think that people come for that as well because there's the physical effect, obviously it's on a physical level ... so you physically feel better, not just absolutely physically but emotionally. You've been cared for for an hour and a half – an hour – whatever – and somebody's pored over you and given you all that attention.

Research participants discussed their pleasures in the smells of the salon and the cosmetics used in the fashioning process. Some smells, experienced when the fashioning routine took place in the domestic space – the memory of the smell of a mother or aunt's powder compact, lipstick, setting-lotion, perfume or even hand-made hair lacquer – were remembered with evident pleasure up to forty years or more after last encountering them. 'Gabrielle', whose visits to the hairdresser have become an important component in maintaining her self-esteem after years of illness, describes how the hairdresser who visits her at home sensitively works with her hair now that it has become 'thin and patchy':

> I like it when she is sort of behind me and she's doing my hair and she'll go like that [gestures as if pulling a lock of hair over her forehead] and brings it downwards with both her hands, and if she doesn't like it she pulls it up a bit and covers – if there's any space anywhere – and you know, really spends time on me.

Revisiting the feminist anthology *Sisterhood is Powerful*[30] I was intrigued by a

Figure 1. Atlantic City, 1968: first mass demonstration and action by Women's Liberation. Picketing and guerrilla theater on the boardwalk. Photograph, Beverly Grant/Newsreel. Reproduced from Robin Morgan, ed., *Sisterhood is Powerful: an Anthology of Writings from the Women's Liberation Movement*, New York: Vintage Books, 1970.

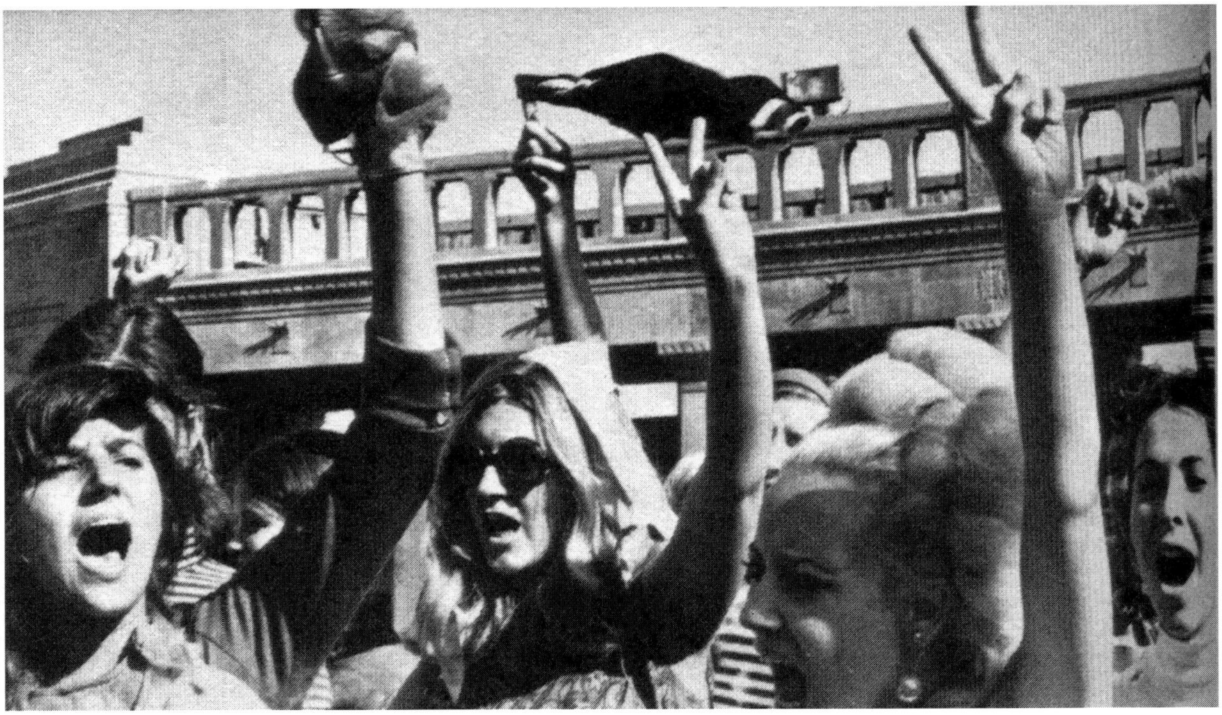

photograph of the first mass demonstration by Women's Liberation in Atlantic City, New Jersey in 1968.[31] Prominently foregrounded is a woman with a large, elaborately coiffed, bleached and excessively feminized 'pompadour' hairstyle, 'panda eyes'[32] and conspicuous jewellery (Figure 1). She is chanting and stridently giving the 'V' sign, flanked by other demonstrators. Just as this photographic record was made, girdles, bras and lipsticks were being ceremoniously trashed in a dustbin labelled 'freedom'.[33] In a symbolic, concluding moment, an effigy of a 'dumb blonde', with caricatured bouffant, is symbolically dumped. The 'bouffanted woman' plays an ambivalent role here, visible as a demonstrator against/witness of the trashing of Miss America, but nevertheless troubling to some later feminists who may seek to suggest that liberation was fought for by women who unequivocally styled themselves 'naturally'. The memories of research participants in my study demonstrate how bouffanting and feminine excess ran counter to normative forms of femininity in post-war Britain. The advice presented in many of the girls' annuals and magazines in this period reveals the divergence between 'natural' models of femininity and those performed by music stars exemplified by Dusty Springfield in the early to mid-1960s.[34] In *Helen Shapiro's New Book for Girls*, an 'annual' published by The Daily Mirror Newspapers Limited (1963), for example, the writer of 'Golden Rule No. 10' in the 'Top Ten Rules of Dress' asks:

> How much make-up should a young girl use? A little in the right place at the right time ... nowadays the shiny look with no powder and the natural look with no lipstick is more likely to be the look you like. Possible pitfall? Too much eye make up. Black ringed eyes wth spiky lashes and beetle brows can turn a pretty face into a joke. At 14 as at 40 make up should be applied with a fairy touch and not a trowel.

In contrast, 'Sandy' remembers both the intense pleasures of identification with Dusty and her father's disapproval of the star's television performances:

> I remember my Dad's hostility towards Dusty. I remember that really, really vividly ... My Dad was angry about her black eyes ... he was saying 'black eyed bugger' and all that ... When Dusty came [after Kathy Kirby] it was like [sharp intake of breath] she was like, sort of, *more*. She was just like *more* ... I can't – I don't know how to describe more but I do remember being struck by the whole image, you know, it was like, you know, her eye makeup and her big hair and a long sort of dramatic dress and the way she sort of [dramatic gestures], you know when she was singing. As well as the voice it was the whole package, she was just really ...

Although never the subject of serious music criticism (or reviews) in the key British feminist magazine *Spare Rib*, Dusty, for many of the research participants, was iconically and narratively remembered as unconventional and subversive in her vocal performances, and for her association with black Motown stars, 'ambivalent' sexuality, 'independence' and fashioning of feminine excess. Dusty described her self-fashioning during the 1960s as designed to be 'as unsexy as possible'.[35] Her later (re)construction of herself in memories (arguably through a 'queered' lens, aware as she was of her own appropriation as 'camp' and a gay-male icon, at least from the early 1980s) is of fashioning 'an over the top parody of stereotyped femininity that did not pose a threat'[36] (Figure 2).

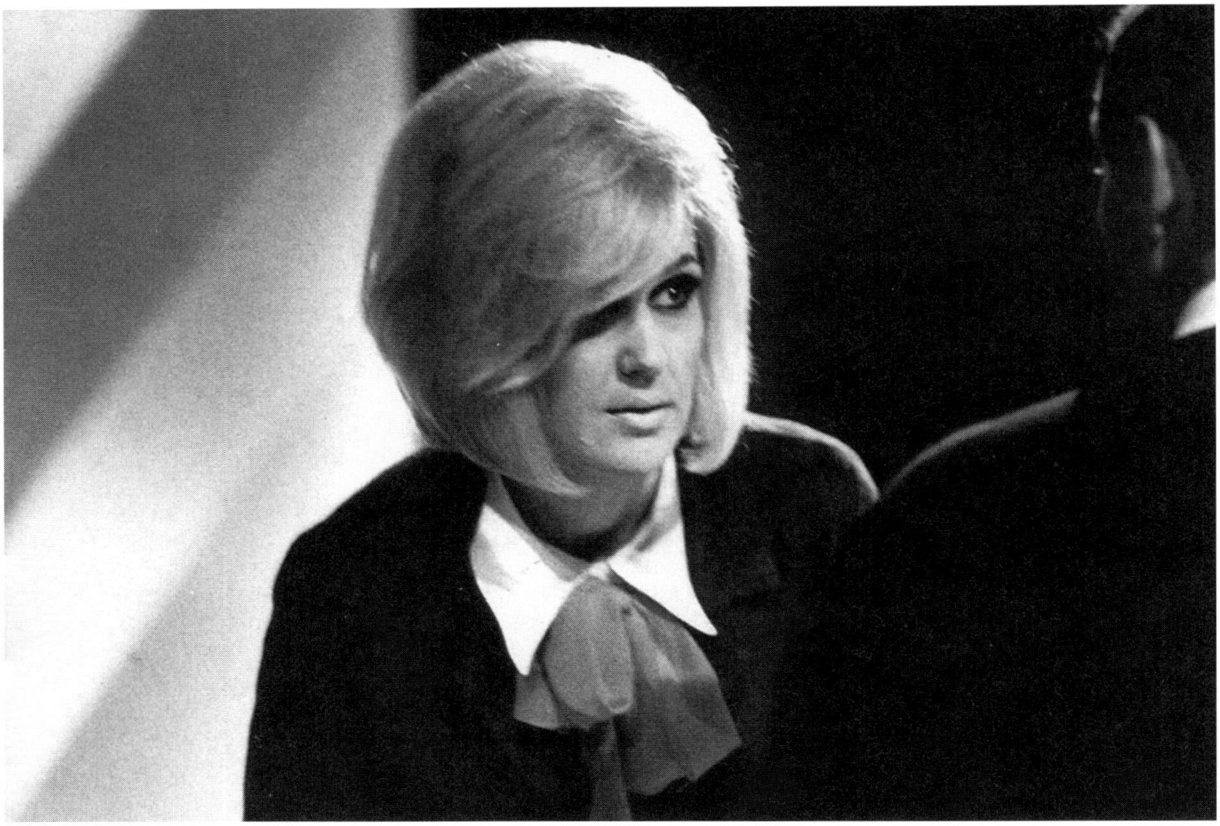

Figure 2. Panda Eyes. Dusty rehearses for *Ready Steady Go!* in 1964. Reproduced from Lucy O'Brien, *Dusty, a biography of Dusty Springfield*, London: Sidgwick and Jackson, 1999.

The 'bouffanted woman' resurfaces as an ironic form in American and European forms of gay-male drag in the 1980s and 1990s (Ru Paul, Lypsinka, Lily Savage, Lady Bunny et al.) but this 'camp' use of 'big hair' was not recognized by the female research participants who described the genealogy of bouffanting and big hair in the 1960s in Britain. For example, 'Elizabeth' noted:

> The idea of camp wasn't ever in my mind and I don't remember it being mentioned ever. I don't ever remember anybody, anyone referring to, well using the word camp and certainly I don't remember any of my female friends who also liked Dusty modelled themselves on Dusty in terms of make up and hairdos even speaking about her in terms of camp or anything like that. No, she was just, she was fantastically well groomed.

However, in the mid-60s, Dusty can be read as challenging the socially sanctioned format for make-up 'advice' to be found in literature for girls with her tip for mascara users, 'You have to spit in it to get the right consistency.'[37] Dusty's own, frequently reciprocated identifications with black female music stars, notably Martha Reeves, is also reflected in many participants' accounts of pleasurable and 'liberating' identifications across ethnicities.[38]

Pleasurable identifications with inappropriate forms of feminine excess that defied the social sanctions on feminine artifice during the 1950s and 1960s were not restricted to the idealized representations of music or film stars. 'Elizabeth', in two extracts, describes the impact both stars and family members may be seen to have had on shaping women's desires to enact *disruptive and disreputable* forms of femininity:

Yes I did wear lipstick and it was very pale pink and I think I was influenced then by the Italian 'thing' in the 1950s, very much influenced by Sophia Loren and oh, of – yes, I remember the first time ... I painted my nails, John, my Dad went absolutely mental because ... it was only prostitutes in his idea, his head that painted their nails, and it was red, I painted them red and that was like, you know, and I just didn't understand why he was so angry ... One time he did say, 'You go out trying to look like bloody Sophia Loren', so I think I must have done a decent job on myself. [Laughter]

Oh yes, I mean it was wonderful for me to think of myself as having an exotic aunty, you know the woman who my mum was ashamed of, even though she looked up to her in lots of ways, she did disapprove of the fact that Josie – I don't think that she hennaed her hair, but it was always bright red so I think that she may have dyed it, and yes, Josie always had very long nails and they were always painted bright red ... and I just thought she was extremely glamorous and terribly daring, yes, and I did want to be such a person myself.

Subordinated discourses of pleasure in self-fashioning

In many accounts, working-class women's memories of performing femininity conform to Bourdieu's differentiation where 'Popular aesthetics are characterised by immediate emotional and sensual pleasure, bourgeois aesthetics are based upon formal and universalised criteria devoid of passion and pleasure.'[39]

'Sandy' remembered fashioning as frequently a collective pleasure, shared with other girls:

I do think that a lot of what we did when we were sort of mimicking people such as Dusty or Kathy Kirby ... it was quite a private thing for us girls you know, like we did, we used to have these little concert things and party things and we used to put these sheets over the washing line and things outside and sort of mimic singing you know and ... we used to leave the window in the living room open to play records so that the noise would come through, you know, just sort of sing along with it, ohhh, and we loved it.

She describes the pleasures of identification she enjoyed as a teenager in constructing highly 'fashioned' hairstyles, identical to her friend's, that were themselves based upon, and named after, female music stars: 'a Dusty, a Clodagh Rogers, a Cilla Black'.[40] Although *escapism* has also been pejoratively linked with the passive consumption (by women) of repressive texts and with narcissistic fantasy, Stacey recuperates this term as one expressive of women's pleasures in such complex identifications: 'Escapism is not merely an individuated process, but rather involves a submergence of self into a more collective identity which could be seen to have a gendered specificity.'[41] Visits to the salon, in that they offer both the 'renewing self-fashioning event' and the pleasures of the salon interior, are analogous to Stacey's interpretation of the routines of cinema-going: 'I would argue that what emerges from these repeated accounts is the importance of moving beyond the pleasures of the text to include pleasures of the ritualised event'.[42]

Although there has been a burgeoning of texts, exemplified by *Stargazing*, that describe the possible pleasures – identificatory, escapist and liberatory –

that spectator/star relationships allow for, more work is required to interpret the pleasurable processes at work in identificatory (fashioning) exchanges between strangers. Some examples offered by participants in this study include those where women have memories of fashioned spectacles by strangers, recalled as 'Elizabeth' does here, over a period of half a century and more:

> Well it would be when I was maybe, I would say about 8, 9, or 10, so that would be the 1950s, and we used to see this woman quite often either on the bus or walking through Sandyfield. She was always on her own and I would say she seemed quite old to me at that time, but I suppose looking back she was only maybe in her thirties, but she was very unusual because she had this hairstyle that I can only describe as being like an eighteenth century [laughter] aristocracy wig. It was – her hair was naturally grey – wasn't tinted but it was always piled up on her head in that pompadour shape and also it had – [laughter] she had two fat ringlets always to complete it, just like you saw in like fairy story books.

For 'Elizabeth', the voluminous curls of women in the fairy stories of her girlhood remain iconic, pleasurable memories, but are frequently interpreted as 'classed'.[43]

My argument is that feminism has failed to offer a context for thorough debate on femininity, frequently reflecting an image affiliated with mainstream Modernist, binary oppositional taste where the decorative, the vernacular and artifice are negatively positioned in opposition to a linear, unadorned, utopian 'style'. In a 1975 *Spare Rib* article entitled 'Tammy Wynette: Peroxide Politics and the Counter Revolution', the rhetorical invocation of the evils of feminine excess and feminized, popular, 'low' culture demonstrates the unconscious proximity of feminist positions to those of conservative patriarchy on this issue, at a critical time in second-wave British feminist politics: 'The passive faithfulness, the mindless ecstasy over trivia that characterises the country music heroine are all too familiar to any readers of women's magazines'.[44]

The construction of 'natural femaleness' construed as embodied by British feminist music collectives, promoted through *Spare Rib*, are in contrast to the more 'encrusted' forms of femininity performed by both black Motown/ Philadelphia and white country-music stars. Not only did *Spare Rib* fail to acknowledge the massive popularity of these 'other' musical and fashioned forms amongst British women in the 1970s, when the magazine was at its most influential in determining the 'tastes' of feminism, but an interview with the pioneering feminist band 'The Stepney Sisters' illustrates the limitations of their identifications with specific 'others'. Interviewer Marion Fudger asks Stepney Sister Ruthie, 'Have you ever thought to take your music into more working class situations?'

> Ruthie: Well, we've had discussions about playing in ordinary pubs where anyone will go, or trade unions where we would be playing to a more working class audience. Perhaps our gigs are rather exclusive in that we only play middle class places. One idea was that if we made a record we'd be able to reach a much wider audience, like women trapped in the home, listening to the radio.[45]

Despite her clearly expressed pleasures in self-fashioning, 'Sandy' describes her move into feminism as both liberatory[46] and paradoxically oppressive in terms of her problematic (re)construction of femininity across class divisions:

> I do remember when I sort of got onto the [lesbian feminist] scene with more middle-class women, I recall, I remember feeling guilty about my appearance . . . I think I was very affected by what I picked up around me, you know, feminist and class things at that time in my life and that how I looked was a compromise between what I wanted and liked and what pleased me and what I thought other people would, you know – how I would fit in.

Much early British and American second-wave feminist politics (and activism) sought to determine the margins of acceptable femininity despite the fact that, as Stern points out, specific forms of femininity *were* permissible to feminists, even within the first utopian texts that frame the popular conception of feminist modes of fashioning. 'Every would-be prohibitionist allows exceptions to his or her own rules and has a different notion of where to draw the line between a seemly degree of elegance and excess.'[47]

The fashioning space as a 'women's space'

Although the provision of 'women's spaces' is routinely understood as a project begun by second-wave feminists flowering from the early 1970s in Britain and diminishing coincident with the rise of Conservatism in Britain in the early 1980s, in some British urban contexts, including Glasgow, women enjoyed relatively few feminist-created or sanctioned spaces.[48] However, like most British towns and cities in the post-war period, Glasgow has been home to hundreds of spaces and places managed and frequented by women, where women's experiences and histories are central, where many of their needs are met and where support, comfort and pleasures are dispensed and consumed.[49]

In response to my first question addressed to 'Ellen', as she was having her hair done in the woman-run hairdressing salon 'Paris', she and hairdresser 'Jean' wove family histories of customer and hairdresser and articulate affectionate recognition of the place of the visit in 'everyday knowledge':[50]

AP:	How long have you been coming here?
Ellen:	Eh God, Jean – how long?
Jean:	What age is Ralph? Before that . . .
Ellen	Ralph was 21, no before that . . .
Jean:	Lisa's 21, before Lisa was born . . .
Ellen:	Yeah, before Lisa was born, so about . . .
Jean:	Well how long have I been down here?
	[General laughter in the salon]
Ellen:	I think it was when you come, Jean!
Jean:	Aye, aye . . .
Ellen:	When Mrs Morrow took over.
Jean:	Well before that.
Ellen:	That's right.
Jean:	So about – we've been here 22 years, so about 22 years. Even before that you came to this salon didn't you?
Ellen:	Yes aha.

Jean: Even before so –
AP: [laughing] So you must like it? You must do a good job! [To Jean]

'Sandy', who began her hairdressing career at thirteen, interpreted the salon as unequivocally 'women-friendly':

I got 50 pence, I got 50 pence for a Saturday morning, you know, but, I mean, I just loved it, I loved the environment. I felt so safe there. It was like, it was just all these regular customers in for shampoos and sets . . . but I just loved it. I mean I loved being in there and the – I felt very safe in there. It probably took me time to get safe, but really, you had to be trusted, you know, it was like, 'What's said here won't go any further' you know, so it probably took time to – for me to be initiated in and be allowed to listen in on the – all the gossip and stuff, but once you were there it was great, you were so trusted.

The salon was a place where she learnt skills that were to equip her for her later academic life and work as a counsellor:

I think, well, I do think that I learnt the basic counselling skills as a hairdresser for sure. Because it was women coming in and you know, building up trust relationships and them confiding in you. It was a place for confidences but it was a place for women to come together in a very feminist way . . . it was all about women going to the salon and calling their husbands, you know [laughter] and that type of thing, you know 'Oh the shit!' or 'Sods!' you know, that type of thing, but being very – but the strong codes of confidentiality and supporting each other and not realising they were supporting one another, you know, so yeah, I certainly learnt a lot about, sort of, how to be with – how to be supportive and how to be with other women from that and it was a lovely time in my life.

'Ettie', the daughter of an Irish Catholic, immigrant mother described her work in a fashionable salon in Glasgow in the early 1960s with its startlingly diverse clientele (ranging as it did from the prostitutes who worked at the Polaris base, to Scottish Television stars including The Beverley Sisters) as a place where her awareness of issues including the realities of marriage and childbirth, contraception, menstruation, abortion and homosexuality was raised in an intimate, supportive, woman-centred environment. Describing her customers and the physical demands of the job, 'Ettie' remembers:

We used to get prostitutes in the morning, maybe some housewives, grannies, babies, children, first hair-cuts; lunchtimes you got the buyers out of Daly's, Copeland's, Pettigrew's, C&A, all the shops on Sauchiehall Street, you used to get office workers as well coming in at lunchtime, in the afternoon again back to housewives, teachers, then after half three, four o'clock you were on your feet – if you are ever taking a picture you can take a picture of my varicose veins!

When asked about the relationship between hairdresser and customer 'Ettie' describes it as reciprocally 'confessional':

So you listened to their sharing, people shared with you things that you wouldn't even share with your . . . I remember one saying, 'I'm haemorrhaging.' I learnt an awful lot in hairdressing as well that kind of held me in good stead for the choices I made. One of them said, 'I'm haemorrhaging', another one she had a coil in, another one . . . I used to think, why are women going through this? Is this what being married and being a woman is about? I don't want any of this. I want to stay healthy you see. Och, we had laughs as well. It was like confession. Where would you offload that kind of stuff? . . .

They shared the deepest – if they miscarried, if they wanted a baby and couldn't have one, they shared the deepest – their affairs or dates or dates that went wrong or somebody giving them a 'dizzy' as they called it then, that's standing you up . . . they shared the deepest hurts, the joys as well . . . We were the counsellors – unpaid.

In order to add to feminist knowledge of femininity, media and women's pleasures in self-fashioning, a more rigorous analysis of issues of *cultural justice* is required in the hope that this will usefully illuminate the subordinated, but meaningful (feminist) practices of women who remain remote from cultural capital. It is clear that women's pleasurable identifications, where they impact on their constructions of themselves and their domestic spaces, can arise through identifications with other women as well as with 'stars' or other mediated representations, and that these may be empowering 'cross-identifications'; between women of different ethnicities, ages and classes. In the context of feminist debate concerning the demise of Women's Studies (and Women's Units) and the turn from Women's to Gender and Queer Studies in Britain, 'unofficial' or culturally subordinated women's spaces continue to function, albeit largely neglected by (academic) feminist and 'high culture'. Femininity can and does form an array of possible options for fashioning, as Stern has already argued. 'Feminist fashioning' is but one form within femininity that is nevertheless equally 'constructed.'[51] The recent vogue for 'queering' forms of feminine excess, and the ongoing denial of the possibility of feminist agency for women who choose this form of self-fashioning, contributes to the mainstream neglect of pleasures and uses of femininity by women. The accounts of research participants in this study indicate that such experiences cannot be reductively and theoretically discounted.

Whilst it is critical that the continual, misogynist lampooning of both femininity and 'feminist style' be challenged in both 'high' and 'low' culture, the complex social, historical and cultural currency of 'feminist fashioning' and its ambivalent links with Modernist 'taste' and antipathy to and consequent neglect of 'feminine excess' justifies a longer look in the mirror.

Notes

1 For example, J. Spence and P. Holland, eds, *Family Snaps: the Meanings of Domestic Photography*, London: Virago, 1991, V. Walkerdine, *Schoolgirl Fictions*, London: Verso, 1990, and A. Kuhn, *Family Secrets, Acts of Memory and Imagination*, London: Verso, 1995.

2 F. Haug et al., *Female Sexualisation, a Collective Work of Memory*, London: Verso, 1987, p.50.

3 Ibid.

4 Noliwe Rooks discussed this concept in a paper called 'Hair Dramas: Bodies and Style in African American Identity', delivered at the Style Conference, Bowling Green State University, Ohio, July 1997.

5 My memories of perceiving particular feminists expressing distaste at my own past fashioning made me concerned that other feminists might also read women who shared my history and taste (and who continued to fashion themselves 'to excess') as insignificant and unlikely to contribute to the development of feminist knowledge.

6 J. Ribbens and R. Edwards, eds, *Feminist Dilemmas in Qualitative Research: Public Knowledge and Private Lives*, London: Sage, 1998, p.12. An excellent example here would be Angela McRobbie's work from the mid-1970s with girls and their consumption of texts. See, for example, A. McRobbie, *Feminism and Youth Culture: From Jackie to Just Seventeen*, Basingstoke: Macmillan Press, 1991.

7 Katherine Stern, 'What is Femme? The Phenomenology of the Powder Room', *Women: a Cultural Review*, vol.8, no.2, 1997, p.184.

8 Stern illustrates mainstream subordination of femininity by citing an array of historical sources including, conclusively, Bloch's study of medieval misogyny. For Bloch femininity is in the detail, the decorative and ultimately all symbolic activity. See R. Howard Bloch, 'Medieval Misogyny', *Representations*, no.20, Autumn 1987, cited in Katherine Stern, ibid.

9 S. Brownmiller, *Femininity*, New York: Carcanet, 1986, my italics. Brownmiller's feminist interrogation of the investment of patriarchy in the construction of femininity is in a feminist best-selling canonical trajectory on this theme, preceded in 1970 by Germaine Greer's *The Female Eunuch* (MacGibbon & Kee, 1970) and followed in 1990 by Naomi Wolf's indictments of the 'atrocities women endure in the name of "beauty"' *The Beauty Myth* (Chatto & Windus, 1990).

10 S. Lee Bartky, *Femininity and Domination: Studies in the Phenomenology of Oppression*, London: Routledge, 1990, p.42.

11 Ibid., p.40.

12 Stern discusses Greer's *The Female Eunuch*, and Wolf's *The Beauty Myth* and argues that these authors and Marxist Feminists have concurred in their historical castigating of 'cosmetic acts'. The 'female eunuch' was, for Greer 'a castrated and emptied out doll-like product of a lifetime's indoctrination, an idiotic ritual' (Greer cited in Stern, 'What is Femme?').

13 Indeed her quest is to recuperate the status of *femme*, arguably the more consciously styled, 'queered' version of femininity.

14 Pamela Robertson subsequently published *Guilty Pleasures: Feminist Camp from Mae West to Madonna*, Durham, NC: Duke University Press, 1996. After Susan Sontag's influential essay 'Notes on Camp' (in *Against Interpretation and Other Essays*, New York: Dell, 1966), camp became associated almost exclusively with gay male culture. Although the meaning of camp is contested (see Robertson, *Guilty Pleasures*), David Bergman has articulated a commonplace understanding that it is a style of objects or the way objects are perceived that favours 'exaggeration', 'artifice' and 'extremity', in tension with popular culture, and that the person who recognizes camp or can camp is a person outside the cultural mainstream. See D. Bergman, ed., *Camp Grounds, Style and Homosexuality*, Amherst: University of Massachusetts Press, 1993, p.5.

15 The term 'excess' is of course relative. In this essay I hope to interrogate 'feminine excess' in at least two distinct ways: the pleasures or routines of cosmetic acts for women in the context of burgeoning anti-cosmetic rhetoric of feminism and the notion of excess as it has been articulated by both mainstream and feminist literature.

16 Robertson, *Guilty Pleasures*, p.18.

17 Stern, 'What is Femme?'

18 Haug et al., *Female Sexualisation*, p.79.

19 J. Stacey, *Stargazing: Hollywood Cinema and Female Spectatorship*, London: Routledge, 1994.

20 F. Kerner Furman, *Facing the Mirror: Older Women and Beauty Shop Culture*, New York: Routledge, 1997, p.168.

21 For example, K. Mercer, 'Black Hair/Style Politics', in *Welcome to the Jungle, New Positions in Black Cultural Studies*, London: Routledge, 1994. See also G Akuba, 'Coming to Voice Through Dreadlocks: Hair Signification and Women of African Descent', paper delivered at the Style conference, Bowling Green State University, Ohio, July 1997, and b hooks, *Black Looks: Race and Representation*, Boston: South End Press, 1997.

22 Mercer, 'Black Hair', p.101.

23 Ibid.

24 Second-wave feminist concerns to construct political identities within academia have problematized the normative (hierarchical, canonical) 'separateness' of theory from the lived experiences of 'othered' groups. Feminist academics, as Stanley points out, are in 'a hybrid condition', occupying a state of liminality that situates them as both 'insiders' *and* 'outsiders', as both 'them' and 'us' (L. Stanley, 'My Mother's Voice? On Being a Native in Academia', in L. Morley and V. Walsh, eds, *Feminist Academics, Creative Agents for Change*, London: Taylor and Francis, 1995, p.85). Some feminist writers have consequently constituted forms of 'intellectual auto/biography', bringing neglected knowledges into the realms of academia. The researcher's aims, methodology and relationship with the 'researched' have been critically interrogated by many feminist writers and this work is ongoing. For an indication of the diverse issues confronted and insights gained by researchers adopting such methods, see, for example, Ribbens and Edwards, eds, *Feminist Dilemmas*.

25 These are Stacey's terms for the distinct ways that women have remembered stars, as nostalgic, remote, idealized 'frozen' images of feminine perfection and/or as an intimate, empowering and enduring representation of our past selves.

26 These texts included the complete run of *Spare Rib*, the (*Manchester*) *Guardian*'s 'Women's Page' (from 1959) and British music and film annuals for girls (1959–75).

27 All the participants quoted in this article do identify or have identified themselves as working-class, and are white. All names are pseudonyms; most were chosen by the participants themselves at the end of the interview. In my doctoral thesis, I include accounts from black and ethnic-minority women and white women's iconic and narrative memories of black and ethnic-minority women and discuss issues concerning fashioning, femininity and ethnicity.

28 J. Stacey, *Stargazing*, p.132.

29 Whilst recognizing the vast, exploitative appropriation of black and ethnic-minority culture/s by whites, the prevalence of pleasurably remembered identifications and intimacies between femininities, between white, black and ethnic minority research participants that cross ethnic boundaries are difficult to read reductively as 'white use of "other" ethnic forms of fashioning equals appropriation', 'black/ethnic-minority uses and identifications with "white" forms equals false consciousness due to racist oppression', for the reasons that Kobena Mercer has described in 'Black Hair'.

30 R. Morgan, ed., *Sisterhood is Powerful: an Anthology of Writings from the Women's Liberation Movement*, New York: Vintage Books, 1970.

31 The 'No More Miss America Pageant' which, significantly, had as its target the notion of the fashioned woman as the embodiment of patriarchal subjugation.

32 This phrase is associated with the style of making up eyes employed by Dusty Springfield in her early years of fame and is extended to describe such encrusted dark modelling of the eyes. See L. O'Brien, *Dusty, a Biography of Dusty Springfield*, London: Sidgwick and Jackson, 1999.

33 As the video record of this event recently uncovered by Laura Cottingham illustrates; see L. Cottingham, *Not For Sale, Feminism and Art in the USA During the 1970's*, Hawkeye Productions, 1999.

34 A chapter of my doctoral thesis is devoted to the constructions of forms of femininity in the 1960s in Britain in relation to the star Dusty Springfield. Dusty is remembered iconically in a mass of participants' memories that link her to notions of feminine excess. I discuss the intimacies of femininity between Dusty and her fans and Dusty the fan of female stars of Motown, Blues and Hollywood.

35 O'Brien, *Dusty*, p.80.

36 *Scotland on Sunday*, 15 February 1998.

37 *Melody Maker*, 'Pop Think In', November, 1965.

38 For a typical Martha Reeves take on Dusty and her role as Motown's champion in Britain see O'Brien, *Dusty*, pp.62–3.

39 P. Bourdieu, *Distinction: a Social Critique of the Judgement of Taste*, London: Routledge, 1979.

40 Lucy O'Brien notes that in the 1960s Dusty named her wigs after stars including Sandie Shaw and Lulu.

41 Stacey, *Stargazing*, p.109.

42 Ibid., p.94.

43 Crudely summarizing 'Elizabeth''s interpretation for brevity here, the thicker and longer the hair, the better a woman's chances and status in the world. 'Elizabeth' remembered the hair of Grammar School girls, ballerinas and female art students as having these characteristics. Thick, unruly, simply fashioned hair of this type was not unlike my own iconic memories of 'what (white) feminists looked like', derived from the photos of authors on the fly covers of women's and feminist press books (of Kate Millett, Germaine Greer, Andrea Dworkin) and, later, in the pages of *Spare Rib*.

44 S. Tyrell, 'Tammy Wynette: Peroxide Politics and the Counter Revolution', *Spare Rib*, no.42, Dec. 1975, pp.44–6.

45 Stepney Sisters interviewed by Marion Fudger, *Spare Rib*, May 1976, pp.6–8.

46 The freedom 'to make choices', the collective pleasures of identification on marches and the permission to articulate her lesbian sexuality.

47 Stern, 'What is Femme?', p.191.

48 As part of the second-wave feminist project to create the space for women to address their oppression and resist patriarchy, 'women's spaces' proliferated in many European and American cities. Symbolic, early projects such as Womanhouse, an art project created by female students at CalArts, Los Angeles in 1971 under the supervision of Judy Chicago and Miriam Shapiro, were followed later in the decade in Britain by Women's Groups and Centres and single-issue, campaigning and 'crisis' organizations such as Women's Aid, Wages for Housework and Rape Crisis, run on feminist principles. For an excellent survey of Women's Liberation activities see E. Setch, 'The Women's Liberation Movement in Britain, 1969–79: Organisation, Creativity and Debate', unpublished PhD thesis, University of London, Royal Holloway College, 2000.

49 A feminist Women's Centre, broadly following the template of collective women's organizations established in Britain in the late 1970s ran in Glasgow, without revenue funding, until the late 1980s. The first Women's Unit in Glasgow was not established until 1990 (and is now closed). Glasgow Women's Library, founded in 1991, remains the sole resource of its kind in Scotland.

50 J. Ribbens and R. Edwards interpret 'Everyday Knowledge' as the epistemological base of women's lives; see *Feminist Dilemmas*, p.12.

51 Stern argues that masculinity is but another; see 'What is Femme?' p.193.

Patricia Holland

Spectacular Values: The Pleasure of the Text and the 'Contamination' of Current Affairs Television

The pleasure of the text: . . . it can say 'never apologise, never explain.' It never denies anything: 'I shall look away, that will henceforth be my sole negation.'[1]

Current affairs and television journalism

At first sight current affairs television may seem like unpromising ground for a discussion of the visual. As a specific television genre, current affairs centres on the journalistic report, and is notable for being led by the spoken word and the flow of argument and information. In a current affairs programme, such as *Panorama* or *Dispatches*, the sequence of images usually matches the flow of a narrating voice on the soundtrack, and may make little sense if seen alone. Depiction takes second place to explanation.[2]

From the early days of television, doubts and worries have been expressed about the visual in relation to journalist-based programmes. The very title of the BBC department which developed the genre we know as 'current affairs' in the 1950s appeared to deny any visual content; it was known as 'Talks', following its predecessor on radio. Over the history of television journalism, the need to come to terms with the visual has given rise to suspicion and fears as well as an excitement about new opportunities. There has been a recurring sense that, if the visual is allowed to predominate, many of the core values of journalism may be lost or, at the very least, need special protection. My aim in this paper is to explore some of those concerns, and to argue that:

a) such doubts and worries are, indeed, justified; the power of the image may well overwhelm the explanatory content in a variety of different ways, and this has special consequences for the journalism of the current affairs genre, *and*
b) nevertheless, it is precisely the complex interplay between the flow of images – of varying power and intensity – and the construction of verbal sense, which gives television journalism its particular strengths.

Recent commentary on current affairs programmes has chiefly dwelt on their expository content. Debates in academia and the press have focused on issues such as journalistic integrity, breadth of coverage, bias and censorship.[3] Truth, authenticity and responsibility have been asserted as central journalistic values, together with the production of forms of public knowledge which will serve an informed democracy.[4] An alternative approach has brought the visual to the forefront by drawing attention to the continuous flow of imagery in the television medium. This tradition of analysis has given an account of a postmodern medium in which truth and authenticity are themselves fictions, and news and current affairs are simply variations in the unstoppable flow of images, all with similar value, none more 'true' than the others. [5]

I want to take something from both these traditions. In the first place I want to insist that truth and authenticity are indeed central to the journalistic project, especially in the public-service framework of British television. Current affairs remains a mainstream, rationalist genre. But I want to place my insistence in the context of the particularly televisual ways in which those values of truth and authenticity are mediated, recognizing that the visual is often primary. I shall also be bearing in mind a tradition in the theory of art which has sought to tease out the relationship between words and images with their radically different ways of creating meaning.[6]

Rather than taking the more familiar perspective of the viewer, or 'reader' of the television text – who, in Fiske and Hartley's account, may select, discard or recombine images from the television flow at will – I will be focusing on the perspective of those who have *made* current affairs programmes or who have in some way or other been responsible for them. In other words I will be considering the *production* of imagery, rather than speculating about its *consumption*. I will explore the debates about what is appropriate for the current affairs genre from the point of view of those who must put their convictions into practice. When making a serious programme, an important part of their concern has been to resist those serendipitous readings described by Fiske and Hartley.

Television current affairs is an unstable genre which has changed considerably over its history. No simple definition is appropriate, as the genre has been constantly reshaped in a tension between the need to impart information and the need to appeal to an audience. At some points producers have preferred lighter magazine-style items, at others they have insisted on greater journalistic 'seriousness' and length. Sometimes the figure of a known and charismatic journalist has had great importance, at other times information has been imparted by an unnamed commentator. Sometimes studio debates and interviews have predominated, at other times programmes have come closer to the documentary style. In tracing the ways in which the visual has seemed to be dangerous or undermining, my approach will be to take into account the constantly changing parameters of the genre. This means looking at how its practitioners have marked it off from other television genres such as news and documentary, and how its boundaries have been policed. As W. J. T. Mitchell points out in relation to art practice, 'Genres are not technical definitions but acts of exclusion and appropriation which tend to reify some significant other.'[7] Practitioners operate with the pragmatics of daily necessity and pressure; they rarely articulate clear definitions. But we can trace a history of debates over what is appropriate to a journalism-based genre, and what properly belongs to other types of programme, and hence should be excluded. Concerns over the visual – as a possible 'other' to journalistic practices – have been central to the ways in which current affairs has developed on UK television, and hence to its very definition.

Throughout the half century of its existence – dating from the mid-1950s with the establishment of *Panorama* on the BBC and *This Week* on ITV – doubts about the visual and the spectacular have been part of the discourse around the current affairs genre. Sometimes they have taken the form of a half-articulated undertow, sometimes they have surfaced in a full-blown dispute. In identifying what should be excluded from the genre, concern has been expressed over both popular-entertainment values and highbrow aesthetic ones. Current affairs has developed into a form that is less austere, more explanatory and more flexible than news, but, unlike documentary, it has not, on the whole, been thought suitable for an expression of the film-makers' art. At the other pole there has been a strongly argued need to defend it against a collapse into 'infotainment'.[8] Contemporary programme styles which deal with the news agenda but diverge from the traditional current affairs format in various ways (examples include *Tonight with Trevor Macdonald* (ITV 1999–) and *MacIntyre Undercover* (BBC 1999)) have been criticized for 'dumbing down' and for not 'really' being current affairs programmes. [9] At various points this caution about the inappropriate has centred on a suspicion of the visual – since both the aesthetic and the entertaining tend towards visual expression. This tendency has increased as the introduction of digital technologies brings a much greater range to televisual forms.[10] Journalism has not been a televisual space in which spectacular values are expected, but it has been an arena in which they have been hotly contested.

This article is a speculative spin-off from a wider project on the history of the ITV current affairs programme *This Week* (1956-92).[11] I want to take this opportunity to explore ideas which might not be expected to have a place in a conventional television history, and yet which seem to be central to it. It derives from nagging worries about the nature of current affairs' claims to seriousness and importance, and about the qualities which have been held to confirm or to undermine that seriousness and importance. One starting point is Jacques Derrida's insight that those very qualities that seem marginal and irrelevant to the topic in hand are those which, on closer inspection, will be found at its centre. As in Derrida's account of Plato's Pharmakon, those poisonous elements that appear to endanger the stability of factual programmes are also their cure, for they are the very elements which convey the televisual message most powerfully.[12] Another inspiration comes from feminist work which focuses on aspects previously thought to be marginal, and which stresses the need to read into the margins and between the lines.[13]

Several writers have documented an antipathy to the visual amongst intellectuals. W. J. T. Mitchell begins his influential *Iconology* – on the relationship between image and text in the visual arts – by admitting that 'a book which began with the intention of producing a valid theory of images became a book about the *fear* of images'.[14] A similar routine antipathy can be detected in the everyday language of television professionals, where visual elements may be disparagingly referred to as 'talking heads' or 'moving wallpaper'. Nicholas Mirzoeff begins his review of contemporary visual culture by pointing out that the antipathy of intellectuals has been a 'displaced hostility to those who participate in and enjoy mass culture'.[15] In the case of television current affairs, antipathies and fears have indeed linked into a wide network of ideas and attitudes which appear to threaten the integrity of the genre – amongst them trivialization, 'tabloidization', feminization and unreliability. Such fears have effected changes in policy and shifts in the ways in which programmes have been produced and are expected to be received.

I will first trace some of those shifts in policy, and will then look more closely at the specific nature of the visual in the current affairs genre. My conclusion will be that, despite a long history of suspicions – or, perhaps, in a strange way borne up by those suspicions – the creative energy of television journalism lies precisely in the tension it brings into play between the pressures of the visual and the imperatives of the verbal. I will suggest that this interplay is a crucial factor when thinking about the expression of truth and authenticity which is central to the journalistic project.

A politics of the visual

News and current affairs are politically sensitive genres. In my consideration of a politics of the visual, I will be drawing attention to politics in its mundane historical sense, by looking at shifts in policy chiefly in the early years from the 1950s and into the 1970s. The context is a wider consideration of the politics of journalism, since news and current affairs on British television are committed to neutrality and factual accuracy, which, as Barrie Gunter points out, also entails a 'moral disposition towards reporting'.[16] In the early days of BBC television news, newsreaders were not seen in vision at all. When they did become visible, partly to compete with the new independent channel which was launched in 1955, the 'visual manner' of the newsreader became an issue. 'If a newsreader were seen while giving the news, any change in his [sic] visual manner, a smile or a lift of an eyebrow might, however little this was intended, be interpreted as comment', wrote Grace Wyndham Goldie, Assistant Head of 'Talks' at the time.[17]

Unlike the BBC, Independent Television of the 1950s was unashamedly populist and all about 'visual manner'. However, by the late 1960s, the companies that made up the ITV network had been criticized by their regulatory body, the Independent Television Authority, for what the Authority described as a 'retreat from culture'.[18] Produced by Associated–Rediffusion, the London weekday station, the early *This Week* programmes had been light and entertaining, mixing short and often irreverent items on politics and current affairs with topics such as pets, fashion and cinema. 'Glamour' was one of the qualities sought by its first editor, Caryl Doncaster.[19] In 1968 the regulator introduced a system of 'mandated' slots for 'serious' programmes. This meant that the current affairs programmes *World in Action* (from Granada) and *This Week* (now from Thames Television) must be broadcast throughout the ITV network at peak viewing times. The reinstatement of 'seriousness' and 'culture' secured the space for the development of classic television journalism during the 1970s. In the case of *This Week* (unlike *World in Action*), the journalist became a central figure.

This Week had already moved to longer, single-topic programmes, under the influence of editors including Peter Morley and Jeremy Isaacs. Jeremy Isaacs in particular has said that he wanted to exploit the potential of the television medium to the fullest extent. That included getting out of the studio – which he saw as 'cold, unfeeling and alienating' – and using film to 'show how people really lived' and to achieve a 'marriage of image and sound'.[20] It was a common feeling at the time that journalists trained in the print medium needed to become more visually literate and learn how to make filmic comments on matters of social concern.

However, in an influential series of articles in *The Times* in 1975, John Birt – at that time Head of Current Affairs at London Weekend Television – together with economics journalist Peter Jay, argued that the pendulum had swung too far in the other direction. They attacked current affairs programmes for a 'bias against understanding'. The phrase was to become infamous, as was their recommended alternative, the 'mission to explain'. Less often remembered than the criticisms themselves are the reasons given by the authors. The 'bias against understanding' was a consequence of a bastard genre, born of an 'unhappy marriage between newspapers and film'. For Birt and Jay it was the film ethos that was to blame, 'contaminating ... not only the choice and treatment of the stories, but also those members of the team on whom the directors rely for their journalistic input – the researchers and reporters'.[21] In their view the verbal had priority over the visual; scripts should be written first and then the pictures should be gathered to illustrate the preordained words.

John Birt was later in a position to impose his preferred style on BBC journalism. When he joined the Corporation in 1987 as Deputy Director General he brought news and current affairs together into one department which would continue to put words before pictures. Back in the mid-70s he and Peter Jay argued that filmic, aesthetic values ran counter to the journalistic drive for authenticity and truth. They described current affairs 'films' as 'polished and ambitious' in which 'film imperatives override journalistic concepts' and where 'the aim is to make a film not to produce a report'. The feared 'contamination' was not from popular-entertainment cinema, but from the prestigious – and visually interesting – field of documentary which was admired by up-and-coming programme directors at the expense of explanatory content.

At the end of the 1970s, after a series of acrimonious disputes around controversial programmes, *This Week* was taken off the air. In the words of Mike Townson, who was brought in to edit the replacement programme *TV Eye*, the journalists had had too much power. Townson strengthened the power of the directors, who were promoted to producers, and said that this meant there were now two journalists – a visual one and a verbal one.[22] He argued that current affairs should be more pleasurable. 'Why is so much current affairs approached as if the nation is being summoned to prayer?', he later wrote in *The Listener*.[23] Townson was criticized for his 'populism' and was described as 'grafting tabloid style and values on to broadsheet journalism'.[24] In these examples, policy-makers had linked the visual to:

a) the biased, the unstable and unreliable;
b) the popular;
c) the pleasurable and emotive.[25]

The central values of journalism remain those of truth and authenticity. From the point of view of some journalists and producers, the audience's apparent craving for visual pleasure seems to pull against those vital intentions – whether, in the criticism made by Birt and Jay, the visuals are of high aesthetic quality, or, as with those who criticized Mike Townson, the increased stress on the visual was thought to be more populist.[26] The visual may be distracting in itself. When it becomes associated with that destabilizing cluster of qualities – the unreliable, the biased, the emotive and the pleasurable – it may be even more so. Concerns focus partly on the *type* of spectacle which is characteristic of current affairs programmes, and partly on the ability of the visual to free the message of a programme from the rigours of verbal explanation. For the current affairs genre this can seem like 'contamination', an invasion of values which belong in other parts of the media, a form of pollution.[27]

In their 1975 article, Birt and Jay went on to criticize the tendency of current affairs to focus on the emotive areas of crisis, outrage and disaster. 'A constant emphasis is placed on society's sores by television feature journalists with little or no attempt to seek the root causes or discuss the ways by which the sore may be removed'.[28]

I will look at one striking example of a programme made in 1973, which they would certainly have seen. The spectacular imagery of *This Week*'s 'The Unknown Famine' deals in the emotions of shock, revulsion, pity and outrage.

The Unknown Famine

Fronted by a young Jonathan Dimbleby, 'The Unknown Famine' (Tx 18 October 1973) opened with one of the most memorable images in current affairs television. The shot lasts for 2 minutes 25 seconds, and follows an introduction in which Dimbleby links the famine in Ethiopia with a famine in the Sahel region of Northern Africa on which he had reported in an earlier programme. The shot moves along a queue of people squatting on both sides of a cracked and dusty track. Using a wide angle that includes both sides of the track, the camera takes the viewer between the rows, each of them up to three or four deep. The waiting people are sparsely dressed in rags which have become the same light brown colour as the surrounding dust. Someone pulls a baby out of the way of the camera; someone flicks away a fly, but apart from that they are eerily silent and still. Whenever the queue seems about to end, another cluster of patient, painfully thin people comes into view and the shot moves inexorably on. The cameraman, Ray Seiman, had simply walked between the long lines of exhausted men, women and children, his camera held low.

The commentary which accompanies the shot is sparse. There are no words for fifteen seconds – a long time in television terms. The first sentences – 'This is a queue for food. These people are Ethiopian peasants. Once they had cattle, land and houses. They sold them all to buy food. Now they have only their rags. They're destitute' – are followed by another pause. This is how the rest of the commentary goes:

Here they receive two meals a day. The food: two handfuls of boiled wheat in the morning and a piece of bread in the afternoon. It keeps them from death, no more.

Last year these people were strong, fit and active. They had known hardship, of course. They had suffered several years of drought. But a year ago, when the rains failed utterly, their crops failed too. This spring the rains failed again. By April this year they were starving. They dragged themselves exhausted into the towns, many of them dying on the way. They have been like this now, surviving, not living, for six months.

[6 secs pause]

There has not been enough food for the last six months. In Wollo alone at least 60 thousand and possibly more than 100 thousand have died from the famine.

[10 seconds silence]

The shot dissolves to the next.

The words offer a re-contexting of the image. The visual dynamism of the moving shot – which multiplies and depersonalizes tragic bodies, one after the other – is matched by another, verbal dynamic which directs our attention to the invisible history of the people we are shown. We are invited to revise our initial impression, to see an image of a process rather than of a state. These people were 'strong, fit and active', but circumstances have brought them to this state. They are not examples of timeless suffering.

But powerful imagery takes on a life of its own. The programme-makers must decide what words to use and how to match the words to the shot. However carefully this is done, several things may happen. First, when the completed film is shown the impression of the visuals may overwhelm that of the words. The viewers may forget that they are also listeners and ignore what is being said. Secondly, at a purely material level, the image may easily be separated from its commentary. The shot may be reused in other films and in many different contexts, as this shot and others from 'The Unknown Famine' have been many times. At the time of its first showing stills from the film appeared in most national newspapers, together with their own accompanying text. Thirdly, the image will almost certainly remind viewers of and refer them to similar images with which they are familiar, and which help them to interpret this one. Finally, as the image gains currency, viewers and critics may specifically reject any verbal information as distracting and even argue that it spoils the emotional impact. If the image of a starving child outrages, the sense of outrage may itself be relished. Viewers may take pleasure in being stirred to action and not be prepared to debate whether that action is appropriate or not. They may not want their emotion to be diluted by qualifications, explanations or doubts. Newspaper coverage of 'The Unknown Famine' demonstrated something of this response. Headlines following the showing of the programme demanded 'Let's *do* something!'

Jonathan Dimbleby has written, spoken and been interviewed about this programme and its sequels, many times.[29] He has frequently pointed out that although he knew of the ongoing political situation in Ethiopia, which helped to turn the effects of the drought into a disastrous famine, he deliberately did not refer to it in the programme, as this would have distracted from the main message about the desperate situation in which the people shown in the film found themselves. The writer Alex de Waal has argued that a closer knowledge of the situation would have shown that the rush to give aid was counter-productive.[30]

The imagery of 'The Unknown Famine' appeared at a time when a body of images of famine and destitution in the Third World, and particularly in Africa, was gaining currency, much of it through advertising campaigns by the aid agencies.[31] 'The Unknown Famine' chimed in with charity advertisements produced by Oxfam and Save the Children, and with documentary photographs by a number of concerned photo-journalists which were appearing in the recently launched Sunday newspapers' colour supplements. Even though the famine in Ethiopia was (more or less) unknown in the West, the intertextual references and a framework for making sense of the image were already being set.[32] A resonant image which centred on starving children, desperate mothers and people who were nothing more than bags of skin and bones in an arid rural landscape was already echoing back and forth throughout the media. But, at the same time, a critique mounted by photographers and critics, as well as by many within the aid agencies themselves, was gaining in influence. They argued that the cumulative effects of this image served to depoliticize the information gained and created the impression of an Africa filled only with starving and incompetent people with no history or culture. By the end of the 1980s the tide had turned. The General Assembly of European NGOs adopted a code of conduct on images and messages. In Britain Save the Children, amongst others, produced detailed guidelines for journalists and photographers arguing that 'the dignity of the people with whom Save the Children works should be preserved ... portraying poverty and dependence as the norm is not accurate ... [they] risk "exploitation by camera" if their identity or opinions are excluded in the promotion of development issues'.[33]

Sequences from Dimbleby's film were extensively used in educational programmes to refocus interest on development issues, as well as in programmes which dealt with the history of Ethiopia and of current affairs journalism.[34] For example, in 'An Ethiopian Journey' (LWT 1998), Jonathan Dimbleby retraced his steps and recounted his long association with the country following 'The Unknown Famine'. The opening shot was shown once more – no longer as a report, but as an image that had gained iconic status. This time its length was interspersed with newspaper headlines and it was matched with a commentary track which described the reactions of the time.

But UK television was not the only context within which the material shot for 'The Unknown Famine' was used. The film caused a deep sense of shock within Ethiopia itself, since the government had effectively covered up the seriousness of the situation. The terrible images from the film were re-cut and shown on local television, interspersed with shots of extravagance and ostentation amongst the rich and powerful, including a wedding cake flown in from London at the cost of £1,250.[35] The image of starvation, used in this very different context, became a political weapon and was instrumental in bringing down the Emperor Haile Selassie.

Aspects of the visual

Spectacular imagery similar to that which characterized 'The Unknown Famine' may be sought by current affairs producers as it builds audiences and brings notoriety and prestige. At the same time, as I have shown, excessively powerful spectacle has been seen as fraught with problems. Although the spectacular is, by definition, the most striking, the most pleasurable and, for that reason, possibly the most threatening aspect of the visual in current affairs television, I first want to discuss an equally interesting aspect, which I shall call 'the routine'. A distinction between 'spectacular' and 'routine' imagery is, once again, a pragmatic one, defined by its usage rather than by any qualities intrinsic to the imagery itself. In the continuous flow of television pictures, all have potentially spectacular qualities, yet, in order to build communicative sense, some must be prioritized over others. The images which I shall describe as 'routine' are those in which the spectacular potential has been repressed. However, a sense of what imagery should be restrained and where the spectacular potential may be exploited is constantly changing. The greater familiarity of shocking imagery at the present day is part of that change.

Spectacular moments only have impact against a background of routine imagery. Yet the body of imagery which makes up the characteristic, unobtrusive daily flow which is specific to television brings its own qualities and creates its own dilemmas. It needs to be studied in its own right, and questions need to be asked about the nature of the routine and why these images, in particular, have been forbidden their spectacular potential. Here I shall look at one example of a 'routine' image – the image of the journalist.

The routine

Television is about people and one of television's most important routine images is the animated human face – whether it appears in drama, talk shows or the news. An increasing number of those who appear on television have the right to face the camera directly, and hence to address the audience directly. However, the essential role of linking and sequencing the flow of television through a direct address to the audience is played by the presenter.[36] Whether newsreader, chat-show host, celebrity or journalist, the presenter mediates between the audience and the huge cast of characters who pass across our television screens. Presenters are professionals who speak to the audience with authority. They thereby carry a certain responsibility.[37]

In a journalism-based programme, the reporter bears the visible weight of the report. The reporter witnesses on the audience's behalf and relays the audience's gaze. Reporters must be seen at the site of the disaster – the earthquake or the plane crash – or wherever the news agenda directs our attention. The body of the reporter must be put at risk and must be seen to be at risk. They must experience the smells and infection of the famine-stricken land and the dangers of the war zone. They must be seen going into Chernobyl (as Richard Lindley did in *This Week*, 18 and 25 April 1991) or being present in the Gdansk shipyard uprising (Julian Manyon in *TV Eye*, 4 September 1980). They must engage in conversation with whomsoever figures on the news agenda –

whether they be people living in poverty, government ministers, health service professionals, law enforcement agents, those suffering from AIDs, criminals or even terrorists. While engaging in these bodily experiences, the journalists must also be performers, and their self-presentation becomes an issue. Journalists may choose to be self-effacing or may develop a celebrity persona, in which case their image may well become a form of spectacle. In either case, it should not be forgotten that the real flesh and blood journalist is never the same as the *image* of the journalist that appears on the screen.[38]

For the audience the current affairs spectacle remains a two-dimensional image, but for the reporter, who must be physically present, it is a complex participatory experience. Jonathan Dimbleby has recalled his feelings when faced with the scenes of the 1972 famine – and admits to contradictory reactions, including pride and excitement because he was aware, at the time, of the huge impact the programme would make.[39] Television journalists, together with the programme-making team, must weigh up the appropriateness of their bodily visibility and their visible reactions to what they are experiencing. Journalists may be horrified by a scene or may treat it with professional detachment, but whatever their personal attitude, their reactions must inevitably be filtered when they reach the screen. Part of a programme-maker's skill is to mediate that original experience so that it will seem convincing when it is wrenched from its physicality and placed within the context of the television flow. Programme-makers must bear in mind television's tendency to deconstruct its own narratives; on the commercial channels, the worst disaster story will be surrounded by advertisements, and on all channels a report will always be preceded and followed by other programmes in a quite different mood. In addition, large numbers of viewers will be moving between channels while a programme is on the air. Within such a context, however desperate the situation reported on, an excessive reaction from journalists may simply not ring true. The audience may interpret it as celebrity figures drawing attention to themselves. For these reasons, the tendency is to expect that the spectacular aspects of the image of the journalist must be repressed.

In current affairs programmes, those who write and speak the words provide a verbal support for the moments of spectacle. They act as moderators and mediators. This puts limits on the degree of spectacular visibility they themselves are allowed. Birt and Jay argued that reporters, too, could be 'contaminated' by the 'film ethos'.[40] When *This Week* was taken off the air at the end of the 1970s, one reason given was that the journalists had become too prominent and too personal, following their own agenda. At that time the consensus was that the image of the journalist, to maintain a 'moral disposition towards reporting', should remain within the routine.

The spectacular

In contrast to the self-effacing, routine image of the journalist, the spectacular seeks out self-conscious, ostentatious display. It draws attention to itself for its own sake. The spectacular has been seen as both a radical and a conservative force. It has been described as subverting the blind onward drive of a narrative by introducing hesitations and space for reflection and speculation. At the same time it has been seen as apolitical and hedonistic, feeding off and re-inforcing divisions such as those of gender and ethnicity.[41] Above all it is about pleasure and affirmation, taking little account of value or morality. Like Barthes' 'pleasure of the text' it says 'never explain, never deny'.[42] A reluctance to detract from the power of the spectacle is also a desire to protect the pleasure of the visual – however perverse that pleasure may be. The spectacle of horror and disgust is a major component of entertainment cinema. The horror and disgust aroused by images of the real world are equally not without their pleasurable component – hence the embarrassment over pleasures which should be kept secret, and the guilt over the production of a spectacle which may be seen as illegitimate. The spectacular is easy to appreciate and popular, yet it may be distracting, inauthentic, amoral.[43]

The spectacular seems the very antithesis of the current affairs ethos, since every element of a current affairs programme must take into account the critical, rational role which characterizes the genre. In current affairs, spectacular elements are intended to reinforce or illustrate the argument. The aim is to confirm truth and authenticity: 'Although one can read about problems, can know about problems, when they're before your eyes in the way that that film so successfully did, then that does give you an added spur, an added commitment. You see very vividly just how appalling it is'.[44]

Spectacular images supply conviction and evidence, but they always offer something else as well, opening up unpredictable vistas. Their excessive emotional power makes them difficult to control and place. A spectacular presentation increases the gap between the viewer and the viewed. It looks for the greatest divergence from the ordinary.[45] Its instability has been seen as needing mediation and anchorage from words.[46] For these reasons, television journalism has traditionally rejected the spectacular and deliberately sought a lower-key range of imagery. However, in recent years the spectacular has become more acceptable and the shocking more familiar.

Recent changes

Recent developments within the current affairs genre have brought a challenge to the accepted balance between the routine image of the journalist and the potentially spectacular nature of the material reported on. There has been a hybridization of genres, and fewer programme-makers seem concerned about potential 'contamination'. New developments have included series in which professional journalists have been encouraged to express opinions and emotions (e.g. *Frontline*, C4 1993); the involvement of journalists in the events they are reporting on (e.g. *MacIntyre Undercover*, BBC 1999); the use of 'ordinary people' in a journalistic role (e.g. *Private Investigations*, BBC1 1994; *Free for All: Speak Out*, C4 1994); and the use of celebrities as journalists (*Children in Need*, BBC). In all of these cases something of the authority of a dispassionate journalistic observer is sacrificed. The relationship between words and images changes when the journalist becomes part of the spectacle.[47]

Spectacular topics and spectacular styles

A particular set of spectacular topics has characterized current affairs programmes, many of them criticized by Birt and Jay in 1975 as 'a constant emphasis ... on society's sores'. They include:

Poverty – with its long tradition of aesthetic appeal,
Horror – the spectacle of pain and victimization, showing broken or wasted bodies,
War – the spectacle of action and excessive violence,
Location – the image of distant places, strange and unexpected events, exotic peoples, landscapes, markets. A range of images which must today be read in a postcolonial context,
The hidden and the forbidden – investigatory journalism seeks to reveal actions that have been kept secret, often using hidden cameras or confrontational styles; or those which have been seen as private or morally dubious – such as abortion.

There has been little doubt that, whatever the dilemmas they give rise to, such topics are at the heart of the current affairs enterprise. A greater source of dispute has been the ways in which such topics, and indeed others, should be presented. In this discussion it will be useful to distinguish the choice of spectacular topics from the use of spectacular styles. Such a distinction can point to styles of programme-making in which the techniques draw attention to themselves, whatever the content of the programme, adding their own quota of visual pleasure. Although there are many eye-catching filmic techniques which have long been an integral part of any programme-maker's repertoire – stylish reconstructions, virtuoso camerawork (such as the long take which opens 'The Unknown Famine'), the use of impressionistic editing – the recent reassertion of the visual has partly been due to the multitude of new, spectacular styles that have become available through digital technology. Programmes now have the option to be based in graphic as much as in photographic techniques, using digitally constructed sequences, which may be multi-dimensional and fragmented, using colour, texture, montage and superimposition. Interestingly, the written word, in the form of decorative text or captions, is now a regular component of the visual image.[48]

Nevertheless, in 'mainstream' current affairs, the use of spectacular styles has been treated with caution. When considering spectacular topics, it has been the moral ambivalence of the pleasure that has given rise to concern. When considering spectacular styles of presentation, the criticisms have centred on 'tabloidization' and populism.

Conclusion

In the balance between restraint and display, there is a flow of interrelated discourses and codes which stand in differing relations to the historical world which is the subject of current affairs programming. Verbal language has a number of recognizable modalities. It can make statements, which may or may not be true; it can weave fictions; it can reflect fantasies. Verbal content may strive for precision – which involves being tentative in its conclusions, offering many qualifications, and being threaded through with expressions of possibility and doubt – or it may assert with a conviction which risks being over-simple or misleading. In contrast with the verbal content, the photographic image is always referential and its communication less subject to rational distancing.[49] Hence words may sometimes be challenged by the visuals, sometimes reinforced by them. Verbal content may be exceeded or destabilized by the heightened emotionality and instability of the imagery, while the visual may be moderated and harnessed by the words. My argument is that, whatever the verbal style, the whole presentation of a television programme is enriched by a complex interplay between word and image. The struggle to keep the imagery in balance with verbal explanation and argument is where the power and excitement of news-based factual programming lies. Negotiations over shifting meanings, and detailed engagement with those visual and verbal elements that make truth-telling possible at all, enable the production of rich and productive multiple truths.

Many writers have found value in concepts such as transgression and resistance, and have sought out the marginal, the oppositional and the counter-hegemonic. But television journalism is a mainstream rationalist genre. I want to find value in its central tenets of authority and authenticity, but also to argue that these can only be sustained if those apparently marginal qualities which cluster around the visual – including its guilty pleasures – are recognized as being part of its centrality.

Notes

1 Roland Barthes, *The Pleasure of the Text*, trans. R. Miller, London: Jonathan Cape, 1976.

2 See Patricia Holland, *The Television Handbook*, 2nd edition, London: Routledge, 2000, pp.91–101. On styles of editing and the relationship between image and sound track in different television genres.

3 On bias see B. Gunter, *Measuring Bias on Television*, Luton: University of Luton Press, 1997; on the current affairs agenda see reports from the Campaign for Quality Television and the Third World and Environment Broadcasting Project (S. Barnett and E. Seymour, *'A Shrinking Iceberg Travelling South ...'; Changing Trends in British Television: A Case Study of Drama and Current Affairs*, London: Campaign for Quality Television, 1999; S. Lay and C. Payne, *World Out of Focus: British Terrestrial Television and Global Affairs*, London: 3WE, 1998); the extended press debate on 'fakery' sparked off by the *Guardian*'s investigation into the Carlton television programme 'The Connection' (October 1996) (including *Guardian*, 6, 7, 8 May and 19 December 1998); and many books and articles on manipulation and misrepresentation (recent examples include T. Allen and J. Seaton, eds., *The Media of Conflict*, London: Zed Books, 1999, and B. Franklin, ed., *Social Policy, the Media and Misrepresentation*, London: Routledge, 1999.

4 P. Dahigren and C. Sparks, eds, *Communication and Citizenship: Journalism and the Public Sphere*, London: Routledge, 1991; P. Dahigren, *Television and the Public Sphere*, London: Sage, 1995.

5 J. Fiske and J. Hartley, *Reading Television*, London: Methuen, 1978; J. Fiske, *Television Culture*, London: Routledge, 1987; J. Fiske, 'Postmodernism and Television', in James Curran and Michael Gurevich, *Mass Media and Society*, London: Edward Arnold, 1991.

6 W. J. T. Mitchell, *Iconology: Image, Text, Ideology*, Chicago: University of Chicago Press, 1986. Thanks to Mary Anne Francis for pointing me to this source.

7 Ibid, p.112.

8 K. Brandts, 'Who's Afraid of Infotainment?', *European Journal of Communication*, vol.13, no.3, 1998, pp.315–35; P. Dahigren and C. Sparks, *Journalism and Popular Culture*, London: Sage, 1992.

9 S. Barnett and E. Seymour, *'A Shrinking Iceberg Travelling South ...'*; P. Holland, 'Authority and Authenticity: Redefining Television Current Affairs', in M. Bromley, ed., *No News is Bad News*, London: Pearson Education, 2001.

10 J. Ellis, *Seeing Things: Television in an Age of Uncertainty*, London: I. B. Tauris, 2000.

11 It is part of a larger project on the history of the current affairs series *This Week*, undertaken by Patricia

Holland and Victoria Wegg-Prosser, currently in association with Bournemouth University. Thames Television, now Pearson Television International, has kindly given access to its archives for the project. I am grateful to the Harold Hyam Wingate Foundation for a grant which made much of my research possible, and to my colleagues Victoria Wegg-Prosser and John Ellis for comments on this article.

12 J. Derrida, 'Plato's Pharmacy' in *Dissemination*, trans. Barbara Johnson, London: Athlone Press, 1981.

13 M. E. Brown, ed., *Television and Women's Culture: the Politics of the Popular*, London: Sage, 1990; J. Thumim, 'Mrs Knight *must* be balanced: Methodological Problems in Researching Early British Television', in C. Carter et al., eds, *News, Gender and Power*, London: Routledge, 1998.

14 Mitchell, *Iconology*, p.3.

15 N. Mirzoeff, *An Introduction to Visual Culture*, London: Routledge, 1999.

16 Gunter, *Measuring Bias*.

17 G. M. Goldie, *Facing the Nation: Television and Politics 1937-1976*, London: Bodley Head, 1977. See P. Holland, 'When a Woman Reads the News', in Helen Baehr and Gillian Dyer, eds, *Boxed In: Women and Television*, London: Pandora Press, 1987, for a further exploration of this idea in relation to women newsreaders.

18 B. Sendall, *Independent Television in Britain*, vol. 1: *Origin and Foundation 1946–62*, London: Macmillan, 1982.

19 V. Wegg-Prosser, '*This Week* and the Introduction of Current Affairs on ITV', in J. Thumim, ed., *Television in the 1950s*, London: I. B. Tauris, forthcoming.

20 Interview with Jeremy Isaacs by Victoria Wegg Prosser, January 1990.

21 J. Birt and P. Jay, 'Television Journalism, the Child of an Unhappy Marriage between Newspapers and Film', *The Times*, 30 September 1975.

22 Author interview with Mike Townson, March 1991.

23 Mike Townson, 'Backchat', *The Listener*, 4 January 1990.

24 R. Bolton, *Death on the Rock and Other Stories*, London: W. H. Allen, 1990.

25 The visual had also been associated with the feminine. The lighter *This Week* of the 1950s and early 1960s had had a few women as presenters and directors. In the more 'serious' period of the later 1960s and 1970s women were almost entirely absent. When *TV Eye* took over from *This Week* in 1979, women producers and presenters reappeared. This may be just a coincidence, but I suspect there may be more to it. I have explored some of the issues around the visibility of women in news media elsewhere (see Holland, 'When a Woman', and P. Holland, 'The Politics of the Smile: "Soft News" and the Sexualisation of the Popular Press', in C. Carter, *News, Gender and Power*). See also Thumim in the same volume.

26 Much of this debate was around what was *said* about Townson's approach. In fact the programmes made for *TV Eye* did not look very different from those made for *This Week*.

27 M. Douglas, *Purity and Danger: an Analysis of the Concepts of Pollution and Taboo*, London: RKP, 1966; J. Langer, *Tabloid Television: Popular Journalism and the 'Other' News*, London: Routledge, 1998.

28 Jay and Birt, 'Television Journalism'.

29 P. Harrison and R. Palmer, *News Out of Africa: Biafra to Band Aid*, London: Hilary Shipman, 1986.

30 Alex de Waal and Jonathan Dimbleby were both interviewed in the BBC2 programme 'The Waking Giant', last in the series *Tourists of the Revolution* (1 April 2000). For a detailed account of the making of 'The Unknown Famine' and the events which preceded and followed it see Harrison and Palmer, ibid.

31 J. Benthall, *Disasters, Relief and the Media*, London: I. B. Tauris, 1993.

32 It was not entirely unknown. Oxfam had already tried to publicize the famine but had failed to capture public attention. See Harrison and Palmer, *News Out of Africa*, p.49.

33 Benthall, *Disasters*, p.182; P. Holland, *What is a Child? Popular Images of Childhood*, London: Virago, 1992, p.156.

34 For example: *This Week*, '35 Years on the Front Line, The Unknown Famine', Flashback Productions for Thames Television: ITV, 12 March 1991; 'The Media and Ethiopia', Open University, BBC2, 1994; 'An Ethiopian Journey'. Dimbleby Associates for LWT, ITV 1998. *Tourists of the Revolution. The Waking Giant*, BBC2, 1 April 2000. This is by no means an exhaustive list.

35 Harrison and Palmer, *News Out of Africa*, pp.61–2.

36 J. Corner, *Television Form and Public Address*, London: Edward Arnold, 1995.

37 K. Kumar, 'Holding The Middle Ground: the BBC, the Public and the Professional Broadcaster', in J. Curran, M. Gurevitch and J. Woollacott, eds, *Mass Communication and Society*, London: Arnold, 1977.

38 S. Chatman, 'Story and Discourse (Introduction)', in O. Boyd-Barrett and C. Newbold, eds, *Approaches to Media: A Reader*, London: Arnold, 1977.

39 J. Dimbleby, 'An Ethiopian Journey'.

40 Birt and Jay, 'Television Journalism'.

41 L. Mulvey, *Visual and Other Pleasures*, London: Macmillan, 1989.

42 R. Barthes, *The Pleasure*.

43 I am indebted to the Warwick University conference, 'Popular European Cinema: the Spectacular', organized by Ginette Vincendeau and Richard Dyer, March 2000, for many of these ideas about the nature of the spectacular, even though the conference was dealing with a very different medium.

44 Timothy Raison MP talking about the famine images shown in 1984 in 'The Media and Ethiopia', OU, BBC2, 1994.

45 P. Bruck, 'Crisis as Spectacle: Tabloid News and the Politics of Outrage', in Marc Raboy and Bernard Daganis, eds, *Media, Crisis and Democracy: Mass Communication and the Disruption of Social Order*. London: Sage, 1992, p.118.

46 R. Barthes, 'The Rhetoric of the Image', in *Image Music Text*, Fontana, 1977; V. Burgin, ed., *Thinking Photography*, London: Macmillan, 1982.

47 See P. Holland, 'Authority and authenticity: Redefining Television Current Affairs', in Bromley, ed., *No News is Bad News*, 2001, for a fuller discussion of these issues and of the changing parameters for current affairs journalists and journalism.

48 'The Essential Guide', part of C4's *Bloody Bosnia Season*, August 1993, was a good example of a full use of graphic and digital techniques.

49 See Mitchell, *Iconology*, for a teasing out of these distinctions, especially pp.42 and 47.

Divya Tolia-Kelly

Iconographies of Identity: Visual Cultures of the Everyday in the South Asian Diaspora

Introduction – definitions of visual culture

In his most recent exhibition in Mumbai (2000), 'Figures, Facts, Feelings: a Direct Diasporic Dialogue', Indian artist Parthiv Shah documents the Indian diasporic experience in Britain.[1] He presents a photographic dialogue about the diasporic communities' positioning in relation to India – a montage of photographs of people's homes and their self-created montage of textual icons of identification with India. The reiteration of 'Indianness' through these materials is central to his recording of socio-anthropological domestic cultures. They reflect the continuing dialogue between Indians in Britain and their sense of belonging to a national territory of India. As an Indian artist observing these points of connection and creating new points for his Mumbai audience, Shah views the diaspora from within the 'Motherland'. His photo-

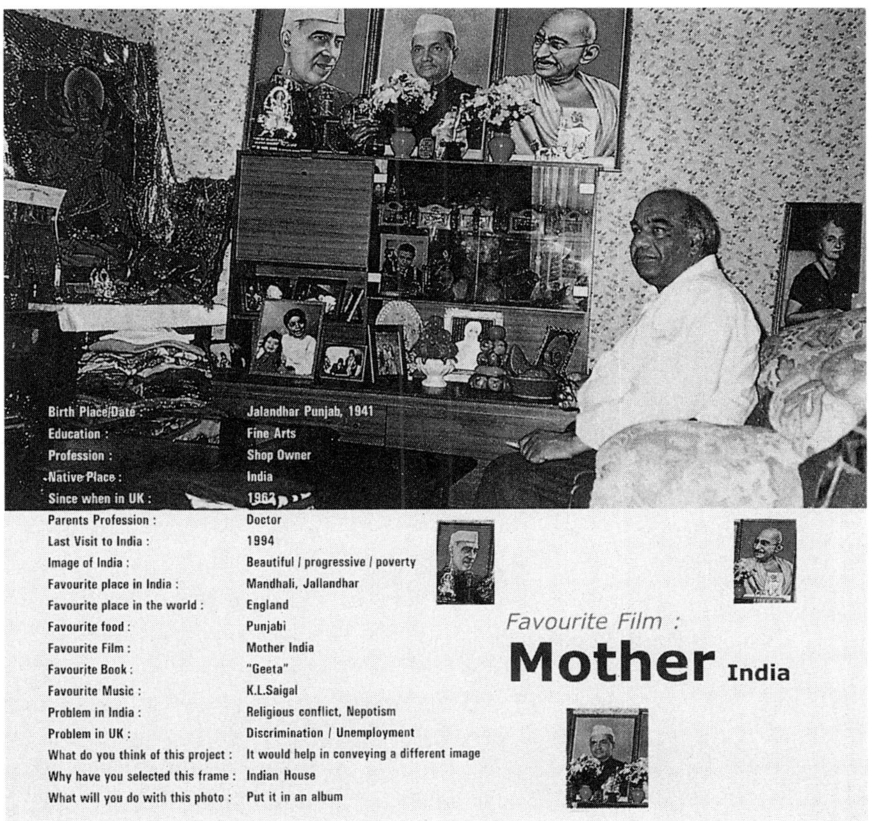

Figure 1. Parthiv Shah, *Figures, Facts; Feelings*, 2000. Reproduced courtesy of Parthiv Shah and CMAC.

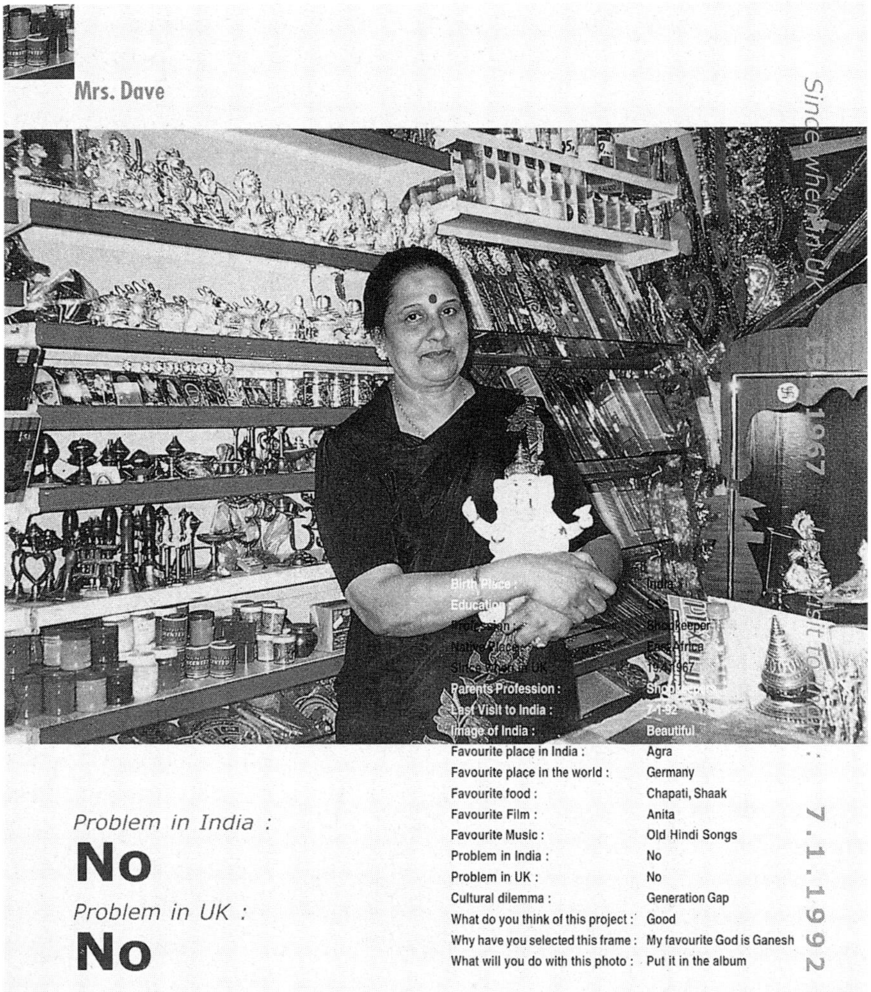

Figure 2. Parthiv Shah, *Figures, Facts; Feelings*, 2000. Reproduced courtesy of Parthiv Shah and CMAC.

graphs (Figures 1 and 2) return the post-colonial gaze through which the diaspora in Britain is defined, recorded and signified, and allow for a shift in the usual flow of visual cultures from India to Britain. This 'returned-flow' raises questions about the way in which 'Indianness' is constructed by the diaspora through visual cultures and objects which, authenticated as Indian, are often part of more complicated commodity routes.

Shah engages with issues of diaspora-identity from outside European art history. He works with a set of structures different from those of Black British artists, who, engaging with theories of identity, also question the political structures and prejudicial practices of art history itself.[2] Studies of visual culture are situated between art history and its 'distancing from the production of living culture', and anthropocentric concerns with the relationship between the visual and processes of subjective/cultural identification and production.[3] This intertextuality requires complex analyses and interpretation from a range of disciplines. Film, video, urban design, photography and advertising are interwoven in our everyday experience of the social world. They matter in their aesthetic and expressive nature, constituting the material realities of the political, economic and social structures of society. Here I consider the positioning of aspects of visual culture in the home as a means of *fixing* and *negotiating* residence in Britain for the South Asian diaspora. There is a politics to the collection and display of these cultures. They express a visual grammar and allow a 'highly individualised presencing' through their existence. I examine the role of these visual cultures in the home in the context of debate about material cultures, consumption and identity.[4]

Visual cultures are central to constructions of identity. Within cultural geography, research has been dominated by their role in discourses of landscape and national identity.[5] There has been a focus, for example, on the canvases of Turner and Constable, and on the more parochial understandings of the social and cultural values of landscape.[6] In these studies, landscape and Englishness have been theoretically linked as a means of contextualizing and deconstructing the function of visual imagery in the narratives of nation, and their role in the relationship between social 'structures of feeling' in the country and the city.[7] Landscape discourse is therefore considered in the construction of geographies of belonging and being.[8] Within geography there has been a particular focus on the effect and development of everyday landscapes and their textures on senses of place and belonging.[9] My concern is with the symbolic landscapes of nation and the local ecologies that shape our connectedness with local landscape. Richard Mabey describes these as a 'uniquely private network of meaning and association that attaches us to them'.[10] This essay examines the effect of post-colonial migration on imagined, material and cultural landscapes of identification. Visual cultures in the home ensure a positioning of diasporic groups through their metaphorical effect, their metonymical value and their accretion of meaning. Signifying remembered landscapes, visual cultures symbolize the experience of a nation, or reflect textures of a specific place. Colour, texture or icons within visual forms can refract memories of the experience of a different continent, a journey or simply a moment. These refracted fragments offer co-ordinates from which members of a diasporic group can *position* themselves in a dynamic connection with the past and future; the place of migration and of settlement; and the expressive cultures of these bounded territories – linked to a sense of national belonging, enfranchisement and the socio-political figuring that this allows within the new country of residence:

> It [identity] is not a fixed origin to which we can make some final and absolute Return. Of course it is not a phantasm either. It is something – not a mere trick of the imagination. It has histories – and histories have their real, material, and symbolic effects. The past continues to speak to us. But it no longer addresses us as a simple factual 'past', since our relation to it, like a child's relation to the mother, is always-already 'after the break'. It is always constructed through memory, fantasy, narrative and myth. Cultural identities are the points of identification or suture, which are made within the discourses of history and culture. Not an essence but a positioning. Hence there is always a politics of identity, a politics of position, which has no absolute guarantee in an unproblematic, transcendental 'law of origin'.[11]

My ethnographic research involved discussion groups with Asian women in North West London, leading to individual interviews in their homes, and the analysis of transcripts and photographs.[12] Research was grounded in the women's own accounts of the aspects of visual culture in their homes deemed central to their sense of belonging. Here I focus on a group discussion of the Bollywood film *Guide* (Hindi), and an analysis of a one-to-one interview with Shilpa.[13] Analysis of *Guide* focuses on the positioning of its text in the memories and social practices of film-going South Asians in Britain. The values and meanings of the film text are considered in the context of a 'triangulation' process conducted by diasporic groups through cultures of identification. Triangulation, a navigational term, describes the way that a ship's co-ordinates can be established by measuring distance from the horizon and due north. A relational measurement, it finds location through use of fixed geographical nodes.

The interview with Shilpa allowed me to explore the value of visual cultures as they are dynamically positioned in her processes of identification and location. Born in India, Shilpa lived in Sudan and Kenya before settling permanently in London. From this interview, visual cultures in the home can be understood as multisensory. The visual becomes material in relation to identification through archival objects of heritage. This visual archive represents a set of co-ordinates through which triangulation, positioning and a sense of locatedness are formed and re-formed through time.

These two very different engagements with visual cultures are examples of the varied textures that have signified connections with a sense of 'home', belonging and a place of identification with 'Indianness'. Discussion of the film *Guide* presents a way of understanding the social interaction that Bollywood offers the Asian diaspora, catalysing memories of events, peoples and places where the film was viewed in the past. The social act of watching therefore consolidates a cultural memory of the practices of being 'Indian', as well as triggering connections with other landscapes and ecologies memorialized in the process of migration. Exploring domestic visual cultures illustrates the very different subjective practices of the everyday, which operate through the complex aesthetic and material textures of daily living. The multisensory nature of visual cultures complicates their effect. Simultaneously visual and material and inscribed with a grammar of symbols, metaphor and aesthetics, they are part of an expressive cultural dialogue, as well as being culturally significant as objects.

Triangulation is the key to sustaining, creating and articulating the multiple nodes of location experienced through migration, settlement and re-settlement in the post-colonial period. The process of cultural identification relies much on the process of location, fixing positions and constructing narratives of appropriation and exclusion within the geographical space around us. Identification with these geographies through domestic visual cultures is a means of engaging with memories, landscapes and a racialized cultural connection with the diasporic network of South Asians.

Nicholas Mirzoeff has called for an engagement with visual culture

> in a far more interactive sense, concentrating on the determining role of visual culture in the wider culture to which it belongs. Such a history of visual culture would highlight those moments where the visual is contested, debated, and transformed as

a constantly challenging place of social interaction and definition in terms of class, gender, sexual and racialised identities.[14]

Engagement for South Asians concerns contestation and debate on the 'structure of feelings' which inform ideas of Indianness. These cultures of the visual resonate with aesthetics and textures of location, affecting colour, media and the cultural aesthetics of national identification. Temporal and spatial contexts of display influence the location of refracted places and fix the identity of the viewer, so that the multisensory nature of visual cultures is crucial in their role in negotiating identity for the South Asian diaspora. Cultures of the everyday are processes through which dislocation, non-identity and memory are negotiated and formed. Understanding of these cultures draws usefully on theorizations of hybridity, in-betweenness and Du Bois's concept of double-consciousness,[15] each of which considers the post-colonial experience as a hybrid cultural identity and as a third space, a non-located and decentred identity in flux. Double-consciousness is a position of seeing oneself through an imposed 'otherness', of being in continual conflict with conscious lived experience. Expressive cultures therefore are a means of interrogating this doubleness. For example, in considering the African diaspora's relationship with musical cultures, Paul Gilroy uses the term 'antiphony' to theorize a social memory of sound that resonates with a slave memory of the African diaspora, an aural texture that triggers the historical past and a means of re-connecting to an oral history of oppression and subjugation.[16]

Textures of identification

For South Asians in Britain, visual networks of culture are made possible through the development of new technologies of transport, communications and the global transmission of TV and film. The textures of memory and heritage ingrained in these visual cultures express negotiations of identity through heritage and geographical imaginings and help to counter dominant discourses of history. Archives of heritage and identity narratives are preserved in the process of self-making. Raphael Samuel's definition of heritage describes a creative process of collection, display and identification with a past landscape through the procurement of domestic objects as central to the sustenance of the self.[17] For diasporic groups, archiving through visual and material cultures preserves connections to various landscapes of migration.

Counter-culture and counter-history are produced through collections, photography and a vernacular based in the everyday, which counter insecurity in a national context – an alternative to modernity but ironically reliant on modern technology and networks of capital, transport and communications. Described by Appurdurai as 'Global Ethnoscapes', they constitute the new non-localized constructions of ethnic identity.[18] These are new landscapes of group identity not based on bounded, territorialized space, and neither culturally homogeneous nor historically unselfconscious:[19] 'The loosening of the holds between people, wealth, and territories fundamentally alters the basis of cultural reproduction.'[20] Through technology the imagination of many other different worlds is possible to a higher degree than ever. Fantasy fuels the way in which we imagine our potential lives, and for diasporic groups transnational networks of cultures offer imagined utopian futures and a myriad of possible configurations in terms of identity and landscapes of belonging.

Self-making through cultures of identification is an important consideration for diasporic groups in Britain. Their heritage is not material in historical architecture or artefacts in national museums or displayed in visual cultures of national history. Their (his)story is marginal and confined to prejudicial discourses of 'otherness' and 'Primitivism'. History-making is on the domestic scale; it therefore becomes a project of collecting the ephemeral.[21] Cultural expressions of past histories or collecting artefacts cannot be carried out in a temporal scale of antiques and relics, but in a scale of decades, as a contemporary activity. Diasporic memory becomes the archive, and everyday relationships with objects become the materials of heritage. Within the politics of national heritage and history, these cultures are integral and not peripheral to an 'indigenous' national culture. Post-colonial cultures are dynamically positioned as a crucial part of the landscapes of the everyday in England, not marginal to them.

These fluid diasporic identities are created and configured through cultural imprints in the form of landscape iconography, through an embodied relationship with visuality. The eye and the body cannot be separated and, instead of individuals gazing at texts, diasporan subjects configure themselves through them. These texts could operate as nodes of belonging, but also as points of reforming identities in Britain, and so the visual becomes a practice of engaging with places, history and/or identity. The point of engagement is privileged, rather than the unified meaning of the text, and the metonymical 'triggers of identification' become a useful way of exploring these practices – representing other places, memories and texts in a visual context of configuration. What follows is an example of the way in which the visual shifts into materiality. The value of seeing an object merges with the other sensory values of touch, hearing, taste, and smell and practices of ocularity and embodiment are continually in flux.

Location, journey and post-colonial negations

The women in this study migrated here from a number of different countries in East Africa and the Indian sub-continent including Kenya, Malawi, Tanzania, Uganda, Sudan, Mayanmar, Pakistan, India and Bangladesh. Their routes to England parallel the migration routes within the British Empire and, as a result, trace the movement of Indian labour during colonial rule in British India. Quite often for post-colonial migrants, especially those expelled from Uganda, material possessions were given up to the state or given to workers on the farms and homes they left behind. Summer dresses specially made to make a good impression, official documents and some small essentials were all that could be transported by the women. So for this particular group there has been a loss, not just of locatedness, but of historical record. Migratory groups are continually omitted from history. The ethnographies of East

African Asians or Indian Asians reveal the experience of in-betweenness, not just in their personal dislocation but also of their social and cultural record. No longer part of Indian history and particularly marginal to Ugandan and British histories, the materials of migration are limited in their expression of their past. Therefore cultural products like films become prisms of location, reflecting iconographies of India, Kenya and Uganda, allowing a connection with textual cornerstones of culture such as literature and language. Film songs are examples of this. But these texts also operate as a place through which the oral histories of migratory groups are refracted. South Asian popular culture such as Bollywood film-making has an importance not only as a cultural phenomenon in its own terms, but in making sense of the diasporic experience of collective dislocatedness.[22] This dislocatedness is not an essential and universal experience for all those re-located through Imperialism, but is crucial for significant numbers of the South Asian population who moved to Britain in the last sixty years.[23] For all of the women I interviewed the memory of the journey is fresh in their minds; it is a crucial point of distancing and of creating their new positionality and identities. They reference the journey as part of their development as individuals and as a point of commonality; it unites them in defining themselves as 'Asians'. The groups I recruited attracted a variety of women and, as their biographies show, their sense of connectedness was not necessarily based on language, religion or social class, but predominantly on their experience of migration from a place which, if not necessarily the same country, is positioned against being in England. At least fourteen different countries are mentioned in the interviews as places of origin/home/birth – constituted through memories, not necessarily as national spaces. Their combined expressions constitute a territory of culture which the women share. Experience of migration solidifies to some degree their creation of the vast place from which they came. Through memory and through refractions in countless forms in visual media, sound and sensual experiences, this place takes on emotional and psychological importance.

The meaning of 'home' is fractured and multiple for these women. Positioned in different ways, home is both a domestic and benign place where children are raised and socialized and an oppressive space of disempowerment and subjugation. Within social anthropology, home is a place where 'structures of feeling' are reinstated and evolve. Cooking, writing, talking, clothing all become crucial fixers of identification, dominated by the culture of the home as an idealized place of security and freedom and a shelter from racism and cultural oppression – a shelter from the rain. Most importantly, 'home' is a temporal and spatial fixer of belonging, security and non-alienation which, in their narratives, operates on different scales of the domestic, local, national and international. It is within this space, simultaneously idealized and material, that the processes of making, belonging and connecting with landscapes of identification operate.

On location with Bollywood

Bollywood film-viewing at the cinema and on TV galvanizes a sense of Indianness, of 'roots' and a collective experience of the diasporic journey.

Film-viewing activates social and cultural networks which operate as 'imagined communities' for viewers.[24] The women describe going to the cinema from childhood as a group experience – and the gelling of social groupings is itself sometimes more important than watching the film itself. Film-going in East Africa and India is described as involving picnics and outings, mostly to open-air cinemas. The smells, sights and feel of the air, the food and the society which were part of the event are central to the experience. These open-air cinemas operated in Mombassa, Nairobi and Malawi in the 1950s, 60s and 70s and the following excerpts are from women remembering those years.

Outdoor cinema-going

Neela – The effect is fantastic and I think we never used to have ordinary cinemas in Mombassa, we always used to go to these.

Anju – It's because it's the open air, a young town watching a film together you know ... it was like a little society.

Shazia – It's like a picnic, but watching a movie sort of thing.

Shanta – In Malawi we did the same ... same thing with driving. We used to do the same thing; we go early, sit there. Tell your friends if you're coming out or not. They decide we leave at the same time, we park nearby, children play and we bring pyjamas with us, so before the picture starts we put them on.

Bhanu – Decide what you're going to cook for each other.

The multisensory experience is clearly evident as an essential context to the film. The community watches together, as an extended family. The cinemas are outside the cityscape and reached literally by entering the jungle and open-land. The journey through the 'wilderness' and the exotic smell of animals are emphasized in their descriptions: one of the Indian women mocks the hyper-reality of the recalled memories. The animals are larger and closer and together the descriptions form almost a diorama of the African wilderness. The auditorium becomes a film set upon which is projected the scene of watching another screen. This is just one of the ways in which present-day cinema-going is a means of connecting to previous films, film audiences and other practices of viewing.

Cinematic dioramas

Manjula – It's not pretty because where we used to go driving, we used to go through a kind of jungle. Where I am saying was always a weird smell, before we entered the drive-in side.

Anju – You could hear the animals ...

Anju – because of the National Parks ... and once a herd of elephants must have come out of the National Park and obviously you could hear ah ... the noises.

Shazia – These people from Africa, as the fashion progresses, their stories will get wilder and wilder! (laughing) ... next the lions will be walking in the cinema, you just wait.

Manjula – ... a thousand cars coming out of the cinema. So there is always a craze, and everybody wants to get out quickly because once you pass a certain, you know, row of trees, you know it's very stinky, very bad smell because it's really outside ... the outskirts of Kampala.

In this sequence the women are talking about two different cinemas – one on the outskirts of Kampala, the other on the outskirts of Nairobi – but in the group discussion they conflate rather than differentiate between these two places, privileging sensual experiences over specific co-ordinates, places and events. Space and time are interwoven in a created memory where the specificity of smell, sound and sight is more important. These are the attributes of a place, constructed through sensory notes, memorialized in the imagination, triggering a sensory memory that is iconographical. Cinemas in Mwanza are described as the same as those in Malawi; Mombassa is the same as Kampala in recollections of the textures of the experience. The value culture of the visual telescopes specific locations and edits reality. The tense is always mixed, past merges into present; the moment is transferable and mutable. It is nevertheless sure in its signification. Separate occasions may be conflated but they function within a visual logic of a particular scene, a constructed landscape of cinema-going through the animal noises, dry savannah and a communal ritual. The heterogeneity of African society, and 'Asianness' itself, are absent from their descriptions. These memories are iconographical, reverent of an idealized landscape of the past.

Cinema-going in the UK

When the women describe their first few weeks away from their birthplace, left behind usually through marriage, their first experiences of cinema-going in Britain are memorable. Cinema was a cultural magnet for the Asian community. It galvanized socially and empowered culturally, offering a sense of solidarity. Seeing a physical presence of Asian bodies was an uplifting experience, reducing feelings of alienation and isolation. At the same time as altering the social geography of Britain, it awakened memories of the social geographies of East Africa and India. These new practices of going to the cinema connected with remembered practices enabled by 'ethnic' trading in the cinema areas where East African and Indian delicacies, clothes, kitchen utensils, fruit and vegetables were soon sold alongside jewellery and cassettes of film songs.

Celluloid home
Manjula – Also the movies reminded us of home, like after coming here, when we used to be reminded of home. Although I'd never been to India when I came here, I still felt as though it was part of me. I used to feel nice when I watched Indian films. You know I felt as if I'd come from there you know. Although I knew I wasn't from there, but my parents were. Somehow I had some kind of attachment to that place.

The women remember the films with poignancy. Tears are shed as films which have been seen over and over again in India or East Africa are reshown in Britain. But for the women it is not the text of the film that is primary, but the actual display of social and cultural aesthetics. Lalita describes her first sighting of an Indian movie after leaving India: she had been living in Montreal for nearly a year when this event happened in autumn 1976:

Reconnecting
Lalita – I said 'What are you talking? which one you want to see? ... Both! ... I don't

want to come home. We'll have our lunch there, we'll have our dinner there and if they repeat the show I'll see that one also ... even if it's the third time.' He said 'O.K.' ...

Lalita – And that's what happened, they showed *Khabhie Khabhie* first 1–4, and then 4–5 was off, and then 5–8 they showed *Bobby* and then everybody wanted *Khabhie, Khabhie* and then some more crowd came and they ran a late night show 9–12 for *Khabhie, Khabhie* and I sat again! ... Because I knew maybe we'll never see it again. It was already five months, six months I was already married and I hadn't seen an Indian wedding or any Indian kind of TV or anything, anything Hindi-speaking. So after that again nothing for two months and then in August they showed one movie.[25]

The emotional response to an Indian event is significant. Lalita doesn't mind which film is shown, but enjoys the whole experience of its language and aesthetics and of being in the cinema with other Asians. Each film is three hours long and she watches three showings in a row, which demonstrates, I think, the power of the meanings of film beyond the textual. The experience is symbolic of the broader cultural practices of Indianness. Senses are stimulated in relation to a cultural appetite, encouraged through the absence of Indian aesthetics and language in the everyday. Satiation is mediated through the film text, but wholly addressed only through the context of watching. Through cinema-going the women are transported to sensory memories of previous cinema-goings – of a different crowd, passing comments with girlfriends, the smell of the Indian cinema: musty, old and tired.

Sensory memories
Lalita – All those things you never think of when you are there. The smell and the darkness and the romance of the cinema is different, because it was in that auditorium it was different ...

Bollywood as a site of memorialization through the film *Guide* (1965)

This cinematic socialization is the process by which the text of the film or the social activity of watching is deemed an essential part of socialization in the family.[26] This is through religious teaching, rites and rituals, language education and simple social morality projected through the filmic text as well as through the process of watching. Reverencing also emerges from symbolic and iconographical imagery and narrative within the text. Cultural products such as films become sites of location, reflecting iconographies of India, Kenya and Uganda. They enable connection with culture through literature and language, as for example in songs. But these texts also operate as a place through which the oral histories of migratory groups are refracted.

All of the women in the study referred to the 1965 film *Guide*, starring Dev Anand and Waheed Rehran. *Guide* was an enormously popular film (based on a novel by R. K. Narayan) with high production values, an acclaimed musical score and choreography – all the ingredients necessary for a Bollywood blockbuster. The opening sequence shows landscapes which the hero, ex-tourist guide 'Raju', is traversing, shot most notably with a 'quasi-expressionistic, garish use of colour and of calendar art sets'[27] (Figure 3). Raju's journey is also a transformation of his own identity and of spiritual metamorphosis. His journey through India is figured as a particular engagement with a montage of the nation. By the end Raju has changed into a spiritual guide and saviour and

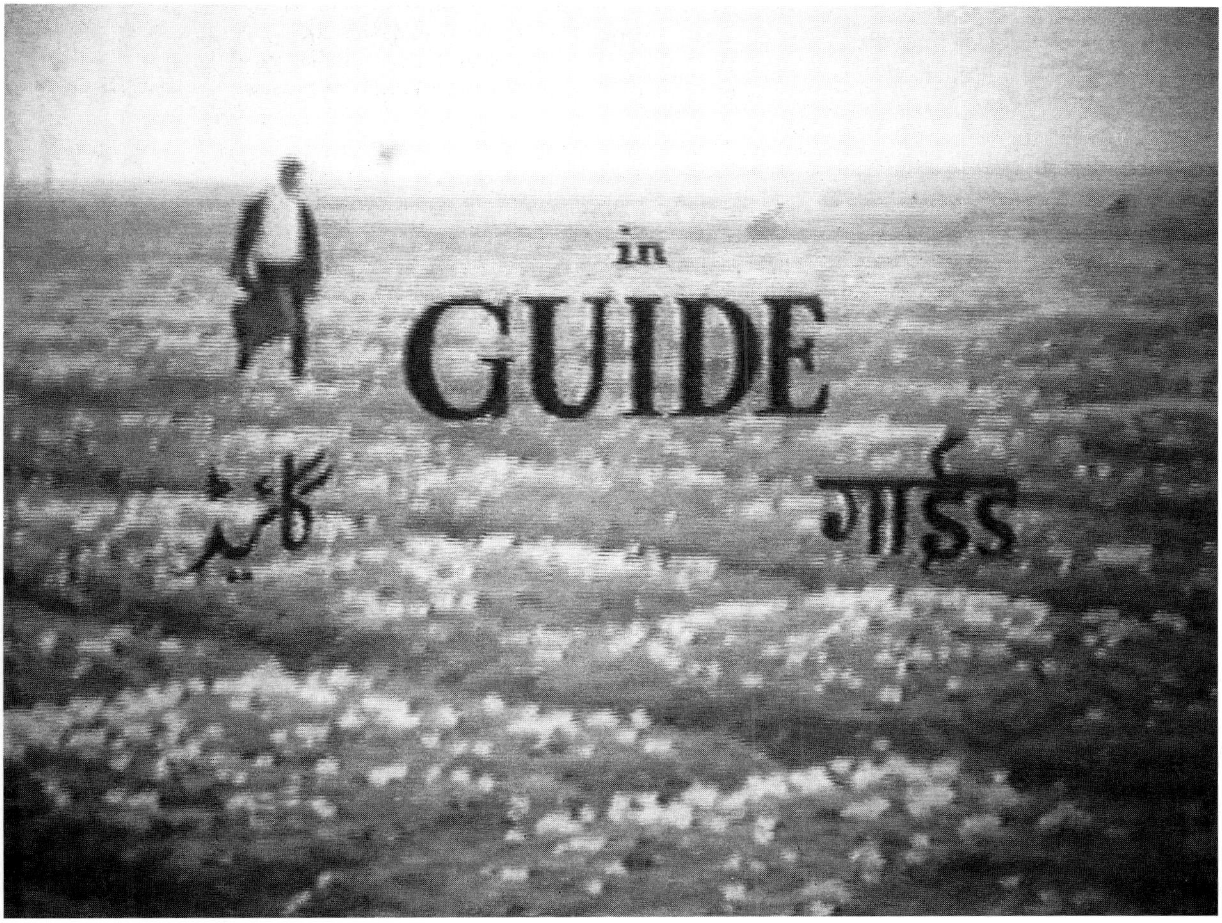

Figure 3. Dev Anand in *Guide*, 1965. Reproduced courtesy of Dev Anand and Navketan Films, Mumbai.

India has become the moral landscape of his identification (Figures 4 and 5). Traversing the landscape cleanses him and provides him with a moral citizenry.[28] *Guide* demonstrates the way that a film's narrative is sometimes secondary to the visual content.[29] The film's aesthetics trigger memories of multiple experiences and oral histories for the viewing diaspora. Sometimes these are memories of memories and not necessarily real and lived experiences.[30] They are symbolic of landscapes, of ecological textures and of even more personal experiences. They are, for the South Asian diaspora, part of a national dialogue, between them – an imagined community of post-migration nationals – and the root source of senses of national identity. This dialogue is a multitextual, multisensory one which shifts and fixes in different moments and different places (Figures 6 and 7).

The Bollywood film crystallizes processes of identification. It simultaneously offers fluidity and fixity, allowing a multidimensional relationship with images that are viewed through the eye but which contextualize the practices of the body. Indian popular commercial cinema has come to represent a kind of psychic investment for migrants from India all over the world. It operates on many different levels. For Sumita Chakravarty, 'the self enclosed romanticism of the gesture of recall, the metonymic substitution of the Hindi film for

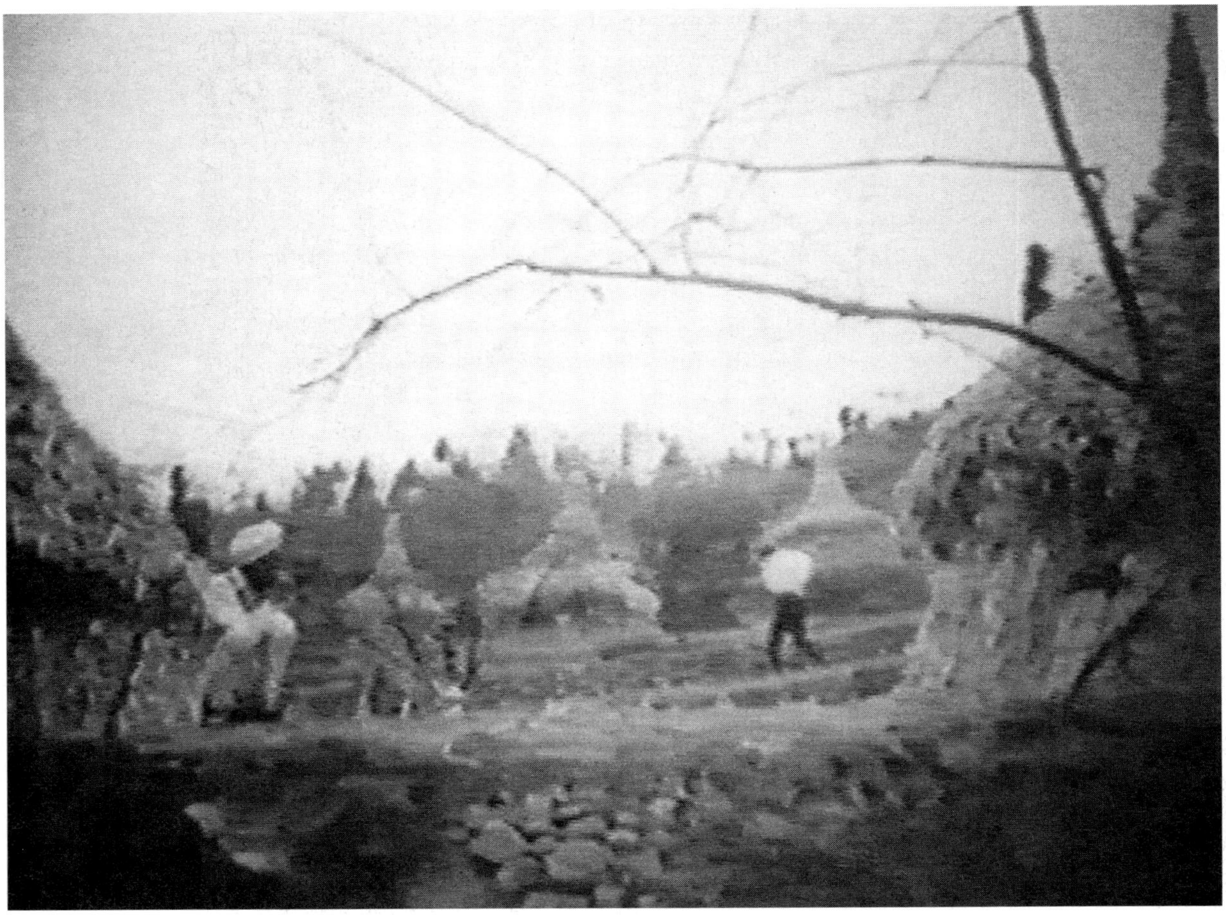

Figure 4. Dev Anand in *Guide*, 1965. Reproduced courtesy of Dev Anand and Navketan Films, Mumbai.

India, is generally a means of effecting closure, of constructing rigid mental boundaries between past and present, parent culture and adopted culture, belonging and exile, nationality and naturalisation'.[31] For all the women in my research this film had a special meaning. For some it was Dev's gorgeous good looks, transporting them back to their teenage years. For others it was memories of loss or of the places where freedom and sensuality were expressed. The film text operates as a prism for all these connections between spatial and temporal localities, connections which are stores for experiences and relationships.

Landscapes in these films become icons of moral order and citizenship as well as aesthetic expressions of a cultural history. The journey of Dev Anand is more than his journey between two co-ordinates; it is a pilgrimage through the icons of Indian landscape which also awakens a sense of spirituality, morality and understandings of individual citizenship. For others it holds more poignant memories:

Memories of loss

Darshna – That clip to me reminds me of how we've all moved through different places ... And when you leave, like you've got 24 hours to leave Uganda, what do you pack in your suitcase? What do you bring with you, to this new place? You've got all your memories, all your family ... anything that's important to you in just one or two bags.

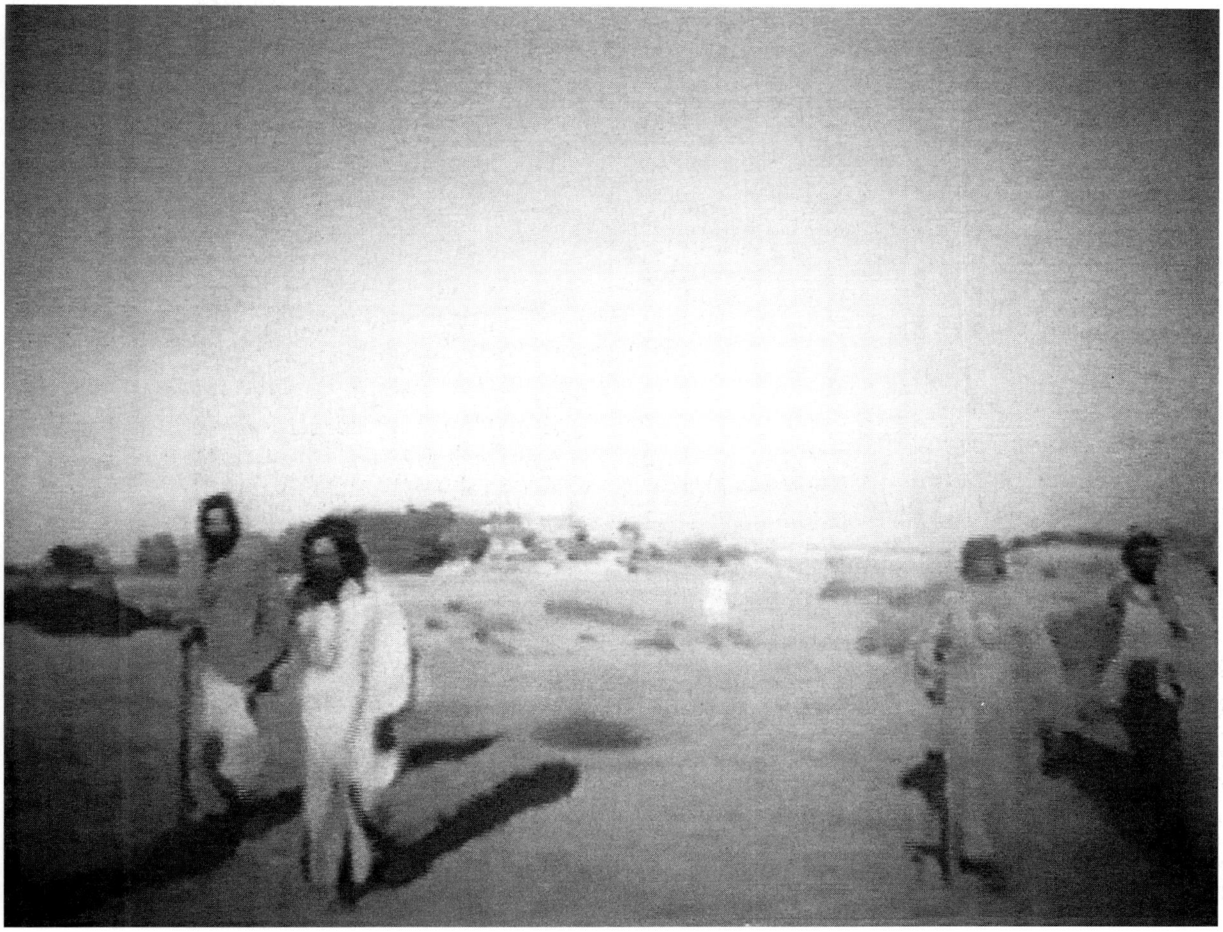

Figure 5. Dev Anand in *Guide*, 1965. Reproduced courtesy of Dev Anand and Navketan Films, Mumbai.

Shaku – [this reminds me of] the innocent life you know without any worries or anything . . . Say like he hasn't got any pressure, him and his mum enjoying life . . . free . . . Now, he's got his potli [knapsack] and that's it.

In the film, the landscapes of Rajasthan are iconographical because they trigger visual memories of India, but not necessarily first-hand experiences. Such epics are superimposed with actual remembered journeys, memories of stories that are visualized and revered as representing a spiritual locatedness in a country that was not necessarily a place of birth. For Chakravarty, *Guide* is an example of a film where impersonation operates. Raju's identity is in constant flux. He offers us an insight into the national psyche. National icons, once closely examined, are not simply bounded representations of actual places, but more political and economic collages of a particular class consolidating a sense of national consciousness. The layers of film text offer a parallel to the workings of memory in the sense, as Toni Morrison argues, that images are stores of memories for those who have no history. Memories themselves are not fixed and true, but are of stories and reflections, what she terms in *Beloved* 'memories of a rememory'.[32]

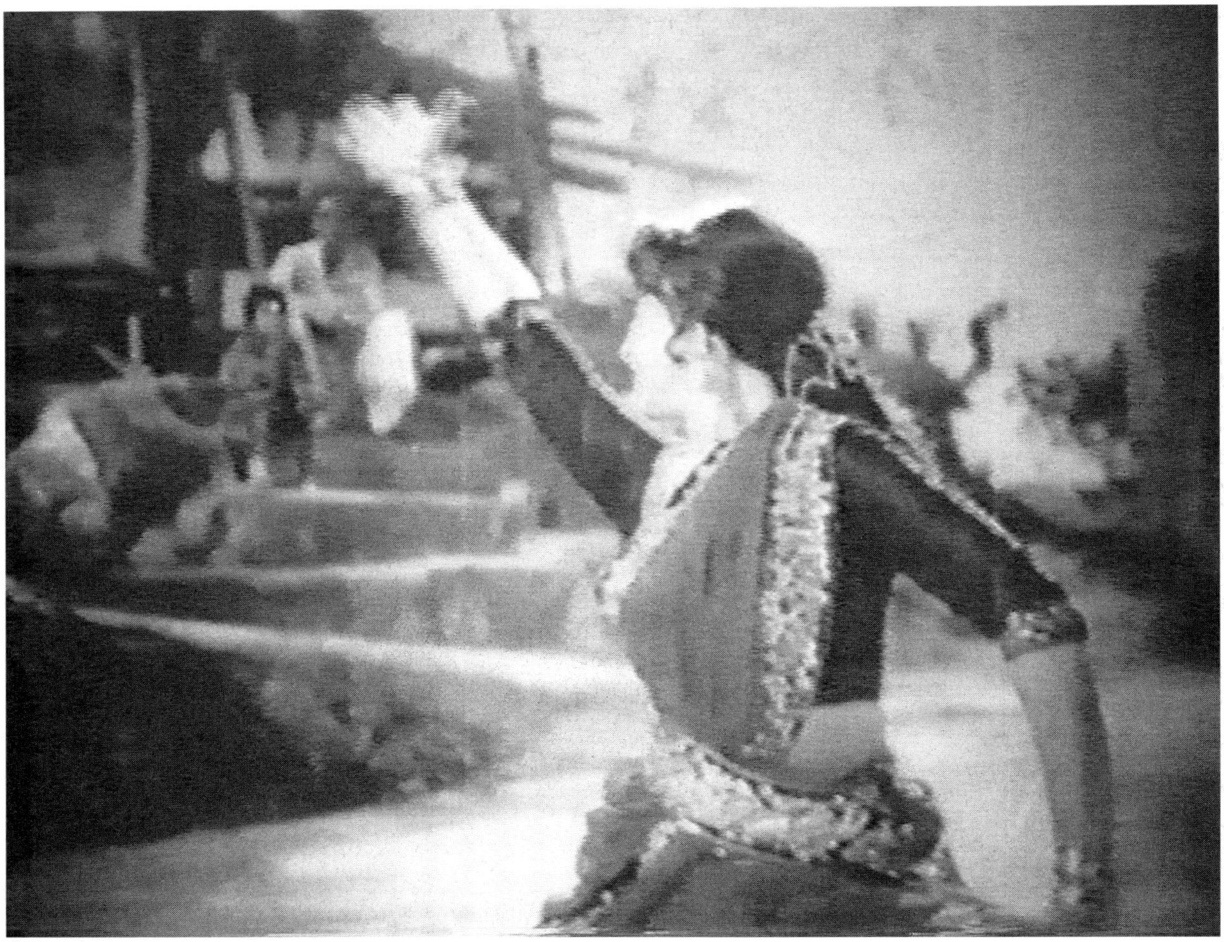

Figure 6. Waheed Rehran in *Guide*, 1965. Reproduced courtesy of Dev Anand and Navketan Films, Mumbai.

Shilpa

My interview with Shilpa serves to illustrate the autobiographical and intimate narrative where objects function as visual, metonymical devices, secured in everyday practices. These are a means of traversing the manifold connections with various 'homes', or places of belonging. The case study stands as a witness to Shilpa's biography, and the influence of its geographies on her engagement with visual cultures in the home.

On 28 October 1999 I interviewed Shilpa in her home. A woman with a rich life-history, she was born in India and was currently living in Harlesden. I asked her to talk about her route to England and used this to access landscapes of 'home', transition and experiences of settlement; this provided a map of formal identification. Shilpa lived in India until she was married, when she left for her husband's residence in Kenya. This marriage failed and she moved back to India.

Shilpa remarried and moved to her second husband's home in Sudan where they lived happily for four years. After the birth of their daughter, she was given the opportunity by her husband to visit her parents in India. He bought

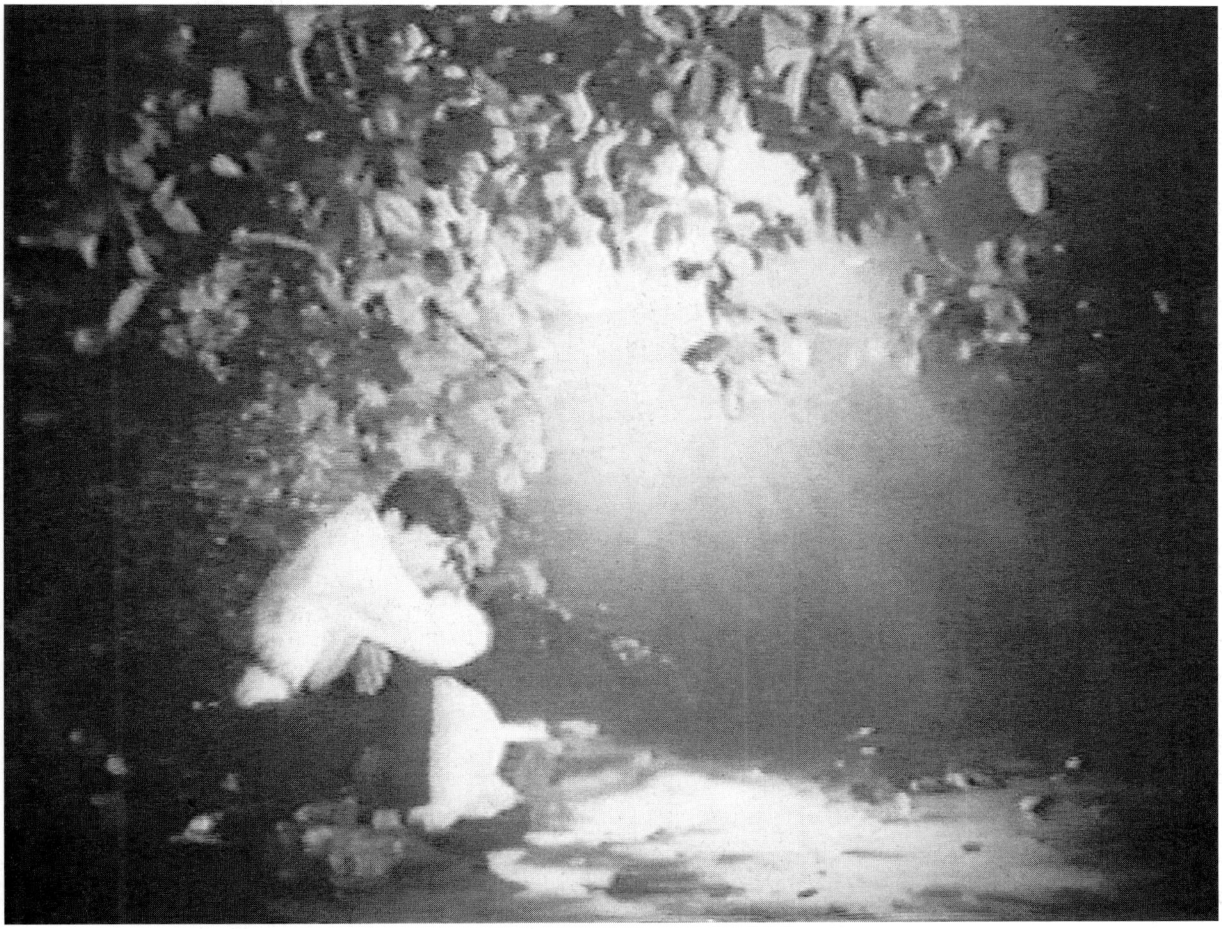

Figure 7. Dev Anand in *Guide*, 1965. Reproduced courtesy of Dev Anand and Navketan Films.

plane tickets for her and she left without her daughter for a trip 'back home'. Whilst in India, Shilpa had a visit from her brother-in-law who informed her that the marriage was over and handed her a suitcase with her belongings. She was consoled by her family who advised her to make a life in India. But Shilpa, then aged 27, soon made tracks to Sudan to 'abduct' her daughter. She regained care of her daughter and fled to England where she rented a small room; from this she was able to apply for Housing Association property. She has lived here for fifteen years without going back to India, Sudan or Kenya.

On a tour of her home, I wanted her to show me aspects of visual culture that were important to her and her sense of 'home'. The first thing Shilpa showed me was a locked cupboard in her 'religious' room in which she keeps things dear to her. She went through photographs of Kenya, some of her wedding, her husband and mostly of her daughter and their life in London.

Next, Shilpa drew out a large, old, suitcase in which her treasured things are kept. It looked fragile; it was bamboo yellow with aluminium fittings. It was from another age and certainly another society. She reverently laid out the contents in the living room. There were pieces of jewellery and toys, attached to which was the story of her younger sister's visit to Harlesden from India about eleven years ago. Shilpa described in detail the markets in her home town where her sister had purchased these items, the temples, shops, her father's clothing business, his sales routes through the local farms, his journeys to Kenya and Uganda, fruits and flowers, kitchens and bathrooms. Her sister had given her a model of an Indian gas stove, an open-fire design used in the back yard of her family home. Shilpa explained how she had used a similar stove in Kenya and Sudan. She described the heat in Sudan, the cold nights and the humidity.

Shilpa became very animated at the sight of a metal bucket in the bathroom which she had bought three years ago in Harlesden. She was so pleased with this find that she bought two: one to keep in case the other got damaged. She explained that she had used a bucket like this in her family home in India, and in her marital home in Sudan. It represented the morning ritual of getting up before dawn, filling the bucket with water for bathing, and setting it on a fire to heat for the whole family. Shilpa's family, and life in India, were evoked through this morning ritual. Since the day it was bought, she and her daughter had been using the bucket to wash in the mornings.

Through this piece of metal Shilpa evoked many different lands and different relationships; the textures of her family home and the environment of Sudan became implanted in Britain. The bucket became a prism through which the intimate, domestic spaces of bathing, cooking and cleaning were evoked. In these refracted cultural landscapes were inscribed a set of aesthetics that connected Harlesden with India, Kenya and Sudan. Shilpa had made reconnections with these places for her daughter: creating an identity, a citizenship, not in the national sense, but as a set of co-ordinates which allow her to map her mother's biography and in turn her family and her cultures of identification. This is what the artist Kitaj terms 'a polygot matrix'.[33] This metaphor offers connection, infinite configurations, but within a community of collected logic.

To be able to particularize this experience as diasporic we must be able to theorize a sense of connections as elastic and constituted through time and space, as in Raymond Williams' term 'structures of feeling'.[34] My premise is that these connections signify pathways to identification through their textures. Is it correct, however, to define the suitcase and bucket – as visual culture? 'Visuality' in this research has become slippery and intangible. Sight is privileged but it is informed by touch, smell, feel, and embodiment. In some senses a 'westnocentric' definition of visual culture is structured around media of expression that privilege sight, each medium in turn being governed by schools of art history and 'laws' of aesthetics. But in a world of memories and landscapes when does 'the mind's eye' get activated in relation to pieces of metal and plastic? Are the bucket and the suitcase visual keys to a past? Can the visual incorporate multidimensional textures that exist in everyday objects? In terms of environmental relationships and citizenship the material and visual cultures in the home are pivotal in identity-making. They enable triangulations that allow for the process of re-territorializing in Britain.

These cultures offer a sense of inclusion, which has aesthetic, sensual, and psycho-sociological dimensions. The landscapes refracted through these objects and texts of home are far from the women's place of residence and citizenship, indicating a sense of connectedness to places outside Britain at the same time as reflecting their relationship with or reaction to belonging within Britain. This examination of the group's relationship with visual media offers insights into what places are desired, safe and owned by this group, and which lead to the points of enfranchisement. Many of the women knew the names of plants, birds and insects and the local ecologies of the Indian sub-continent, East Africa, Yemen and Sudan. These were intimate knowledges and connections not translated to the place of permanent residence – England.

Conclusion

Through the example of the Hindi film *Guide* and my interview with Shilpa, I have illustrated the relationships between the social networks that operate through the practice of watching a film, and the connections between metaphor in the film with the metonymical character of visual cultures in the home. Through experiences of migration – sometimes enforced migration – diasporic groups experience a sense of non-identity and dislocation within the formal structures of national identity and the geographies of England. The experience of the post-colonial migrant has been the focus of much of the work by cultural theorists.[35] I emphasize the everyday meanings and resonances of the visual cultures within the home, a core means by which diasporic groups in England make meaning of their geographical positioning. Most importantly, diasporic landscapes of belonging and identity are fixed and framed through negotiations of national cultures of citizenship and imagined cultural geographies that are constituted as safe, secure and free. These cultures of identification are pivotal to unveiling the relationships that diasporic groups have with national landscapes, nature and environment. Cultures of the visual are prisms through which iconographies of enfranchisement, belonging and memory are refracted. These relationships are continually dynamic and are not an essentializing process for the definition of South Asian culture and identity. Metonymical visual signifiers resonate with the past, but are positioned in the present. The memory of the journey continues to figure within daily cultures, but exists in relation to a sense of non-identity, fracture, loss and exclusion: a relational configuration locked into the marginal position of the post-colonial subject in national dialogue.

Thank you to the women who participated in this research, who were co-ordinated by the Asian Women's Resource Centre, Harlesden, and Sangat Advice Centre, Harrow, in London.

Notes

1 Parthiv Shah, ed., *Figures, Facts, Feelings: a Direct Diasporic Dialogue*, exhibition catalogue, Centre for Media and Alternative Communication: Mumbai, India, 2000.

2 See, for example, Rasna Bhushan (curator), 'Telling Tales: of Self, Nation, of Art', an exhibition held at Castle Museum and Art Gallery, Nottingham, in March–May 1998, five Asian women artists looking at post-colonial identity; also see Roshni Kempadoo and Paloumi in 'Translocations' exhibition, held at the Photographers Gallery, London, in March–April 1997. See also Paul Gilroy, 'It ain't where you're from, it's where you're at: The Dialectics of Diasporic Identification', *Third Text*, no.15, Summer

1991; Rasheed Araeen, 'The Other Immigrant: the Experiences and Achievements of Afro-Asian Artists in the Metropolis', *Third Text*, no.15, Summer 1991.

3 Griselda Pollock, ed., *Generations and Geographies in the Visual Arts*, London: Routledge, 1996.

4 Landscape iconography is the development of the theorization of visual culture of landscape representation revealing political and national iconographies, which inform cultural practice. Stephen Daniels contextualizes the production and consumption of these images, unravelling the multifarious historical narratives and meanings which are yielded by the visual representations he considers. See Stephen Daniels, *Fields of Vision: Landscape and National Identity in England and the United States*, Cambridge: Polity Press, 1993.

5 Ingrid Pollard, *Pastoral Interlude Series*, 1987–8, researched by Phil Kinsman in *Renegotiating the Boundaries of Race and Citizenship: The Black Environment Network and Environmental Conservation Bodies*, Nottingham: University of Nottingham, 1994; Phil Kinsman, 'Landscape, Race, and National Identity: the Photography of Ingrid Pollard', *Area*, vol, 27, no.4, 1995.

6 See Stephen Daniels, *Fields of Vision*, and also David Matless, *Landscape and Englishness*, London: Reaktion, 1998.

7 See Raymond Williams, *The Country and the City*, London: Hogarth, 1993 (also published London: Chatto & Windus 1973); David Lowenthal, 'British National Identity and the English Landscape', *Rural History*, no. 2, 1991, pp.205–30; Stephen Daniels, *Fields of Vision*; Phil Kinsman, 'Landscape, Race, and National Identity in Contemporary Britain', unpublished PhD thesis, University of Nottingham, 1997.

8 Yi-Fu Tuan, 'Thought and Landscape', in D. W. Meinig, ed., *The Interpretation of Ordinary Landscapes*, New York and Oxford: Oxford University Press, 1979. Tuan describes the relevance of landscape as being part of a universal desire for an 'ideal and humane habitat . . . Such a habitat must be able to support a livelihood and yet cater to our moral and aesthetic nature . . . landscape allows and even encourages us to dream'.

9 Humanistic geography has considered the phenomenology of *being* and *dwelling* in the landscape as a point of engaging with the experience of landscape as an intimate *home*. See E. Relph, *Place and Placelessness*, London: Pion, 1976; David Ley and Marvyn S. Samuels, eds, *Humanistic Geography*, London: Croom Helm, 1978; and D.W. Meinig, ed., *The Interpretation of Ordinary Landscapes*.

10 Richard Mabey, *The Common Ground*, London: Hutchinson, 1980. Although Mabey's argument is for ecological preservation, he situates this in the cultural meanings of local landscape ecologies, and their essential place in the well-being of human beings. See also Phil MacNaughten and John Urry, *Contested Natures*, London: Sage, 1998, chapter 4.

11 Stuart Hall, 'Cultural Identity and Diaspora', in Jonathan Rutherford, ed., *Identity, Community, Culture, Difference*, London: Lawrence and Wishart, 1990, p.226.

12 Jacqueline Burgess, Carolyn Harrison, and M. Limb, 'Exploring Environmental Values through the Medium of Small Groups, 1: Theory and Practice', *Environment and Planning A*, vol. 20, 1988, pp.309–26, and Jacqueline Burgess, Carolyn Harrison, and M. Limb 'Exploring Environmental Values through the Medium of Small Groups, 2: Theory and Practice', *Environment and Planning A*, vol 20, pp.457–76, 1998.

13 Vijay Anand (dir.) *Guide*, 1965, 183' (120'), colour, Hindi.

14 Nicholas Mirzoeff, *Visual Culture Reader*, London: Routledge, 1998.

15 See Homi K. Bhabha, *The Location of Culture*, London: Routledge, 1994; Homi K. Bhabha 'Cultures In-between', in Stuart Hall and Paul Du Gay, *Questions of Cultural Identity*, London: Sage, 1996; and W. E. Du Bois, *The Souls of Black Folk*, New York: Bantam, 1989.

16 Paul Gilroy, *The Black Atlantic*, Cambridge, Mass.: Harvard University Press, 1993.

17 R. Samuel, *Theatres of Memory*, Verso: London, 1994. See also Robert Hewison, *The Heritage Industry*, London: Methuen, 1987, and Patrick Wright, *On Living in an Old Country: The National Past in Contemporary Britain*, London: Verso, 1985.

18 Arjun Appurdurai, *Modernity at Large: Cultural Dimensions of Globalisations*, Minneapolis: University of Minnesota Press, 1997.

19 Ibid., p.48.

20 Ibid., p.49.

21 See Rasheed Araeen, 'From Primitivism to Ethnic Arts', *Third Text*, no.1, Autumn 1987; Paul Gilroy, *Small Acts: Thought on the Politics of Black Cultures*, London: Serpent's Tail, 1993; Edward Said, *Culture and Imperialism*, London: Vintage, 1994.

22 'Bollywood' describes the Bombay-based film industry, as opposed to other film production in the Indian sub-continent. Bollywood remains the most popular film culture within the South Asian diaspora.

23 Avtar Brah, *Cartographies of Diaspora*, London: Routledge, 1996.

24 Benedict Anderson, *Imagined Communities: Reflections on the Origin and Spread of Nationalism*, London: Verso, 1991.

25 Yash Chopra (dir.), *Khabhie, Khabhie*, 1976, starring Amitabh Bachchan, Sashi Kapoor, Waheeda Rehman.

26 See A. Brah, *Cartographies of Diaspora: Contesting Identities*, London: Routledge, 1996; also Marie Gillespie, *Television, Ethnicity and Cultural Change*, London and New York: Routledge, 1995.

27 Quoted in Ashish Rajadhyaksha and Paul Willeman, *Encyclopaedia of Indian Cinema*, London and Oxford: British Film Institute and Oxford University Press, 1994.

28 See D. Matless, 'The Art of Right Living: Landscapes and citizenship 1918–39', in Steve Pile and Nigel Thrift, eds, *Mapping the Subject*, London: Routledge, 1995; and Matless, *Landscape and Englishness*.

29 This is discussed in much Cultural Studies material; see, for example, David Morley, *Television, Audiences, and Cultural Studies*, London and New York: Routledge, 1992.

30 Toni Morrison, 'The Site of Memory', in Russell Ferguson, Martha Gever, Trinh T. Minh-ha and Cornel West, eds, *Out There: Marginalisation and Contemporary Cultures*, Cambridge, Mass.: MIT Press, 1990.

31 Sumita S. Chakravarty, *National Identity in Indian Popular Cinema 1947–1987*, Oxford: Oxford University Press, 1996.

32 Morrison, 'The Site of Memory'.

33 R. B. Kitaj, in N. Mirzoeff, ed., *Introduction to Visual Culture*, New York: Routledge, 1999, p.36.

34 Raymond Williams, *The Sociology of Culture*, New York: Schocken Books, 1982.

35 See work by Stuart Hall, Homi Bhabha, Guyatri Chakrabharty Spivak, Paul Gilroy, Rasheed Araeen and the journals *Third Text* and *Diaspora*.

Darren Newbury

Telling Stories about Photography: The Language and Imagery of Class in the Work of Humphrey Spender and Paul Reas

Who are these people going up to the North of England and bringing back these images of what they think the North is like?[1]

This essay argues that class has been a central problematic in visual representations of social life in Britain during the twentieth century, and that critical analysis of photographic practice has neglected this question. The relationship between claims about the world and the visual forms in which these are presented is a central issue for documentary, but this should not be seen simply as a question of the accuracy or adequacy of representations. Class is experienced and understood through the way it is represented in both language and images. Bernard Waites, in his study from the period of the First World War, refers to the 'language of class', which 'expresses the social actor's lived relationship with the everyday world of work and neighbourhood'.[2] It may be true in this context that 'pictorial representations are only an incidental source' of the imagery of class, but from a wider cultural and historical perspective visual images of class are immensely important.[3] In common with literature, television drama and film, during the twentieth century photography has contributed to the creation of a social and cultural imagery of class, which has shaped the ways in which class is understood and experienced as an aspect of national and regional identity.[4] However, in comparison with film and literature, still photography has been largely absent from broader cultural histories. Stuart Laing's detailed account of the representation of working-class life in the late 1950s and early 1960s, for example, makes no reference to photography.[5] This essay therefore contributes to the study of the role of documentary photography in the visual imaging of class.

My second argument is that the *practice* of photography as an engagement with and interpretation of social life has not been given the critical attention it deserves, compared to the reception of images. The position of the photographer is framed in terms of individual creative development, or as a servant of ideology. I argue that photographers are neither mere 'imaging technician[s]',[6] in the sense of being objective recorders of social life, nor neutral channels through which the values of a culture or class are given visual form.

Instead, various discourses inform photographers' understandings of their practice, internalized language and perceptions of the role of photographic images. Also, particular social-class interactions shape the photographic encounters from which images of working-class life are created. Documentary photographs result from interaction between photographer and subject. The 'vision' of the photographer is constrained by having to negotiate his or her presence in a particular context; influenced by his or her relationship to that context. In part determined by the institutional contexts in which the work takes place, this also operates on a more individual level; how the practice of documentary is understood and subjectively experienced by photographers. Ian Walker points out in his discussion of documentary in the 1930s that 'the collection of evidence can never stand alone, can never attain a self-sufficient scientific "objectivity". It must inevitably be intermeshed with the subjectivity – indeed, the desires – of the person collecting the evidence',[7] particularly where visual 'evidence' is collected in cross-cultural or cross-class encounters.

Here I analyse photographers' own accounts to explore the subjective impulses that have contributed to the making of photographic representations of working-class life. The Oral History of British Photography Collection held at the National Sound Archive in London contains life-history interviews which provide a rich and complex picture of the lives of a substantial number of British photographers and the development of their practice, a unique resource for exploring the biographical as well as the social and cultural contexts which informed the ways in which photographers saw and documented the social world.[8] This article uses interviews with Humphrey Spender and Paul Reas and exploits the new insights provided by this material.

My concentration on Spender and Reas is framed by a wider interest in exploring the link between photography and what might be termed the visual public sphere. The emergence of photography alongside the industrialization and urbanization of the nineteenth century has meant that working-class lives have long been a staple subject of photography. Early forms of social documentary that 'sought to illuminate the dark corners of society and make visible the underprivileged and unsightly in order to prick the conscience of the powerful',[9] are perhaps understandable within the terms of 'instrumental realism'.[10] But later documentary practices are subject to a more complex articulation with politics and society. The circulation of images of social life in documentary film and photography increased during the 1930s – a time of intense social and political interest in issues of class, and Spender's most productive period. New picture magazines and the widespread use of film and photography to record and show social life can be seen as part of the emergence of a more socially inclusive discourse about British society. Stuart Hall suggests that the 'social eye' of *Picture Post* contributed to the consensus for social and welfare reform in post-war Britain, whilst limiting a focus on the underlying structural causes of inequality.[11] Peter Hutchings sees John Grierson's documentary films as 'intended to explain various social processes to a mass audience in order, supposedly, that the members of this audience might become more informed participants in a social democracy'.[12] This linkage between the visual and the socially enlightening is problematic, since the act of looking carries with it connotations of power and pleasure. The term 'citizen-voyeur' captures the tension implicit in this licence to photograph the private spaces and lives of individuals in the name of the public.[13] This underlines the importance of placing the photographer's social vision alongside an understanding of the subjective practice of documentary. Spender's interview (1992) offers an insight into the tensions and conflicts between his upper-class background, his desire to place photography in service of socialist political goals and his interaction with working-class subjects.

Reas' interview (1993) betrays a different trajectory. From a working-class background, his photography reflects a more recent rethinking of class identities in the context of consumerism, where faith in the social value of documentary has disintegrated and where, in many of its forms, it is viewed as irredeemably voyeuristic.[14] Working at a time when class has seemingly disappeared from public view, Reas' later work can be read as a reflection on the impossibility of representing class except as an aspect of history – even though there are probably more high-profile photographers from working-class backgrounds now than ever before. In one sense, then, Spender and Reas mark, respectively, the beginning and the endpoint of a particular way of thinking about the value of photographing working-class lives.

Humphrey Spender

Humphrey Spender is seen retrospectively as one of the key figures in the emergence of the documentary tradition in British photography. Yet during the 1930s, described by John Taylor as 'the moment of "documentary", in which (largely middle-class) eyewitness accounts and apparently factual photography brought to light the living spaces of the urban working class'[15] – no such clarity of position was possible. Evidence suggests that Spender himself had only a vague sense of the significance of his own work, and that it was only Tom Harrisson's interest in his Mass Observation images that stopped him from throwing them away.[16] This suggests that there was no accepted understanding of the production and reception of social-documentary photographs in the 1930s. Taylor contrasts the position of the urban documentarist with that of the tourist. For tourists, he argues, there was anxiety about failing to see or feel what they should, whereas documentarists derived authority from being there and bringing back what they saw.[17] My argument here is that Spender's photographic work is the result of his occupying a number of complex, and at times contradictory, positions. But if there was no readily available framework for showing the Mass Observation photographs in their entirety, either as a visual social study or as the body of work of an individual photographer, neither were the images produced in a visual or an ideological vacuum.[18]

Tom Jeffery argues that the project can be seen as a critique of the established press, accused of failing to provide the public with information and of treating them with contempt.[19] Spender's work during this period for the *Mirror* was similarly an implied critique of a press photographic practice that set up images (which he referred to as 'the £5 note photograph') and relied on stereotypes rather than observation. Although this was facilitated by changes in photographic technology, the ideological changes are equally important. Mass Observation was conceived as an anthropological project, but Jeffery argues that looking at working-class life in the north of England cannot be understood merely as a project of middle- and upper-class curiosity, scientific or otherwise. Instead, it was committed to public education, closely tied to politics (Harrisson viewed the project as an interface between government and people).[20] Jeffery argues that this 'need to know' about the wider population informed the documentary movement of the 1930s, underpinned by a need for national unity rather than class conflict. The original reference to Bolton – the focus of a Mass Observation study as 'Northtown' and subsequently as 'Worktown' – indicates the initial placing of the project in the context of North–South economic, class and cultural divisions.[21] The intertwining of this general cultural and social project with the concerns of those through whom it operates is of considerable interest, particularly in the case of Mass Observation's accounts of social life by artists, poets, and photographers, as well as 'ordinary' people, which deliberately made use of what were referred to as 'subjective cameras'.[22]

Spender was influenced in his choice of subjects and his photographic approach by two frames of reference: the notion of objective sociological or anthropological observation and 1930s left-wing politics. Spender often saw his photographic work as serving political goals, though his socialism involved a general humanism, rather than commitment to any explicitly political analysis. Importantly, the social distance between Spender and his subjects, often dominant in his discussion of his own practice, sat uncomfortably with both the anthropological and political frames. This tension is a key to understanding the production of the images, though perhaps not their subsequent reception.

Born in 1910, into what he describes as an 'intellectual, cultured family', this consciousness of his privileged background permeates Spender's discussion of his early life and his photographic work. In a discussion of his childhood he refers to his 'envy of people like Henry Moore, who came from under-privileged backgrounds and were forced to do things that a privileged child is not'. Contact with 'the lower classes' was taboo during his childhood and, as a result, he sought encounters with young working-class women.[23] Spender was, in his own words, 'haunted' and, I would suggest, fascinated by class differences. A number of writers have emphasized the honesty and empathy in Spender's photographs,[24] whereas his own accounts and discussions of his work suggest an acute sense of social awkwardness, embarrassment and anxiety in his cross-class encounters.

Spender's understanding of the significance of his work was influenced by the use of photography in anthropology and he believed that documenting various cities and towns for *Picture Post* was 'serious sociological research'.[25] This is evident in the photographs themselves. For example, David Mellor refers to Spender's *The Wayside Pulpit, Bolton* (1937) as 'evidence on the manner in which agrarian rituals like Harvest Thanksgiving are sustained in an industrialised society'.[26] A theme of many of Spender's images from this period is collective behaviour – political meetings, football matches, leaving the factory and so on (Figure 1) – recording the interactions surrounding events rather than the events themselves. Although Bolton was referred to as 'Worktown', the images suggest a much broader study of its social life, images of work being only a minor part.[27] Spender had no clear sense of the sociologi-

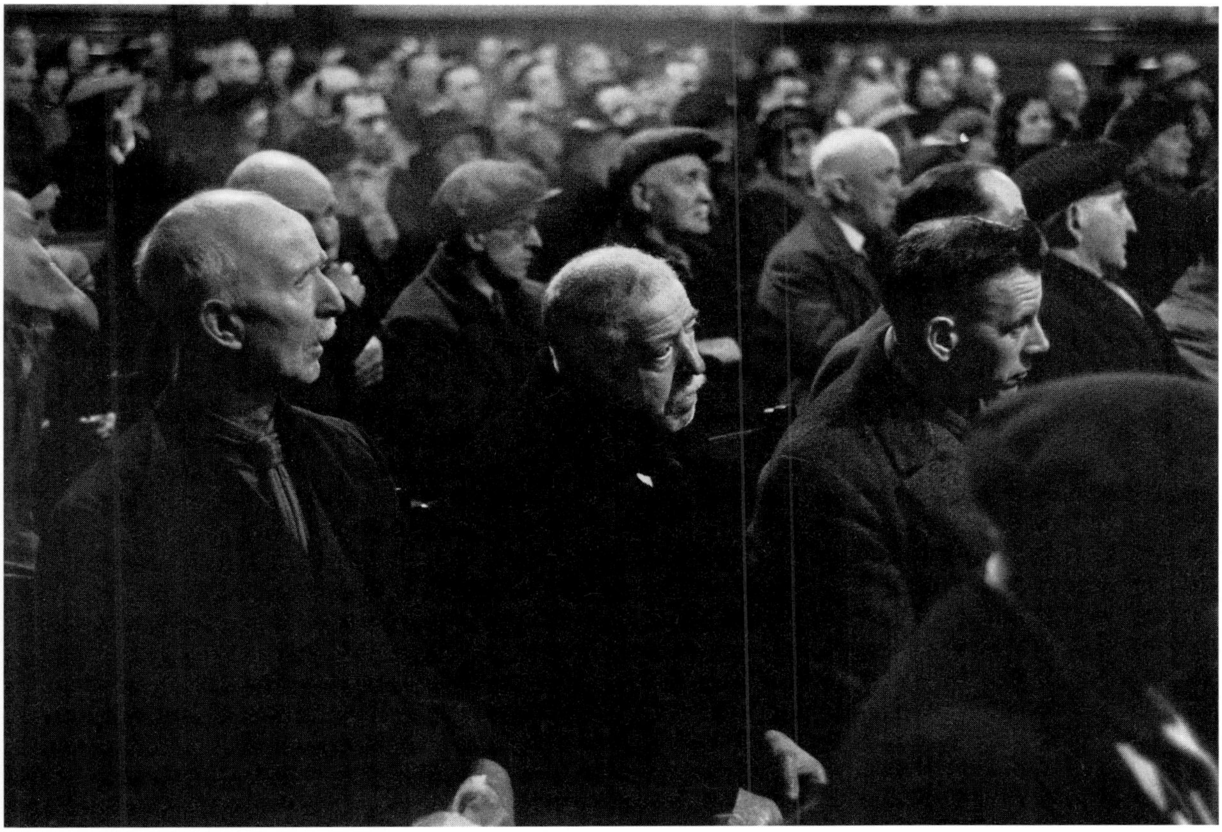

Figure 1. Humphrey Spender, *National Government Meeting, Bolton, 1937*. Reproduced courtesy of Bolton Museum and Art Gallery.

cal or anthropological importance of his photographs, depending on others for an understanding of how they might be useful and for the frameworks within which they were viewed. His work in 1934 in Stepney was at the request of Clemence Paine, a probation officer who used the images in court, analysing the relationship between living conditions and crime. Similarly, Spender depended on Harrisson to supply the intellectual context for the Mass Observation work in Bolton.

The idea of the unobserved observer dominated much of Spender's thinking. He talks about the idea that photographs only counted as 'true, useful and informative' when they were made without the subjects' knowledge. Possibly a critique of established practices in press photography and a result of Harrisson's anthropological influence, it was also intellectual justification for Spender's desire for anonymity. Brinsford contrasts Spender with Bert Hardy: 'Spender was keen to remain invisible, to be secret and keep any contact with his Other to a minimum. Hardy made friends and contacts within the communities within which he worked ... For Spender, the working-class districts and individuals were foreign, chaotic and unintelligible, whilst for Hardy they were familiar.'[28] Raphael Samuel comments on the visual consequences of this stance:

figures are typically seen from the rear or sideways ... Faces, where they are seen in close-up, are lined with worry. Images of entrapment abound, nowhere more so than the pub, where the drinkers are literally cornered. Whippet-like men fill the stands at the greyhound racing track. A long shot of a woman whitening the doorstep has her face – and that of a watching child – a mere blur. A bird's-eye view of Blackpool beach has all the faces out of focus, as though even on holiday relaxation was a forbidden luxury.[29]

Spender was acutely aware that photographing surreptitiously had the potential to bring him into conflict with his subjects, as, for example, once in a public house in Bolton.[30] In this incident, Spender appealed neither to the scientific nor the political importance of the work he was doing, but to the law and the freedom to photograph 'entirely for my own pleasure, life in an industrial town'. The fragility of his scientific and political justifications leads Spender to a discourse of looking that owes more to class difference and power. Interestingly, though, Spender did explore more open approaches. Photographing a family in Stepney in 1934, he tried to become an unobserved observer by building trust and familiarity. This is different in practical and ethical terms from the covert photography he engaged in for Mass Observation.

In her recent book Deborah Frizzell says, 'Like many of his generation, Spender became committed to helping give voice to the concerns of the underclass, which had been excluded from all debate and decision-making positions, invisible in the press or any other media, except perhaps as caricature'.[31] However, the idea of photography contributing to a visual public sphere remains vague and undefined, justifying, in Spender's case, the argument that 'the documentary movement as a whole ultimately lacked the necessary language and political consciousness to make invisible social relations visible'.[32]

Spender discusses his coverage of the Jarrow march; the photographs in Stepney and the work for Mass Observation as linked to his left-wing political stance.[33] The fact that his work was unpaid is what marks it out. Ironically, as Spender was well aware, it was his private income and class position that enabled him to do this work unpaid as an indication of his commitment and 'out of conscience'.[34] But if left-wing politics influenced what he chose to photograph, there was no guarantee that the subjects would understand or even recognize this. Spender recounts the resentment of the Jarrow hunger marchers who saw an exploitative element and lack of commitment in his joining the march ten miles outside of London to take photographs. Spender's explanation for why he was persuaded to work on the Mass Observation project – Tom Harrisson was an extremely funny man who convinced him the work was important, and the fact that the work was unpaid fitted Spender's notion of worthy and radical work – indicates something of the character of his engagement with the documentary work of the 1930s.

Social and cultural differences between Spender and his photographic subjects have an aesthetic dimension. Writing on architecture, Ken Worpole argues that it is possible to talk about a social-democratic aesthetic: 'focused on collective provision allied to modern design and strongly predicated on a belief in the benefits of clean water, sunlight and fresh air – based primarily on public health and the reform of the stunted, malnourished bodies of the worker and his family'.[35] Photography, as the metaphorical bringer of light to the dark areas of working-class existence, could be seen as part of this formation. Although Edwards interprets the endorsement of the idea of 'a clean, managed and efficient order' as a failure of radicalism and an expression of the class interests of the documentary observers,[36] Worpole's argument that this aesthetic represented an alliance between modernism and social-democratic politics is more convincing:

> Certainly, the principal actors involved in both movements had little in common personally, one suspects: the social democratic politicians were more likely to have emerged from trades unions, nonconformist religious backgrounds and left-wing social movements; the modernist architects were more likely to have come from well-educated, bourgeois families, rich enough to afford the lengthy academic and technical training. While it lasted, however, the two forces together created a whirlwind that changed forever the faces of towns and cities throughout Europe.[37]

Spender's work certainly links visual modernism with social documentation. Having trained as an architect, he was influenced by European photography. He spent considerable time in Germany in the late 1920s and early 1930s and was influenced by the *Neue Sachlichkeit* (New Objectivity) photography of that period. He cites the influence of Russian photography's inclusion of workers, and its emphasis on unusual angles and vantage points – but as an exploration of the visual, not an exercise in 'working-class self-authorship' (Figure 2).[38]

Figure 2. *Humphrey Spender, Midway Clowns, Blackpool, 1937.* Reproduced courtesy of Bolton Museum and Art Gallery.

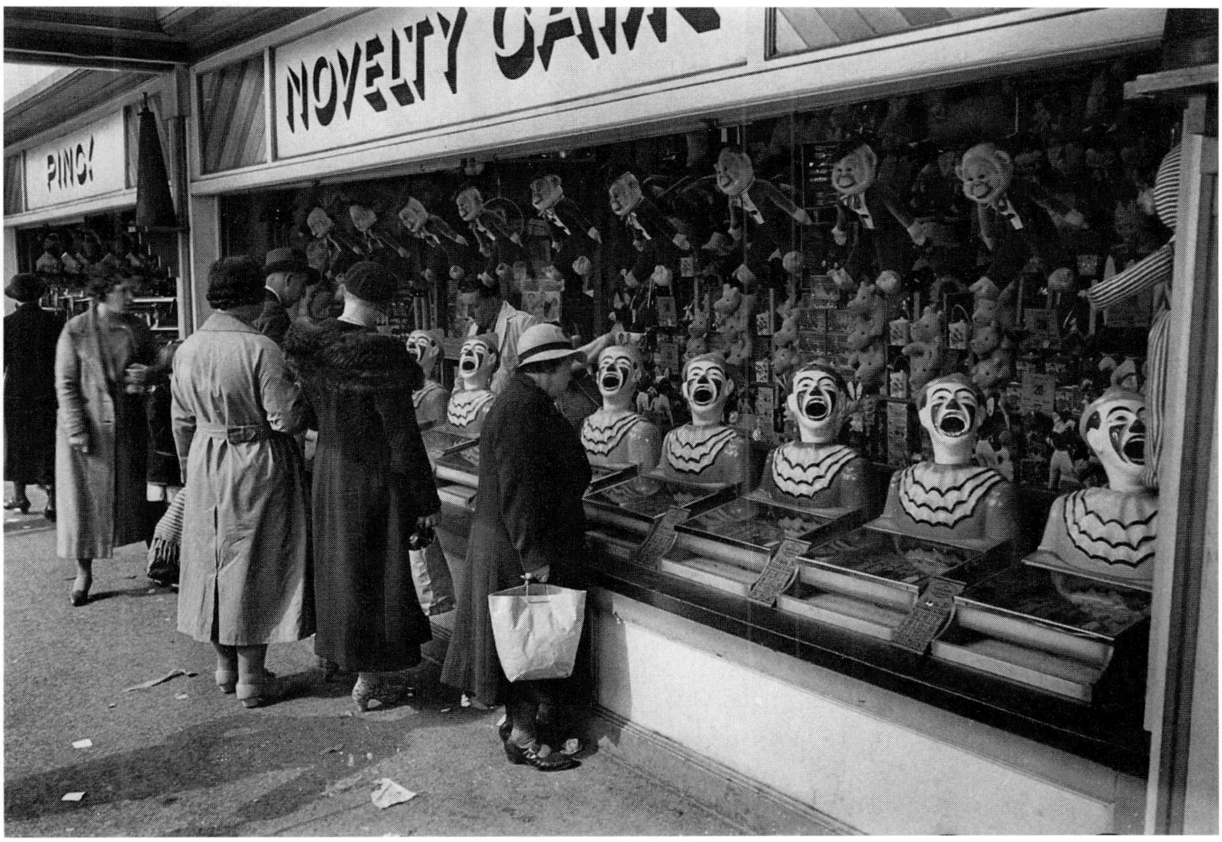

Unlike architecture, documentary photography concerns the present rather than a vision of the future, endorsing an interest in the visual qualities of the current conditions of the working class. If the visually more mundane photographs of the workings of the political process represent the serious project of Mass Observation to inform and educate, then the images of the working-class population of Bolton on holiday in Blackpool represent an interest in the visual and aesthetic pleasures of working-class leisure.[39] Spender's aesthetic response to the unfamiliar working-class environment was characterized by ambivalence, and he often refers to a sexualized image of the working class: 'sexually attractive, possibly slightly unwashed, possibly leading a much more natural life'.[40] He also speaks of Bolton's depressing atmosphere and recalls the 'smell of ghastly frying fat' that permeated the house where the Mass Observation group were based. Spender's photographic work can thus be understood as contributing to a form of vicarious class-tourism on behalf of later viewers (Figure 3).

During the early 1980s, at a time when unemployment was again a major political issue and when traditional working-class culture was at a point of crisis, Spender describes himself, then in his seventies, dressing down in order to blend into the surroundings, and walking into a Newcastle pub – to replay the Mass Observation experience. He describes the 'wave of anxiety, and nerves' that accompanied his fear of being recognized. The fact that he chose to

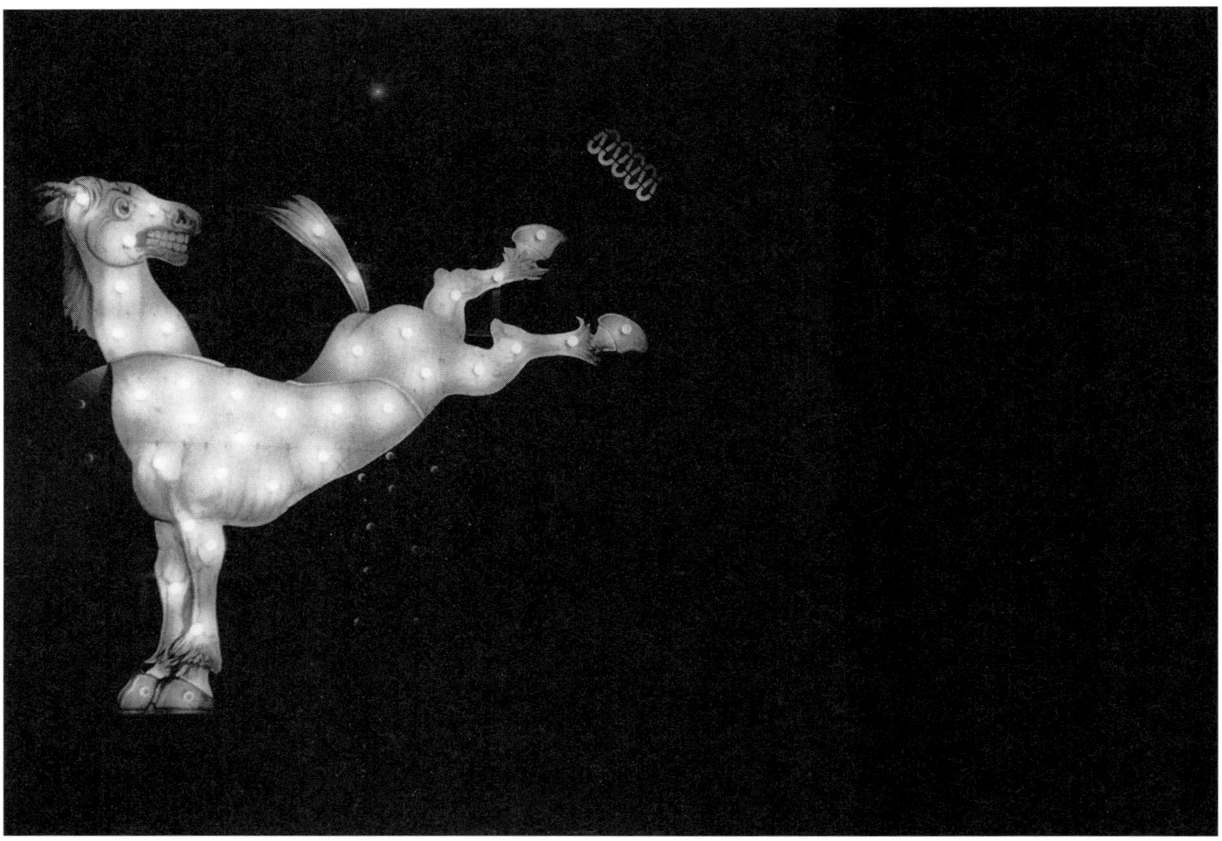

Figure 3. Humphrey Spender, *Blackpool, 1937*. Reproduced courtesy of Bolton Museum and Art Gallery.

replay experiences that induced feelings of anxiety, guilt and fear suggests the significance of his fascination with working-class life at a time when his photographic work was given an important place in British photography.

Paul Reas

Paul Reas stands in sharp contrast to Spender. He was born in Bradford in 1955 and lived on the Buttershaw council estate where, at the time of the interview in the OHBP collection (1993), his mother still lived.[41] His involvement with photography represented a move away from working-class life as much as an engagement with it, and was not framed by the idea of exploring the unfamiliar or 'other'. He saw in photography images of 'situations that were similar to my experience, where I lived and the kind of lifestyle I had'.[42] Reas states his reluctance to discuss his own childhood for fear of it sounding like a caricature.[43] The interview carries a sense of the lasting impact of class on Reas, from his early experiences of education – 'like all working-class kids really, in school you are constantly told ... that you are not going to achieve and you start to believe that early on' – to his involvement in the photographic world.

The 1970s saw the emergence of a more autonomous and self-confident photographic culture from which both Spender and Reas benefited. Photojournalism and magazine photo-essays remained important, and photographic galleries and book publishing supported the notion of the photographer as an individual creative artist, which was important to the re-evaluation of Spender's 1930s work, as were the parallels being drawn at the time between the mass unemployment of the two periods. This autonomy provided the framework for Reas' career as a photographer, but at some personal cost: 'I've learnt to talk in a way that allows me to operate in the circumstances and climate that I now move in ... that's really why I no longer fit back on the Buttershaw estate.' This reflects the complexities and contradictions of a working-class photographic practice for those who emerged from British photographic higher education courses in the 1980s and 1990s and have a direct relationship with their working-class subjects (others would include Nick Waplington and Richard Billingham).

Reas is also working in a social and cultural context that is utterly changed, even from the early 1980s when Spender's work was resurfacing and Spender himself was replaying his experiences of Mass Observation. The working-class communities and forms of organization and culture that provided the focus for many photographic studies were disappearing. The Miners' Strike of 1984 provided the focus for a wealth of documentary activism[44] and photography played an important role in recording the struggle for survival of working-class communities. More important to an understanding of Reas' work is the increased importance of consumption to the formation of identity, accompanying changing patterns of employment and leisure. Traditional forms of working-class culture disappeared from 'the national cultural stage'[45] signalled in photography by a new colour documentary school. Paul Graham's work in dole offices is one of the few prominent bodies of colour work from this period that did not focus thematically on new forms of consumption or employment.[46]

But the relationship between social and cultural change and its representation is not straightforward. Valerie Walkerdine argues that for cultural theory 'the respectable white working class got dropped while the new theorists of mass consumption went shopping'.[47] British photography shifted its focus towards those sections of British society whose values were becoming dominant, and towards the representation of the privatized sphere of consumption.[48] From the mid-1980s working-class lives became less visible, but to conflate this with the decreasing significance of class is a mistake. As Thrift points out, this does not 'imply that working class culture is dying out'. Instead 'it has taken on a new, more consumption-orientated, and probably a more privatized, form'.[49] In the early 1980s, Jeremy Seabrook questioned the ability of photography to represent contemporary experience of class disadvantage. Compared with the 1930s, 'unemployment seems to have become a personal tragedy for people, and not a public scandal ... the site of the struggle has been removed to a less accessible place'.[50] If this renders an emphasis on the public and the visible ineffective, one might suggest that class is perceived as less visually interesting. Reas shares the concern to record the new consumer society, but his focus is on working-class people.

Reas' book *I Can Help* attempts to document the tension between the consumption of images, the fantasies that people are being invited to purchase and the reality, for many, of consumption as anxious and stressful rather than pleasurable.[51] Rod Jones emphasizes the analytical dimension of *I Can Help* and, 'Reas' grasp of its wider implications – the development of the out-of-town supermarket and the new housing estates with quick access to the motorways make us aware of the new patterns of consumption, urban development and transportation as a series of inter-locking initiatives'.[52] Many of the images are also sharply critical, and in his interview Reas talks about his discomfort with the aggressive masculinity of his class background. One of the photographs shows a father in combat trousers choosing wallpaper with military imagery while his young son looks on. Another juxtaposes images of farmyard animals with a supermarket meat counter in vivid colour. Reas questions the values that are being bought along with commodities. Again, Reas is ambivalent about his subjects' complicity; there is neither the empathy and intimacy evident in Waplington's work, nor the condescension implicit in Martin Parr's images of New Brighton (Figure 4).[53]

Whilst, at the time it was produced, Spender's making visible of working-class lives could be seen as a socially valuable contribution to public debate, the 1980s saw a move away from this understanding of documentary photography's commitment to the real, towards more subjective, personal accounts of working-class life. Furthermore, to Susan Kismaric, 'These photographers have lost faith in the simpler solutions and programmatic political stances of early documentarians. Their commitment is to the description of the world at hand, to their intuitive sense of the quality of lives lived in Newcastle and Middlesborough in the depressed North East of England, in Northern Ireland, and elsewhere in Britain's vast post-industrial landscape.'[54] This uncoupling

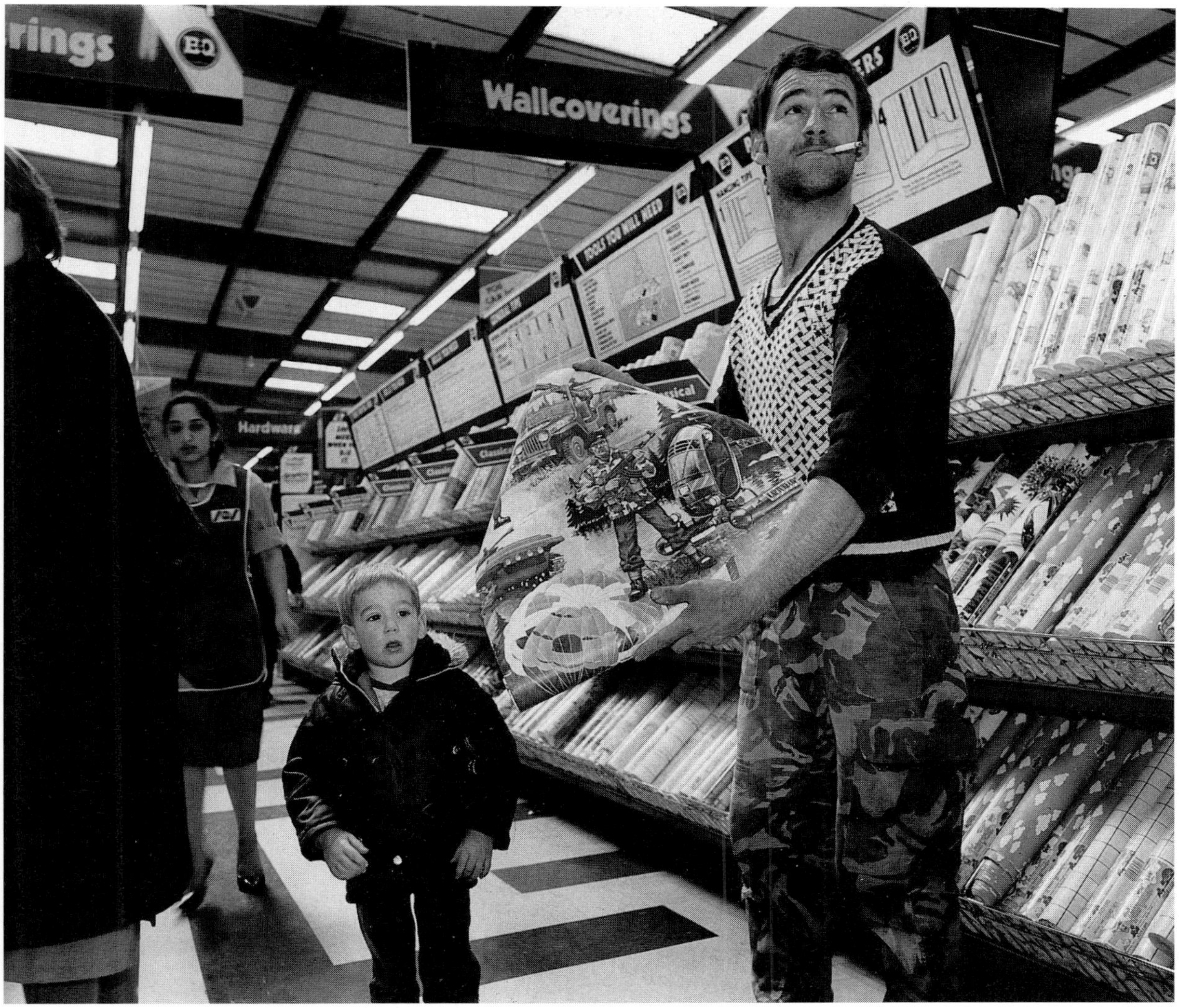

Figure 4. Paul Reas, *Military Wallpaper, B&Q*, from *I Can Help*. Reproduced courtesy of the photographer and Network Photographers Ltd.

of documentary from social or political responsibility was now common. Although some photographers in the late 1980s still aligned themselves with the Griersonian tradition of documentary as the 'creative interpretation of reality', many did not.[55] For example, Chris Killip was concerned that his joint exhibition with Graham Smith at the Serpentine Gallery in 1985 would be dismissed as 'just the north of England'. Some more recent photographers dispute that their photography is about working-class life at all.[56] However, in his study of representations from the 1960s, Stuart Laing makes an interesting point about the shift away from social realism in television drama, to a form which draws on the characterization and humour of music hall: '*Coronation Street*'s relation to northern working-class life was then not so much the reproduction of its routine experiences as of its characteristic forms of entertainment.'[57] Documentary photography also needed to find a more expressive and less 'worthy' vision than the strict, austere black and white documentary of the 1970s – a new social aesthetic more representative of the times.[58]

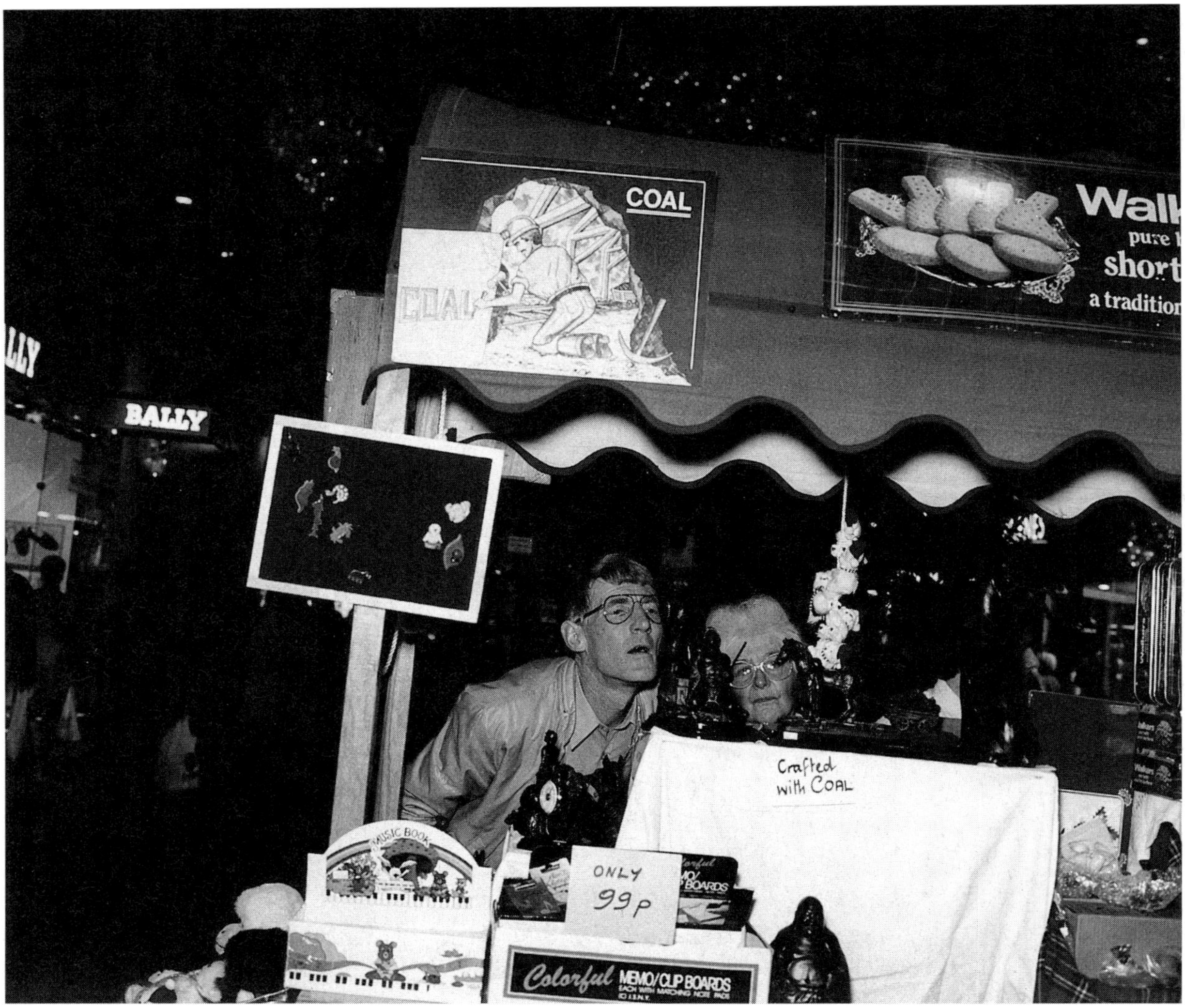

Figure 5. Paul Reas, *Post Industrialism 1, Metro Centre Shopping Mall, The North East of England*, from *I Can Help*. Reproduced courtesy of the photographer and Network Photographers Ltd.

Reas' later work considers the transformation of working-class lives into visual commodities to be looked at aesthetically and purchased out of a sense of nostalgia. Already in *I Can Help*, for example, one photograph taken in the Metro Centre shopping mall in Gateshead (Figure 5) shows objects crafted with coal. Another shows a heritage image on the wall of a supermarket built on the site of a Bradford car factory. Here, Reas' photography is reflexive, turning back on earlier photographic images of working-class lives as they are reinvested in heritage representations. As Reas argues, 'Photography creates all these myths that the heritage industry is largely about... that notion of Northernness which is perpetuated in places like Beamish in County Durham. A lot of the imagery that you encounter comes straight from Humphrey Spender, Bert Hardy, Chris Killip, Bill Brandt.' It is indicative of the transformation that has taken place in the perception of class that, in a period of less than ten years, Chris Killip's work has been assimilated into this longer history of photographic representations of working-class lives.

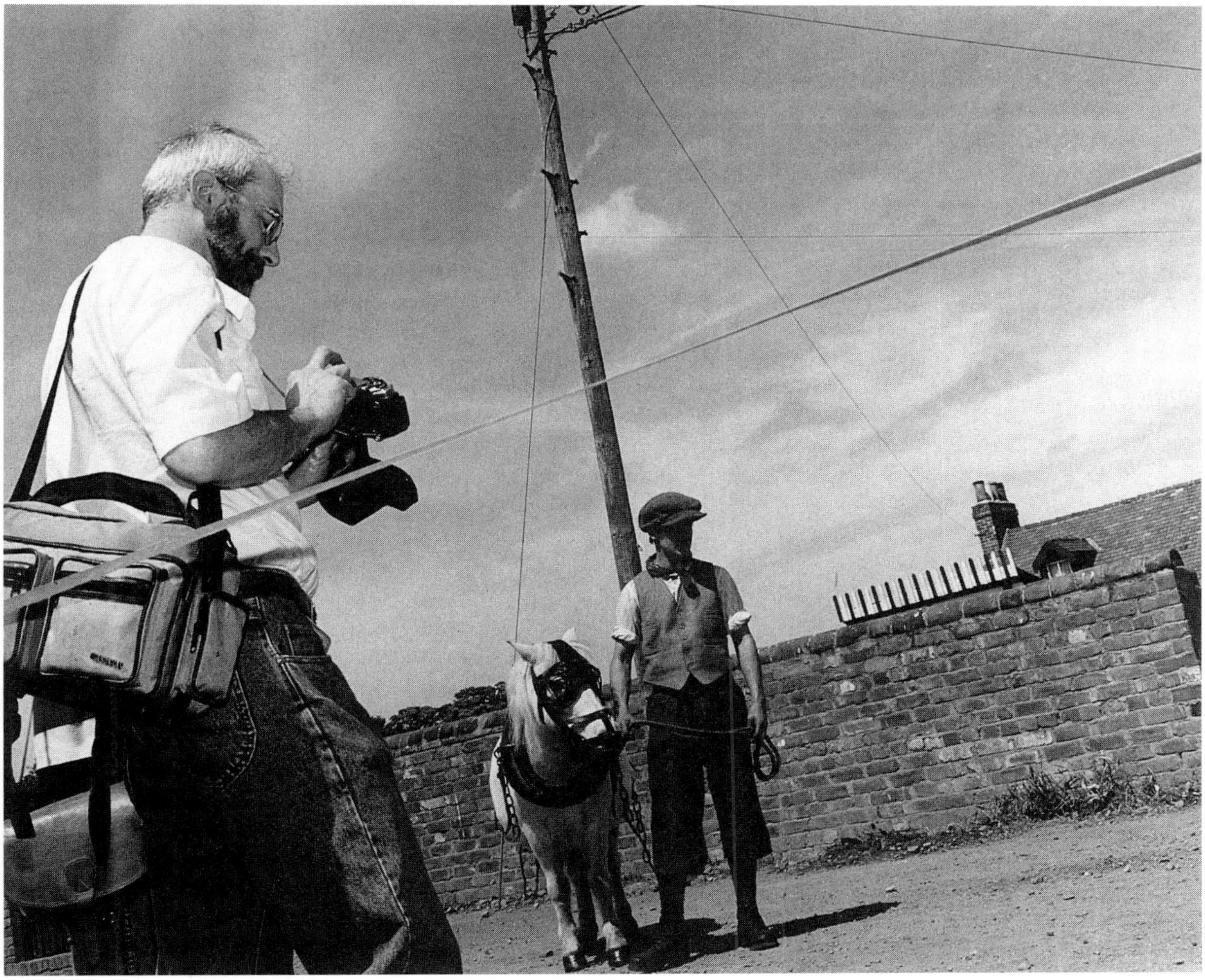

Figure 6. Paul Reas, *Great Northern Experience, North of England Open Air Museum, Beamish, Durham*, from *Flogging a Dead Horse*. Reproduced courtesy of the photographer and Network Photographers Ltd.

In *Theatres of Memory*, Raphael Samuel criticized Reas' photographic book on the heritage industry – *Flogging a Dead Horse*[59] (Figure 6) – as 'a sustained essay in disgust':[60]

> it is not the teashop ladies, those ancient targets of macho abuse, but the spectacle of the Northern working class – young and old, men and women – which excites sexual disgust. In the camera's eye they are no less repellent when smiling than when scowling, and it is difficult to imagine them doing anything which might make them appealing, or earn them a modicum of dignity and respect . . . The idea that the masses, if left to their own devices, are moronic; that their pleasures are unthinking; their tastes cheapo and nasty, is a favourite conceit of the aesthete.[61]

Reas' background does not guarantee a progressive vision, nor is he uncritical of working-class taste, and his work may fit the intellectual trend of 'heritage-baiting'. But for Reas seeing the imagery of working-class heritage sites as a kind of debased spectacle is not, as Samuel suggested, the 'conceit of the aesthete' or the condescension of the 'high-minded' towards working-class taste. Reas is not the voyeur that Samuel assumed him to be, confusing the reception of the images with their production in projecting a smug condemnation of heritage culture from an assumed audience onto him. Like Richard Hoggart in *The Uses of Literacy*, wherein the working class is complicit in the debasement of its own culture,[62] Reas feels no injunction against criticizing the taste or attitudes of his class. To some extent Reas' work has to be seen as a critique of the kind of vicarious class tourism for which Spender and others provided a template. Reas was fully aware that the commodification of working-class lives in the form of heritage follows the residualization of their cultures. As Hewison says of Beamish, 'while this charming world was being created, the life of the North East was being destroyed'.[63] He articulates two relevant concerns in his life-history interview: that heritage does not represent 'a serious attempt to talk about the experience', for example, of mining; and that heritage offers 'pretend' as opposed to 'real' jobs for those areas that have suffered in the process of de-industrialization.[64] Both points indicate a concern born out of Reas' sense of class identity, even if this is not easily discerned from the visual work.

Conclusion: class, cultural memory and visual representation

It is often argued that class is no longer an issue. The social changes that occurred during the 1980s have been consolidated and subsequently absorbed into 'commonsense' perceptions of British society. In political and social debate and policy there has been a move from class-based understandings of the distribution of life chances towards 'an individualization of social inequality'.[65] This demise of class analysis is mirrored in discussions of visual culture. The major themes that have dominated the visualization of working-class life – the visual spectacle of industrialization, the 'poetics of labour',[66] the extremes of poverty and large-scale political mobilization – have passed into history. If (*pace* Hoggart) Britain has become more culturally and visually classless, a lack of interest in class in photography is the natural corollary of social change, as is a rejection of documentary, where 'the object of analysis and its conventional means of representation have both been assumed to be exhausted'.[67] From this point of view, Reas' heritage work signals both the end of the kind of imaging of working-class life initiated in the 1930s, and the end of class itself. Why, then, is it important to look at these images now?

Despite the submergence of traditional class themes in the redefinition of regional identities in contemporary Britain, I am arguing that traditional notions of class are important to the formation of identity in the present. The imagery of class therefore must be seen as an important resource of cultural memory. But even if the consumption of heritage images of class is predicated on their being safely contained in a way that does not disrupt the present, a more positive interpretation than Reas' view that they are inevitably a form of 'gross nostalgia' is possible. The idea of cultural memory recognizes that the imagery of class is important beyond the initial context of its production. Class identities are formed historically as well as under present social and economic conditions. Despite massive changes in economic circumstances between the times of Spender and Reas, class has 'remained a chief metaphor for defining oneself and other people'; and, as Joanna Bourke goes on to argue, 'crucial to this continuity was the power of historical construction. Men and women calling themselves "working-class" were drawing upon an identity based not only on their current position within society, but also on a position inherited from their parents and grandparents.'[68] Photographic archives such as John Gorman's extensively researched collection of images from working-class life – which he describes as 'a photographic remembrance ... a keepsake impression of the life and times of the organised working class' – therefore represent important resources for working-class cultural memory.[69] In this respect the rediscovery of the work of Spender's and Reas' heritage images are part of the same phenomenon – the former providing the raw material through which traditional working-class culture can be rediscovered and reinvested, the latter commenting on this process. It is not only in photography that one might make such an argument. In his discussion of representations of traditional working-class culture in contemporary British film, Roger Bromley characterizes class as an absent presence, 'the theme that dare not speak its name'.[70] A number of popular British films, including the recent *Billy Elliot*, can be read as a series of obituaries for 'the high working-class tradition'.[71] Bromley argues that instead of signalling the end of class, they can be seen as an indication of the contemporary salience of class, that people have been led 'to recognize that, notwithstanding their patterns of consumption or occupation, economically they are "working-class"'.[72] The reception of these images of class is in itself an interesting focus for further research.

The recognition of the contemporary value of documentary images is, however, not an uncritical endorsement of past practices. Photography has contributed to the formation of symbolic locations of working-class life, which, following Marc Augé, one might refer to as 'places of memory'.[73] Consider, for example, the excitement with which Daniel Meadows greeted his arrival in working-class Manchester to study photography: 'it was better than Brandt, it was better than Orwell ... I could walk into the homes of people who looked like they'd just stepped straight out of Bill Brandt's photographs or off the pages of *The Road to Wigan Pier* and talk to people about their lives and photograph them.'[74] Because the work of influential photographers such as Spender dominates the way in which the past has come to be viewed this demands careful and critical scrutiny. Recent photographic history and criticism has taken a simplistic view of documentary as inevitably voyeuristic and condescending. What I hope to have demonstrated here is not that the motives of documentary photographers are pure and well-intentioned, but that the relationship between photographer and photographed is a complex one. Who is doing the photographing, and whose stories of photography and class are being told, are important factors.

If Reas' heritage work can be seen as a point of closure, is there a future for a documentary engagement with working-class life, outside of the recycling of historical images? I want to argue that in spite of recent photographic theory, documentary forms have an important role to play in the representation of contemporary social life. I am not persuaded by Frosh that one should respond to the collapse of faith in the social value of the visual with 'the strategic refusal to photograph – and to look'.[75]

In his critique of 1930s documentary, Edwards points to the photomontage practice of John Heartfield as an alternative to realist documentary which, following Stuart Hall, he suggests was 'capable of revealing social contradictions'.[76] In British photography this view has come to dominate recent thinking on documentary, leading to what Roberts argues is a suppression of 'questions of social reference ... in the interests of privileging the avant-garde critique of representation'.[77] An alternative line of development, with its roots in the work of 1930s and informed more recently by John Berger's collaborations with Jean Mohr, remains committed to a form of realist representation.[78] Its emphasis is on the photographic representation of coherent and integral ways of life, asking how individuals and communities maintain coherent selves and identities despite the disruptions of modern life and capitalism.[79] Although documentary has often been presented as theoretically naïve, the practice of telling stories can take a deliberate and political stand against the fragmented display of images of life in (post)modern societies. Roberts, although ambivalent on the issue, recognizes that the rejection of documentary is ultimately self-defeating:

> such critiques have legitimised photography's retreat from what photography is supremely skilled at doing: generating a visual archive of the look of the material world. The return to the studio then in the 1980s in the name of 'deconstruction' and 'allegory' was absolutely central in clearing away the positivistic prejudices of much of the classist character of social documentary (for example, the heroicized male worker), but at the same time it weakened the empirical link between the photographic process and the visualisation of class relations in the material world.[80]

One direction for social documentary might lie in the visualization of those marginalized by the value systems of mainstream British society, focusing on the more individualized forms in which class disadvantage is currently experienced. Bromley describes the contemporary films of Ken Loach similarly, arguing that he 'is not claiming to depict *the* working class as such', but 'individuals for whom their class position is a crucial dimension of their experience'.[81]

If one equates images of working-class life with images of workers and the industrial process – the focus of 'worker-photography' both in the 1930s and in its 1970s reinvention – then the absence of such images in the present can be seen as a withdrawal from the representation of working-class life. If, on the other hand, one includes the fascination with working-class culture evident in Spender's work for Mass Observation, then there are points of continuity. The enthusiastic reception of the work of photographers such as Nick Waplington and Richard Billingham in the 1990s, though not unproblematic, reflects an aesthetic interest in the visual qualities of particular working-class environments:[82] in the case of Billingham, the rich, if also abject, visual quality and texture of domestic life for a family living on a West Midlands housing estate; for Waplington a more positive vision of life lived in the context of long-term unemployment in Nottingham.

Although there are considerable differences between Spender's engagement with a working class which he found both fascinating and frightening and Reas' representation of a world he knew from personal experience, both were informed by the idea of 'photographing the ordinary'. If one accepts that life chances, values and culture continue to be structured by the social relations into which individuals are born, then, as important as historical images are to the visualization of class, the challenge for documentary photography is to re-establish 'the empirical link' with the social and material world, to find ways of telling new stories about contemporary social life.

Notes

1 Paul Reas interviewed by Val Williams, 1993, Oral History of British Photography Collection, National Sound Archive, London.

2 B. Waites, 'War and the Language of Class', in P. Joyce, ed., *Class*, Oxford: Oxford University Press, 1995, p.336.

3 Ibid.

4 See for example Peter Hutchings' review of visual respresentations of the North East; P. Hutchings, '"When the going gets tough . . .": Representations of the North-East in Film and Television', in T. E. Faulkner, ed., *Northumbrian Panorama: Studies in the History and Culture of North East England*, London: Octavian Press, 1996, pp.273-90.

5 S. Laing, *Representations of Working-Class Life, 1957-1964*, Houndmills: Macmillan, 1986. Laing does acknowledge this absence from the work.

6 J. Brinsford, 'Citizens of the Secret Machine: Elements towards a Bakhtinian History of Photographic Representations of the British Working Classes in the Twentieth Century', unpublished PhD thesis, Sussex University, 1997, p.21.

7 I. Walker, 'Phantom Africa: Photography between Surrealism and Ethnography', *Cahiers d'Études Africaines*, vol.147, no.XXXVII–3, 1997, p.646.

8 V. Williams, R. Perks and M. Barnes, eds, *Talking Photography: Catalogue of the Audio and Visual Collections at the British Library National Sound Archive*, London: British Library National Sound Archive, 1998. The collection was initiated in 1989 by the Oral History Section of The British Library National Sound Archive. It now contains interviews with over 100 photographers, curators, collectors and other influential figures working in British photography since the 1920s. The emphasis of the project is on collecting life-histories; as a consequence the interviews do not just offer insights into particular individuals' active involvement in photography, but also on their early years, their education and many other aspects of their lives.

9 P. Frosh, 'The Public Eye and the Citizen-Voyeur: Photography as a Performance of Power', *Social Semiotics*, vol.11, no.1, 2001, p.46.

10 Allan Sekula, cited ibid., p.46. Foucauldian analysis seems an increasingly blunt instrument with which to analyse photographic practices.

11 S. Hall, 'The Social Eye of *Picture Post*', *Working Papers in Cultural Studies*, no. 2, Birmingham: Centre for Contemporary Cultural Studies, 1972.

12 Hutchings, '"When the going gets tough"', p.281.

13 Frosh, 'The Public Eye', p.50. Frosh's focus is more on the viewer than the photographer. The general sway of his argument is also to suggest that the linkage between the visual and citizenship is a legitimating discourse and little else. He therefore ends negatively on the notion of a 'strategic refusal to photograph – and look' (p.56).

14 This has been accompanied by a more self-consciously subjective documentary practice, of which Reas' work is indicative. What in Spender exists as an undercurrent, partially obscured by the linkage between photography and discourses of social progress, is instead brought into the open and celebrated. See I. Walker, 'Documentary Fictions?', *Art and Design*, vol.10, no.9/10, 1995, pp.29–33.

15 J. Taylor, *A Dream of England: Landscape, Photography and the Tourist's Imagination*, Manchester: Manchester University Press, 1994, p.152.

16 Humphrey Spender interviewed by Grace Robertson, 1992, Oral History of British Photography Collection. Subsequent quotations, or references to Spender's views, are from this interview unless otherwise stated.

17 Taylor, *A Dream of England*, p.152.

18 Between 1940 and 1975 the pictures were left untouched and unseen, and many left unprinted in rolls of uncut film. They came to light in the mid-70s, first in a limited edition print run (100) produced by students of Spender's at the Royal College of Art (*Britain in the 30s, Photographs by Humphrey Spender*, with introduction and commentary by Tom Harrisson, London: The Lion and Unicorn Press, 1975), and subsequently in an exhibition organized by Derek Smith at Sussex University in 1977 where the Mass Observation archive was established; see John Taylor, *A Dream of England*, pp.162–4.

19 T. Jeffery, *Mass Observation: A Short History*, Occasional Stencilled Paper, Birmingham: Centre for Contemporary Cultural Studies, 1978.

20 This was not of course unproblematic, and the invasiveness of Mass Observation techniques was itself the subject of public debate and criticism in the press, though the controversy revolved as much around the notion of covert listening-in as it did around looking.

21 Bolton was originally described as 'Northtown' in the report on the first year of Mass Observation's work; see C. Madge and T. Harrisson, eds, *First Year's Work 1937–38 by Mass Observation*, London: Lindsay Drummond, 1938, p.66.

22 Ibid.

23 The sexual dimension to Spender's perception of class difference was something that I had not anticipated, and is not referred to in the literature on Spender, though as a dimension in cross-cultural encounters it might be a predictable enough theme.

24 See D. Frizzell, *Humphrey Spender's Humanist Landscapes: Photo-documents, 1932–1942*, New Haven: Yale Center for British Art, 1997, p.16.

25 He recalls attending a course given by Raymond Firth in preparation for a further project planned by the founder of Mass Observation, Tom Harrisson, though this project was never actually carried out.

26 D. Mellor, 'Mass-Observation: the Intellectual Climate', in J. Evans, ed., *The Camerawork Essays: Context and Meaning in Photography*, London: Rivers Oram Press, 1997, p.136 (originally published in *Camerawork*, vol.11, September 1978).

27 S. Edwards, 'Disastrous Documents', *Ten.8*, no.12, 1984, p.23.

28 Brinsford, 'Citizens of the Secret Machine', p.30.

29 R. Samuel, *Theatres of Memory*, vol. I: *Past and Present in Contemporary Culture*, London: Verso, 1994, p.331.

30 See the discussion of the pub incident in H. Spender and J. Mulford, *Worktown People: Photographs from Northern England 1937–38*, Bristol: Falling Wall Press, 1982, p.127.

31 Frizzell, *Humphrey Spender's Humanist Landscapes*, p.15.

32 Jeffery, *Mass Observation*, p.45. This is Jeffery's summary of the argument put forward by Stuart Hall. For a further elaboration of this argument see Edwards, 'Disastrous Documents'. Although in respect of the work of Humphrey Spender, Edwards' article covers similar territory to this essay, there are a number of substantial differences. What is referred to as 'the documentary discourse of the 30s' is given a sense of coherence that is, I suggest, inconsistent with the evidence presented here.

33 Although the Jarrow Crusade has become a symbol of mass unemployment in the 1930s, it was in fact a relatively small march and different in a number of ways from many of the other hunger marches of the period. This difference was central to the fact that the Jarrow march was the subject of official visual recording whereas others were not; 'the "respectability" of the march and its co-operation with the authorities earned it more sympathy and publicity than any other' (J. Stevenson, *British Society 1914–45*, Penguin: London, 1984, p.291).

34 Spender did paid photographic work for the *Mirror* national newspaper during this period.

35 K. Worpole, *Here Comes the Sun: Architecture and Public Space in Twentieth Century European Culture*, London: Reaktion, 2000, p.10.

36 Edwards, 'Disastrous Documents', p.22.

37 Worpole, *Here Comes the Sun*.

38 'Changing the everyday as a revolutionary experience meant more than the use of strange perspectives and unusual angles, it also meant a radical change in who was behind the camera. The theory and practice of working class self-authorship asserted the de-academicisation of the everyday in terms of the proletarian reordering or rewriting of the categories of the real' (J. Roberts, *The Art of Interruption: Realism, Photography and the Everyday*, Manchester: Manchester University Press, 1998, p.48).

39 Although one might argue that class voyeurism is an important dimension in the making and, perhaps particularly, the reception of the photographs, the Mass Observation visit to Blackpool was also more complex. Interestingly, as well as involving mass-observers from Bolton, some of whom were working-class, it also included those based at Blackheath, amongst them a significant number of young women from working-class backgrounds. I am grateful to Nick Stanley for this information. Twenty-six of Spender's photographs of Blackpool were published under the title 'The Fifty-second Week: Impressions of Blackpool', in *The Geographical Magazine* in 1938 with text by Tom Harrisson.

40 The sexual dimension to cross-class encounters recurs at several points in the interview; for example, Spender refers to Christopher Isherwood as saying 'I went to Berlin to have sex with working-class boys.'

41 The Buttershaw housing estate provided the setting for the film *Rita, Sue and Bob Too* (1987), written by Andrea Dunbar and directed by Alan Clarke. The film focuses on the relationship between two teenage girls and a married man, with the working-class housing estate as a backdrop. Although ostensibly a comedy, the film perhaps has a more serious point about life and opportunity for those

living on working-class housing estates in the 1980s. In relation to a discussion of this film and its writer Andrea Dunbar, who also lived on the estate, Reas talks about the impact of the idea that it was possible to make something about his own experience.

42 Paul Reas interviewed by Val Williams, 1993, Oral History of British Photography Collection. Subsequent quotations or references to Reas' views are from this interview unless otherwise stated.

43 Reas references the caricatured version of working-class life offered in the Monty Python sketch 'We had it rough'.

44 See the Northern Film and Television Archive, *A Catalogue of Films and Videotapes produced during the 1984/85 Miners' Strike*, Gateshead: Northern Film and Television Archive, 1986. The catalogue also lists photographic exhibitions and collections. The rapid change in thinking around documentary photography that occurred in British photography at this point might explain the relatively little attention these bodies of work have subsequently received.

45 N. Thrift, 'Images of Social Change', in C. Hammett, L. McDowell and P. Sarre, eds, *Restructuring Britain: The Changing Social Structure*, London: Sage, 1989, p.22. A question that seems worth asking here is whether or not there was any significant or coherent photographic activity around the idea of the affluent worker in the 1960s, which might be seen as a precedent for the photographic interest in consumption that became dominant in the 1980s and 1990s.

46 See, for example, M. Parr, *The Cost of Living*, Manchester; Cornerhouse, 1989; M. Parr and N. Barker, *Signs of the Times*, Manchester: Cornerhouse, 1992; and A. Fox, *Work Stations: Office Life in London*, London: Camerawork, 1988.

47 V. Walkerdine, 'Subject to Change without Notice: Psychology, Postmodernity and the Popular', in S. Pile and N. Thrift, eds, *Mapping the Subject: Geographies of Cultural Transformation*, London: Routledge, 1995, p.322.

48 Thrift refers to the making of what he calls 'service-class culture' and its dominance in the 1980s; see Thrift, 'Images of Social Change'.

49 Ibid., p.22.

50 J. Seabrook, 'The Changing Face of Unemployment', *Ten.8*, no.11, 1983, p.5. The idea that class disadvantage took on a less visually accessible, and perhaps less visually interesting, form from the mid-1980s was an argument also suggested by Murray Martin in a recent interview with me (interview with Murray Martin, 12.10.00).

51 P. Reas, *I Can Help*, Manchester: Cornerhouse Publications, 1988.

52 Rod Jones, 'Foreword', in ibid.

53 Parr 'liked the idea of Britain in decline' and sought images to illustrate this, 'the fact that there was all this litter hanging about and the fact that people were quite happy to sit in the litter, and the place was falling apart and decaying' (Martin Parr interviewed by Val Williams, 1991, Oral History of British Photography Collection). In a gallery talk, Parr indicates his emphasis on a distance from rather than engagement with the individuals represented in his photographs: 'I usually think in terms of a given scenario, whether it's a supermarket or a dinner party, and I think of that situation and I then if you like find examples of people to put in those situations to try and illustrate it, so in one sense the photographs are quite depersonalized, even though I personally like people and enjoy talking to them, in my depictions in photography they're almost like examples of people that you can identify with and understand, and you just recognize them as people that you would see around' (talk at Photofusion, London, April 1992, Oral History of British Photography Collection).

54 S. Kismaric, *British Photography from the Thatcher Years*, exhibition catalogue, New York: Museum of Modern Art, 1990, back cover.

55 Graham Smith cited in ibid. Unremarked is the influence of Weegee on the work of Smith, particularly in his images of pub interiors in South Bank, and subsequently Chris Killip.

56 Richard Billingham, for example, sees his own work as dealing with more aesthetic and spiritual themes. Nevertheless, I would argue that the social-class dimension in various forms is an important feature in the reception of Billingham's work, even if he himself does not wish to recognize this aspect.

57 Laing, *Representations of Working-Class Life*, pp.190–1.

58 Martin Parr, for example, is a collector of seaside postcards, and their visual influence can be seen in his colour imagery.

59 P. Reas, *Flogging a Dead Horse: Heritage Culture and its Role in Post-Industrial Britain*, Manchester: Cornerhouse Publications, 1993.

60 Samuel, *Theatres of Memory*, vol. 1, p.263.

61 Ibid., p.267.

62 I am grateful to one of the reviewers of this article for this suggestion. Although there are similarities in Reas' and Hoggart's position, there are also a number of differences. Hoggart's perspective is that of someone who, from a working-class background, has made the transition to becoming an authority on high culture. Photography does not have the cultural status of literature.

63 Cited in Thrift, 'Images of Social Change', p.38.

64 In many respects Reas might be thought to occupy a position similar to that described by Marc Augé: 'What they see projected at a distance is the place where they used to believe they lived from day to day, but which they are now being invited to see as a fragment of history', cited in N. Stanley, 'Museums and Indigenous Identity: Asmat Carving in a Global Context', *Pacific Arts Association Special Conference*, Field Museum, Chicago, 20–24 October, 1999.

65 G. Marshall, *Repositioning Class: Social Inequality in Industrial Societies*, London: Sage, 1997, p.16. This is Marshall's characterization of the postmodernist position, whereas he remains convinced of the empirical validity of class analysis.

66 Samuel, *Theatres of Memory*, p.217.

67 J. Roberts, *Renegotiations: Class, Modernity and Photography*, Norwich: Norwich Gallery, Norfolk Institute of Art and Design, 1993, p.8.

68 J. Bourke, *Working-Class Cultures in Britain 1890-1960: Gender, Class and Ethnicity*, London: Routledge, 1994, p.25.

69 J. Gorman, *To Build Jerusalem: A Photographic Remembrance of British Working-Class Life 1875–1950*, London: Scorpion Publications, p.17.

70 R. Bromley, 'The Theme that Dare Not Speak its Name: Class and Recent British Film', in S. Munt, ed., *Cultural Studies and the Working Class: Subject to Change*, London: Cassell, 2000, pp.51–68.

71 R. Hoggart and R. Williams, 'Working Class Attitudes', in J. McIlroy and S. Westwood, eds, *Border Country: Raymond Williams in Adult Education*, Leicester: National Institute of Adult Continuing Education, 1993, p.117.

72 Bromley, 'The Theme', p.53. In this respect John Hill's reference to the *The Full Monty* and *Brassed Off* as 'delayed 1980s film[s]' is perhaps to miss the point; see J. Hill, *British Cinema in the 1980s*, Oxford: Oxford University Press, p.168.

73 For Augé, 'places of memory' are those locations with which our relationship is increasingly mediated or experienced only as text; for example, historic places experienced as motorway signs that are passed regularly but never visited, tourist destinations that are referred to time and time again on television game shows; see M. Augé, *Non-Places: An Introduction to an Anthropology of Supermodernity*, London: Verso, 1995. Maurice Halbwachs' notion that our present concerns determine the kind of past we remember may also be useful here; see M. Halbwachs, *On Collective Memory*, Chicago: University of Chicago Press, 1992.

74 Daniel Meadows interviewed by Alan Dein, 1995, Oral History of British Photography Collection.

75 Frosh, 'The Public Eye', p.56.

76 Edwards, 'Disastrous Documents', p.23.

77 Roberts, *Renegotiations*, p.3.

78 See, for example, Berger's work with Jean Mohr on the lives of immigrant workers, J. Berger and J. Mohr, *A Seventh Man: A Book of Images and Words about the Experience of Migrant Workers in Europe*, Harmondsworth: Penguin, 1975.

79 One might consider the work of the photographers' and film-makers' collective Amber/Side in Newcastle as offering current examples of such a practice.

80 Roberts, *Renegotiations*, p.8.

81 Bromley, 'The Theme', p.54.

82 For a discussion of Waplington and Billingham see D. Newbury, 'Photography and the Visualization of Working Class Life in Britain', *Visual Anthropology Review*, vol.15, no.1, 2000, pp.21–44.

Fionna Barber

The Instability of Otherness: Gender, Irishness and Identity

In 1999 to 2000 the major touring exhibition '0044: Irish Artists in Britain' was shown in various venues in Ireland and the United States. The title refers to the telephone dialling code for Britain from the Republic of Ireland, and the exhibition comprised the work of twenty Irish artists working in England or Wales. Important questions about identity were raised, in that the diversity of artistic practice shed light upon the problematic character of attributions of ethnicity or nationality. As the exhibition's curator, Peter Murray, wrote in the catalogue introduction:

> If there is a theme to this exhibition, it is not about Ireland, or England, and the interminable political wranglings that constitute their relationship ... It is about the personal fractures, fault lines and dislocations, less significant perhaps on the grander political stage, but that nevertheless constitute the reality of people's lives and the attempt to repair these traumas.[1]

Introductory essays help to set an agenda for the viewer's engagement with the works in exhibitions, yet there is a problem in identifying the trauma of diasporic experience as enacted and resolved at a personal level alone. To do so obscures the role that actual instances of profound loss have played in the historical formation of anxiety and displacement experienced by individuals.[2] Indeed, as Luke Gibbons has argued, the colonial relationship of Britain to Ireland has been characterized by instances of historically repressed trauma, whose symptoms can be found in the work of contemporary Irish artists such as Philip Napier or Alice Maher.[3] The colonial expropriation of lands belonging to the indigenous population was followed by the massive loss of life incurred during the Famine of 1845–1849; this itself became the catalyst for the large-scale emigration of the surviving peasantry, which became a major feature of Irish society from the mid-nineteenth century onwards.[4] Yet, until recently, memory of the Famine has been largely evacuated from narratives of Irish identity, becoming, in Gibbons' words, 'a phase of history that could now be confined to the communal Prozac of the heritage industry'.[5] The violence of political conflict in Northern Ireland has also left deep psychological wounds and the consequences for art practice still require further investigation.[6] However, Irish emigration to Britain is increasingly seen in terms of economic and cultural opportunity and certainly many Irish people have benefited in this way.[7] Such positive experiences of emigration should not obscure the historical underpinnings of trauma and loss, whose negotiation, I argue, have become a part of the cultural experience of Irishness in Britain.

Historically, as I discuss below, signs of Irishness in British culture have been encoded in representations of the body. These were produced in response to the influx of working-class Irish immigrants after the Famine and racist definitions of Irishness which continued to appear during political struggles for Ireland's independence. Yet they were dependent on an interaction between both visual and verbal designations of Irishness – in specific kinds of appearance or physiognomy or in relation to the sound of the Irish voice. Easily identifiable Irish accents provided grounds for racist categorizations which were not possible on the basis of skin colour, since most Irish people are white. These bodily identifications have become a particularly durable means of categorization of Irish people in Britain, culturally embedded to such a degree that they have become unconscious. In this context it is significant that several artists in '0044' – an exhibition specifically concerned with the consequences of the Irish diaspora for art practice – engaged with issues of identity at the level of the body or its traces. These included Andrew Kearney's photographs of the fragmented male body and Kathy Prendergast's *The End and the Beginning II* (1997), which incorporates human hair with other found elements. I want, however, to focus on two other pieces from the exhibition, Daphne Wright's installation *Indeed Indeed* (1998) (Figure 1) and Mo White's video work *At the Table of Fine Graces* (1999) (Figure 2) which also involve a concern for embodiment. Both of these engage with visual and verbal constructions of the gendered Irish body in relation to issues of identity and representation. The subtle degree of interaction between these issues in the two installations works to make visible the difficulty of stable attributions of Irish 'Otherness'. Yet they make for uncomfortable viewing in different ways; both works appear to register something disturbing within the formation of Irish diasporic identities, troubled by the spectres of trauma and loss.

Constructing Irishness in Britain

The exhibition was first shown in the United States, where it seems to have raised issues around the problematization of Irish identity. The construction of Irish ethnicity in the States has taken somewhat different forms to those in Britain, due to different patterns of assimilation of the Irish diaspora since the mid-nineteenth century. This is linked to a tendency to read Irish art within a narrow set of expectations based on a reductive ethnicity. During the summer of 1999, '0044's exhibition in New York at PS1 coincided with two other shows of Irish art, the retrospective 'When Time Began to Rant and Rage: Figurative Painting from Twentieth-Century Ireland' and 'A Measured Quietude', which consisted of works on paper.[8] The titles of both of these shows were derived from poems by W. B. Yeats, also the subject of a small exhibition at the New York Public Library.[9] In an attempt to review all these shows for the *New York Times* – not an easy task, admittedly – Roberta Smith resorted to anchoring Irish culture safely in the primacy of the literary, through allusions to the short stories collected in Joyce's *Dubliners*.[10] After identifying the most 'interesting' Irish work on show as also derived from the early twentieth century – notably the perhaps inevitable Jack B. Yeats and the cultural nationalism of Sean Keating – the review lapsed into a fairly pedestrian account of more-contemporary Irish art. A few artists from '0044' were singled out by name,

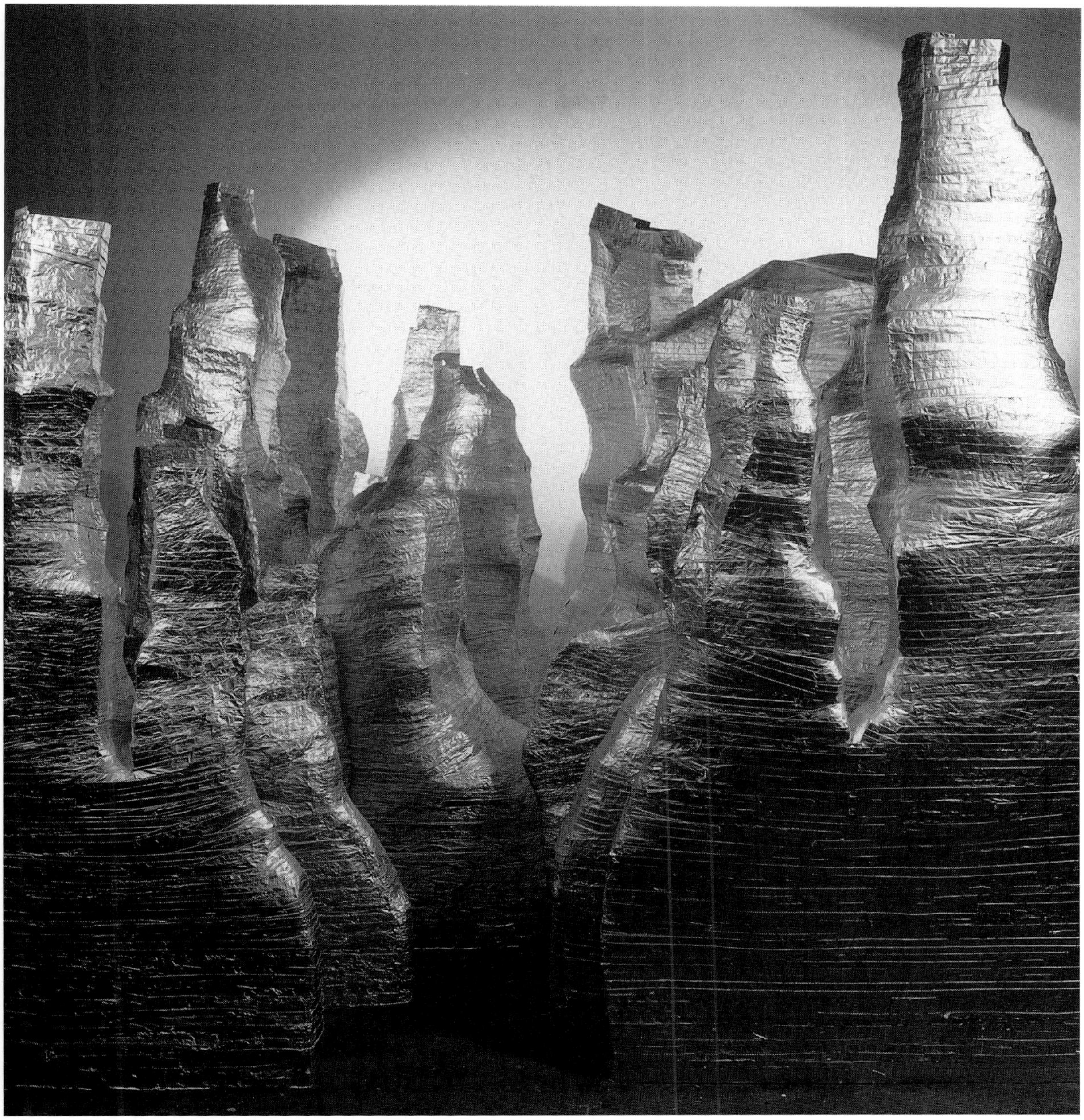

Figure 1. Daphne Wright, *Indeed Indeed*, 1998, tinfoil, sound, glue.

including Daphne Wright's 'fairly original Post-Minimalism'. The point, however, is not that more-recent Irish art is less interesting, or that it is merely a question of the adaptation of international visual languages in the exploration of the 'personal', as Smith also suggests. Since the turn of the last century the dominant paradigm for Irish culture has been literary rather than visual. It is, however, the *reformulation* of this relationship, as a critical engagement between the visual and the verbal, that can allow searching questions about Irish ethnicity to be posed in the work of some postmodernist practitioners.

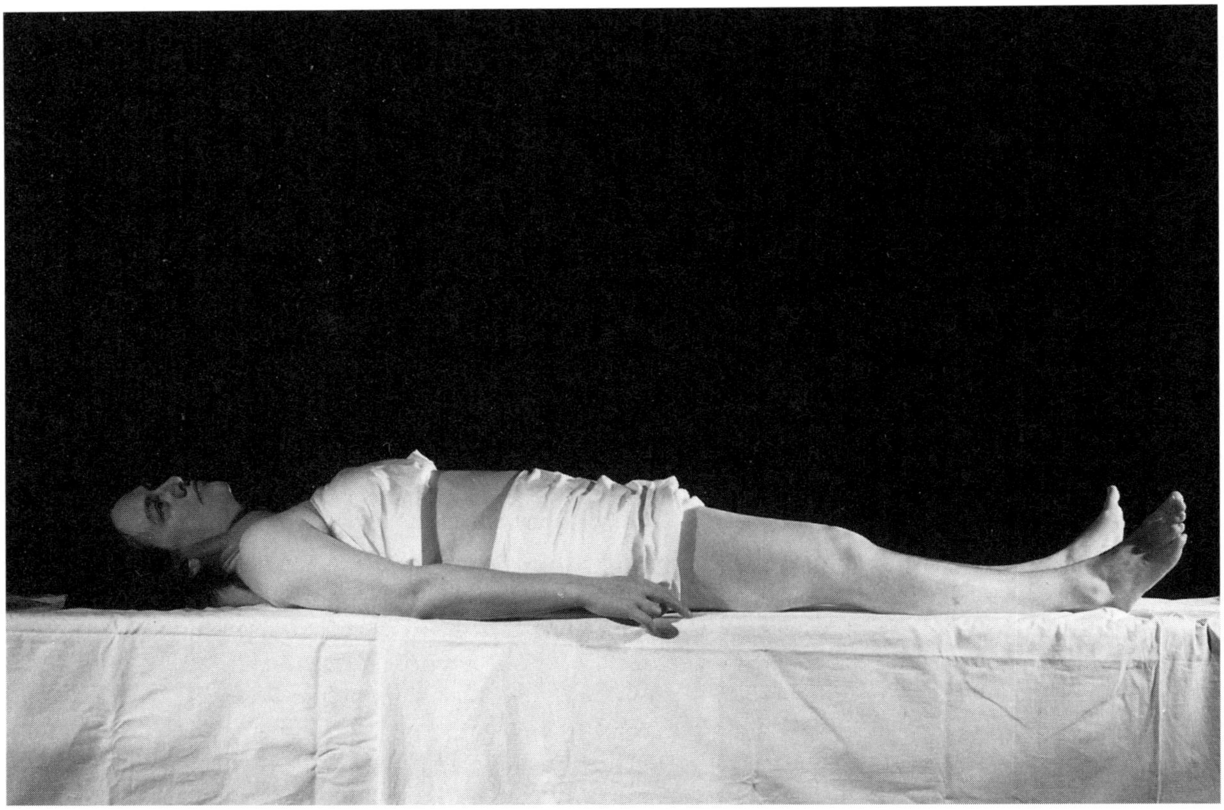

Figure 2. Mo White, *At the Table of Fine Graces*, 1999, production still. Photogapher: Gary Kirkham.

However, an implosion of referentiality from global to personal also bypasses any significance of the cultural domain within which the works in '0044' were produced. This was a show consisting of work by Irish artists in Britain in the late 1990s, yet identifications of 'Irishness' in the works are difficult to make with any confidence. This is the case across the diversity of work included, from Siobhan Hapaska's fibreglass sculptures *Land* (1998) or *Here* (1995), to Nicholas May's semi-abstract painting *Virtually Painted Landscape (after 2001)* (1998), or the collaborative performance and video work of Anne Tallentire and John Seth. Significantly, these works by Hapaska and May evoke issues of landscape, a form of painting that gained prestige in Ireland during the 1920s and 1930s, when the Irish Free State was both established and consolidated. In the work of artists such as Paul Henry, the landscape of the West of Ireland became a main site for the ideological construction of a reactionary ethnicity promoted by the Free State's government. The West was the region believed to be least affected by British rule; the survival of the Irish language and folk traditions there were mobilized within the regressive nationalism of the newly independent Free State. Henry's depictions of the Connemara seaboard as a timeless zone of mountain, bog and sky helped to perpetuate such readings. Both Hapaska and May's work uses ironic strategies to open up a distance from these associations of landscape within an Irish context, and the function of landscape as a trope of Irish identity is an issue to which this discussion will return.

The experience of emigration is often contradictory. Although it is frequently underpinned by economic necessity, the resultant trauma and loss are countered not only by economic opportunity but by the chance to construct identities less readily available within the structure of society in Ireland. Indeed for many Irish immigrants, particularly women, the experience of reconstruction of identity within a new culture is a positive one, despite its pervasive contradictions.[11] Most Irish artists now working in Britain belong to the generations that have arrived since the early 1980s and, as such, they exemplify the more recent Irish immigrants identified by Breda Gray as increasingly well educated and aspirational.[12] Yet Gray has also argued that the contradictions around Irish identity in British society are common to immigrants from a range of different backgrounds. Although impelled less by economic factors, the relocation of Irish artists to Britain is also characterized by a similar dualism: the loss of the familiar is superseded by assimilation into a more expansive, and potentially exciting, diversity of art in Britain. As the sculptor Maud Cotter observed, when interviewed for the catalogue of '0044': 'Exile is fantastic ... You get to a point where you can remove both from where you are and where you came from ... I never felt as fully engaged with Ireland as much as I did when I was in London because you are free of the context, so you are totally free to examine it.'[13] Cotter's statement evokes a sense of 'creative exile' more readily associated with the position of James Joyce as emigré Irish practitioner; however, the distinction between exile as a state of *modernist* consciousness and that experienced within postmodernism requires further investigation.[14] Displacement can involve an initial unpicking of the affective bonds of genealogy and location; although this may be painful, it also facilitates an interrogation of determining histories and constructions of ethnicity which is more difficult when part of lived experience. Yet it is precisely these issues of displacement and the formation of identity which constitute the basis of some of the more radical practices of a pluralist postmodernism. As a result, cultural practice can potentially strike resonances with the heterogeneous experience of Irish people in Britain, while avoiding any one privileged definition of Irishness.

The relationship between two contradictory forces of difference and assimilation, according to a recent essay by Bronwen Walter, consistently determines the construction of Irishness in Britain, with considerable effect on Irish people's lived experience.[15] On one hand the maintenance of ethnic difference is derived from the long-established history of Ireland as England's 'Other', yet at another level this difference is also denied in that Irishness is continually included within British nationality. This assumption of a shared ethnicity based on whiteness works to exclude more recent 'Others'. As Walter observes, it is notable that Ireland was excluded from the Immigration Acts of the 1960s.[16] This paradoxical yet durable model emerged in the mid-nineteenth century, as a means of negotiating the increased immigration of the working-class Catholic Irish after the Famine. Yet what is particularly significant is that it is a discursive formation operating through signs of the gendered body and its physiognomy. During the conflicts over Irish Land Reform and Home Rule, the British popular press, drawing on developments in physical anthropology, increasingly designated the physiognomy of Irish men as simian. In John Tenniel's cartoon *Two Forces* (1881), produced during agitation by the Irish Land League, the Irish male anarchist has a protruding upper lip and shallow lower jaw. Meanwhile the girlish Hibernia, the idealized symbolic form of the Irish female body, cowers upon the bosom of a classicized and upright Britannia. She, in turn, both tramples the Land League underfoot and brandishes the sword of Justice against the weapons of the Irish apeman, a primitive pile of stones.

As L. P. Curtis has argued, these visual designations of Irishness lost their effect by 1914; with the outbreak of war, the demands for Irish Home Rule were superseded by other more pressing imperialist concerns.[17] Yet conflicts around Irish ethnicity in Britain have obviously continued. Despite the persuasive rhetoric of ethnic homogeneity in the interests of a unified British nation, Irish cultural difference insistently returns. According to Walter, this is once more enacted in terms of the corporeal, in the form of the Irish voice.[18] A dialectic of exclusion and assimilation is played out at visual and verbal levels – Irish people in Britain frequently suffer racist assumptions on the basis of how they speak. The voice becomes an ambivalent signifier of identity, both positive and negative. Significantly, it is this interplay between verbal and visual, the presence and absence of Irishness, that in very different ways marks the two works by Daphne Wright and Mo White that I now want to consider.

'Like a penknife in my heart . . .'

The questions raised in Daphne Wright's installation *Indeed Indeed* over assumptions of ethnicity and identity are consistent with a process of interrogation that began somewhat earlier in her work. Born in Ireland in 1963, she initially studied sculpture in Sligo and Dublin before moving to England in 1989 to take up a postgraduate course at Newcastle Polytechnic. Apart from a year spent at the British School in Rome in 1992, she has continued to live and work in England. Much of Wright's work during the 1990s was concerned with a critical investigation of the increasingly atrophied identity of Anglo-Irishness. The rural Anglo-Irish, a group which to some degree constitute Wright's family background, were the ruling elite from the early eighteenth century until Ireland's independence from Britain in 1922. At this point, as Protestants, they became marginalized within the Catholic Irish Free State, and have struggled subsequently to maintain what can be seen as an increasingly archaic cultural identity.[19] During the political stability of the early eighteenth century, as Roy Foster suggests, the building of grand rural residences surrounded by cultivated demesnes signified 'an obsession with putting a mark on a landscape only recently won and held'.[20] Political power was accompanied by the establishment of cultural hegemony as a specific identity began to take shape for the Anglo-Irish Ascendancy. Despite their relatively recent English or Welsh antecedents and connections, this class increasingly regarded itself as Irish. Yet, as is clear from the bitter satire of Jonathan Swift, even during this period Anglo-Irish identity was far from secure. And, as such, the Big House was a cultural embodiment of the values of the Anglo-Irish, in both dominance and decline. In the ironic strategies of Maria Edgeworth's *Castle Rackrent*, published in 1800, the physical deterioration of the house itself became an allegory of the atrophy of the class that inhabited it. This book is generally recognized as the first 'regional' novel in English, yet it was also an early satire on the moral degeneration of the rural Anglo-Irish.[21]

Something similar is at work in Daphne Wright's installations, in the synthesis of the domestic with elements of the gothic. One of her recurrent concerns has been with the destabilizing of Anglo-Irish identity through the decay of the Big House. It is literally the fabric of the building's construction that is significant in Wright's practice – the plaster that lines its interior spaces, supporting the spectacle of the painted and papered surface. Her use of plaster in earlier works acknowledged its role within the domestic interior, as in *Domestic Shrubbery* (1994) (Figure 3), where the trellised wallpaper stood free of the wall and was made of the plaster that would otherwise support it. This plaster lattice also suggested the equally regulated exterior space of the cultivated garden, a domain further evoked in the architectural structure of *Still Life: the Greenhouse* (1995).[22] Yet, significantly, the plaster was not merely associated with the decorative as feminine; hidden among the latticework roses were occasional small, anatomically correct hearts that looked as if they

Figure 3. Daphne Wright, *Domestic Shrubbery* (detail), 1994, plaster, sound, wire.

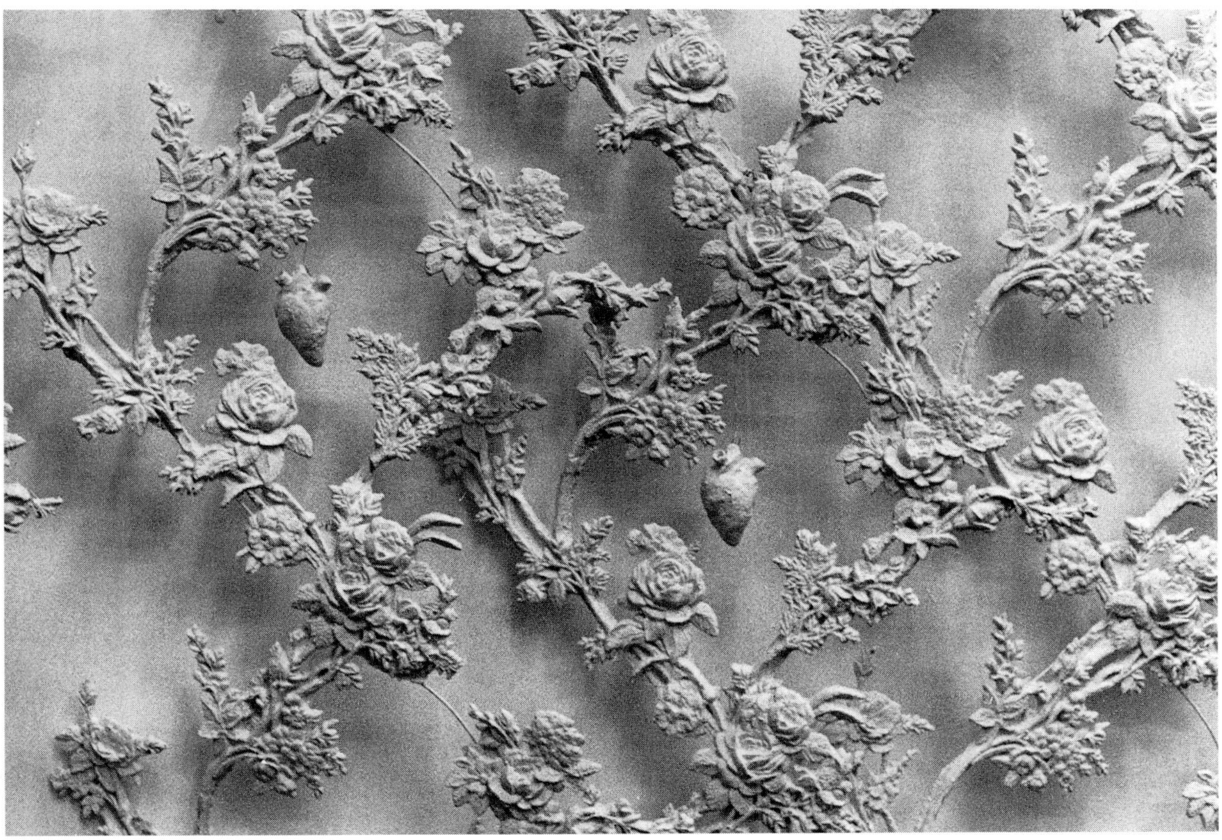

had recently been removed from the body. Like something leaking through the wallpaper, there was a definite sense of Anglo-Irish identity as marked by symptoms of a repressed trauma, that can only be experienced as horror. A similar concern for the visually disturbing in the midst of seductive spectacle was also found in Wright's later *They've Taken to their Beds* (1997), where eviscerated bird carcasses hung among the tinfoil roses.

A similar combination of seduction and horror also characterizes the tinfoil installation, *Indeed Indeed* (1998) (see Figure 1). This consists of several constructions with a fairly indeterminate form, which delineate a space where the viewer can stand, surrounded by foil monoliths. To some extent their contours evoke the presence of the human body, but the more immediate frame of reference is with landscape. The resemblance to eroded seastacks or icebergs is reinforced by tiny gulls that appear to float above the foil structure, but are really attached by visible wires. This theatrical quality is echoed in other key elements of the piece: the tinfoil structures are arranged as in a stage set, a device also used by Wright in the earlier plaster *Looking for the Home of the Sickness* (1991–1992) to determine the viewer's engagement with the work (Figure 4). Yet *Indeed Indeed* differs from this earlier piece in that it is no longer

Figure 4. Daphne Wright, *Looking for the Home of the Sickness*, 1992, plaster, sound, metal.

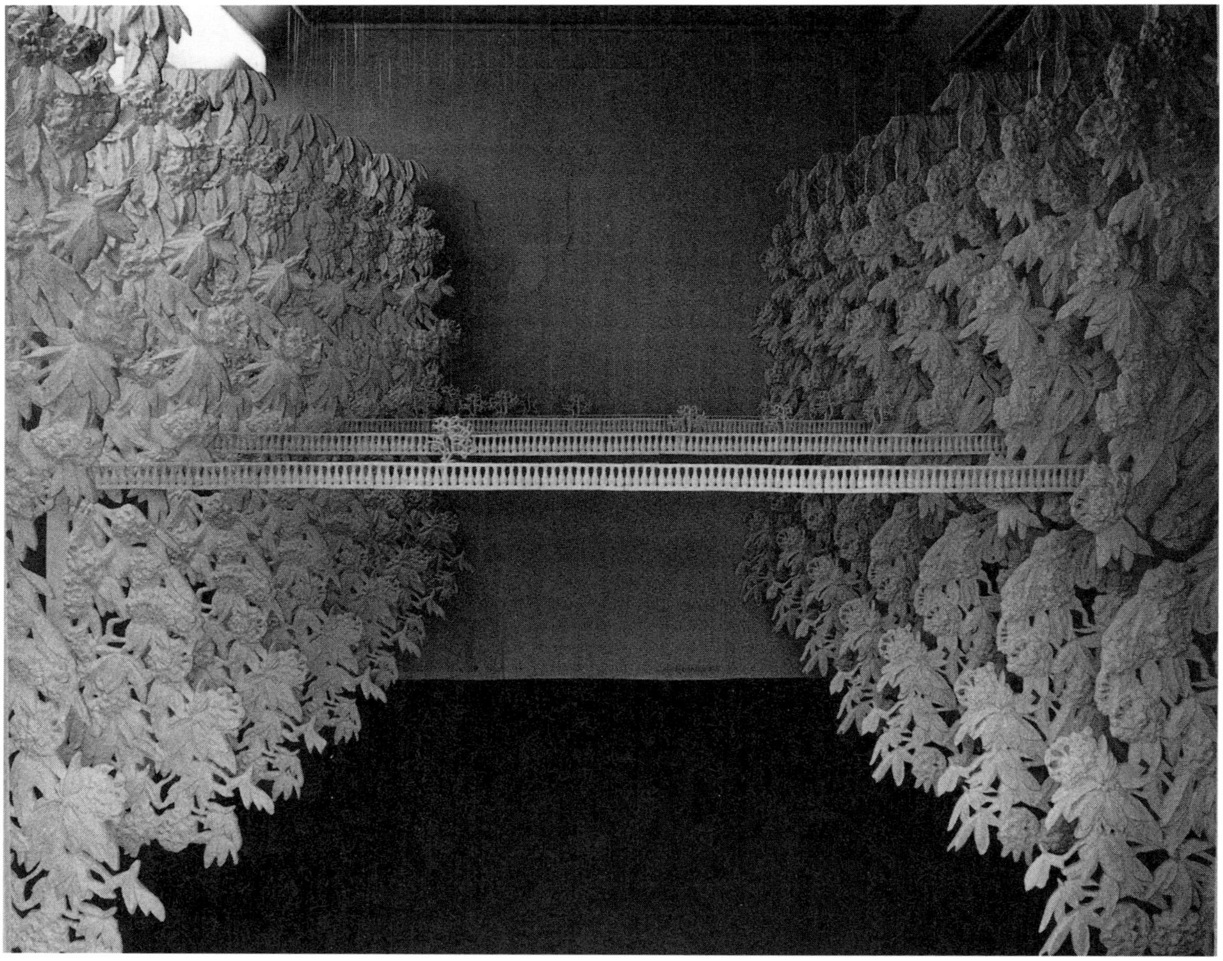

overtly concerned with the deconstruction of Anglo-Irishness. The shift from plaster to the reflective foil implies that different interrogative processes have been set in train, as Wright herself has suggested: 'I give a spectacle and take away the gush of emotion.'[23] Literally self-reflective, as Fiona Bradley has observed, this is an identity more closely bound up with narcissism.[24]

The accompanying soundtrack reiterates this degree of self-absorption, as a stage Irish male voice repeatedly recites a nonsense rhyme:

> When my back began to smart
> Like a penknife in my heart
> When my heart began to bleed
> 'Deed indeed, I was dead indeed
> Deed n'deed n'double deed . . .[25]

In Wright's work the destabilizing of Anglo-Irish cultural identity has been, at least in part, a function of her use of sound.[26] The Irish voice is recognizable as a signifier of cultural difference through accent and intonation. Significantly this voice is male, and it was around masculinity as a public presence that nineteenth-century racist definitions of Irishness were formulated in Britain, while the public presence of Anglo-Irish power in Ireland was also gendered as masculine. Yet for all its theatrical projection this voice lacks appropriate authority. It is rhythmic and circular; mimicking the cadences of maternal speech, it can, in turn, be read as evoking the repressed memories and sensations of the maternal body. Traces of this early relationship can also be suggested by the uncanny associations of the biomorphic foil sculptures of *Indeed Indeed*. The indeterminacy of these sculpted forms implies a lack of boundaries. During the infant's early life it is the process of separation from the mother, of establishing boundaries, that is an important stage in the eventual acquisition of subjectivity. For Kristeva, this is also the site of formation of the abject: the infant perceives the maternal body as ambivalent, both nurturing yet threatening to reabsorb it. The infant's survival is dependent on establishing a separation from her – reincorporation only means death. It is this fear that catalyses the abject.[27] Yet Kristeva also stresses the symbolic significance of abjection as an indeterminate state threatening to undermine the basis of all culture and power. ''Deed indeed, I was dead indeed . . .' – the implicit horror of this voice is that it speaks from an impossible position, as having itself been abjected. But it also can be read as menacing to the power and authority that it seems to emulate, played out through reference to the trauma of abjection associated with the maternal body.

The spaces of the feminine have, in this case, been displaced from Wright's earlier work from the domestic to the corporeal. Notably, the maternal characterizes the most durable female icon of nationalist Irishness, Mother Ireland, who has continually signified Irish identity through signs of a gendered symbolic body.[28] Yet Wright has also identified the shifts in her more recent practice away from Anglo-Irishness: 'The new work doesn't refer to me or my identity. It's about things vacillating, shifting, being circular. For artists who work on identity there's got to be a way of broadening, of moving. It's necessary.'[29] Rather than these sculptures being about the insistent reworking of the trauma of Anglo-Irish identity, the myth of origins, the traces that remain are subsumed into the representation of issues more relevant to the negotiation of Irishness in Britain, also enacted at a corporeal level. In *Indeed Indeed* the visual and verbal work together in a continual corporeal dialectic of identification and rejection of tropes of Irishness. These include elements of the archaic identity of the Anglo-Irish in Ireland, the public gendered construction of Irish ethnicity in Britain (the male voice) and the equally reductive, gendered tropes of femininity within Irish nationalism (the female body). Identification works through both the voice and the visual connotations. This takes the form not only of the encoded signification of the maternal body but also, in its references to geological features, the predominance of landscape as a trope of Irishness within visual representation. Indeed, these readings are mutually reinforcing in that landscape itself has been discursively constructed as feminine; Catherine Nash, for example, has argued for the specific significance of the construction of both place and gender within the formation of Irish national identities.[30] Readings of rejection, on the other hand, rely on the use of horror and the grotesque which permeates Wright's work, conveyed at an auditory level, although in conjunction with disturbing visual elements. The representation of Mother Ireland has been regarded with some ambivalence by recent Irish women artists and commentators. Rita Duffy's painting *Mother Ireland* (1989) is, despite her powerful presence, weighed down by the related demands of children, nationalist ideology and Catholicism; the companion piece *Mother Ulster* (1989) also indicates the complementary pressures experienced by women in loyalist communities in Northern Ireland. *Mother Ireland* has been seen as ambivalent even by republican women engaged in the struggle to remove the British presence from Ireland. Some of the women interviewed in Ann Crilly's 1988 production for Channel 4, 'Mother Ireland', such as the former republican activist and editor of *An Phoblacht/Republican News* Rita O'Hare, identified the notion of Ireland as a mother as positive and nurturing. The opposite view was proposed by Mairead Farrell, who was part of an IRA unit killed in March 1988 by the SAS in Gibraltar some months after her interview for Crilly's film. Her words 'Mother Ireland get off our backs!' demonstrated how much the republican women with whom she was imprisoned in Armagh resented the weight of such a stereotype.[31]

Queering whiteness

In Mo White's video installation *At the Table of Fine Graces* there is a different engagement with issues of Irish ethnicity. Notably the only exhibitor in '0044' to fall into the category of second-generation Irish in England, she was born in 1957 in London to Irish parents and studied at Stourbridge College of Art and Technology, with subsequent periods of postgraduate work at both Birmingham and the University of Ulster in Belfast. White might be viewed as a practitioner less overtly concerned with the trauma of displacement within diaspora, yet the degree of alienation in the language of the video piece, *I Object* (1996) was informed by her sense of cultural dislocation during her study in Belfast.[32] This, in turn, reinforces the degree of critical distance which is one of the more general features of Mo White's practice. Many second-generation Irish people experience difficulties in claiming an identity whose signifiers are less apparent. The lack of a distinctive accent takes away the means whereby the body is marked as Irish; the loss of a specific identity is accompanied by the danger of being subsumed into an undifferentiated white Britishness. This, in turn, has some bearing on the relationship between the visual and the verbal which provides a key focus for the articulation of identity in White's *At the Table of Fine Graces* (Figure 5). Indeed, she herself has described the sense of ambivalence associated with second-generation Irishness:

> For me, problems arise in simply saying I am Irish when I don't have the accent, or I wasn't brought up or born there ... So I think that although it is an experience of Irishness, it's one that's quite specific as well as complex. I certainly don't think of myself as particularly English either ... my experience of Irishness is, in some ways, an experience of Englishness as well.[33]

In the context of an exhibition about the work of Irish artists in Britain, White's work raises questions about Irishness and assimilation. This includes

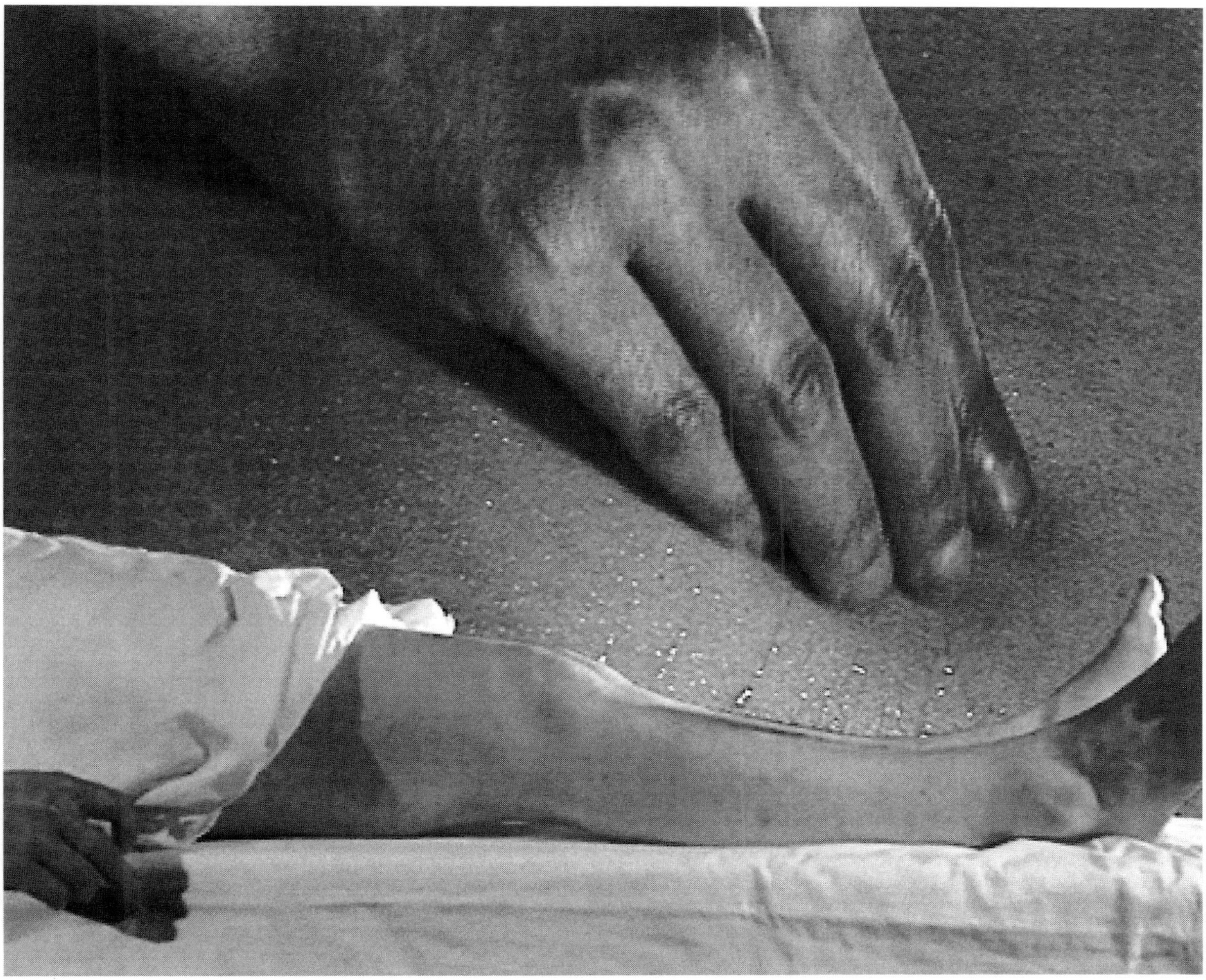

Figure 5. Mo White, *At the Table of Fine Graces*, 1999, excerpt from single screen video projection.

the role of the Irish voice as an index of ethnicity, but her work also engages with other notions of embodiment in relation to gendered representation and queerness. What gradually emerges is an account of identity that is increasingly fluid and disparate, closer to the possibilities suggested by Avtar Brah as contained within 'diaspora space', 'where multiple subject positions are juxtaposed, contested, proclaimed or disavowed'.[34] In some sense this represents a shift from her involvement with the Burginite photographic practices and debates of the 1980s. Since then her work has moved away from the rigorous theorization of the body in favour of a representation that is more concerned with sensory responses.[35] Although theoretical issues continue to inform the work, they are displaced from its surface and combined with other interests. Describing the larger research project of which White's video work *I Object* formed a part, Val Williams identified a relationship of cultural theory to visual practice as involved in the production of 'a dialogue which extends women's art beyond the political and into metaphysics and sciences of understanding'.[36] In this piece, however, the text itself is fragmented, running along the bottom of the image: in *At the Table of Fine Graces* the narrative function is to some degree undertaken by the body itself.

The short video piece *At the Table of Fine Graces* is divided into four sections, each of which consists of a shifting relationship between the whole body and a fragment seen in close-up. Each features the same tracking shot of White's motionless body, partially draped in white and viewed in profile on a white-covered table. Variations occur in the fragmentary close-ups and within the soundtrack. The first section focuses on a hand rubbing an eye, followed by a mouth whose teeth bite gently on a finger held between them. In the final two sections the hand rubs a navel, subsequently caressing the side of a stomach. Initially visceral, the insistent rubbing of the eye by the finger is uncomfortable viewing; it reiterates similar concerns in White's earlier slide projection *Mouth Piece* (1994) (Figure 6). Discomfort is gradually overtaken by the increasing sensuality of the hand's movement over the body; in the final section, the skin is wet with beads of sweat or water. The sound consists of White's voiceover; her words foreground the process of looking:

> I want this body to tell a story right before your eyes. I want this body to remind you of the experience of looking at that body that you might have seen before, right before your eyes. I want this body to stand in for that body that you might have seen before. And while standing in, which, as it is, after all, lying before you, as lying is something to which I will return again and again. [sic]

Both visual and verbal combine to focus on the capacity to provoke narration. The horizontal format of the body invites such a reading, a body whose meanings are continually in production, as suggested by its repeated tracking throughout the piece. The element of sound here continues the destabilization of subject positions on levels that relate closely to questions of ethnicity. What is said is both speculative and uncertain, undermining the voiceover as the locus of authority, just as the meanings of the image itself are shifting and unstable; the combination of the two indicates a difficulty in fixing the body in language in that it is continually evasive and slippery. Yet what is obvious in these unstable readings is that the voice itself is not 'Irish' in either accent or

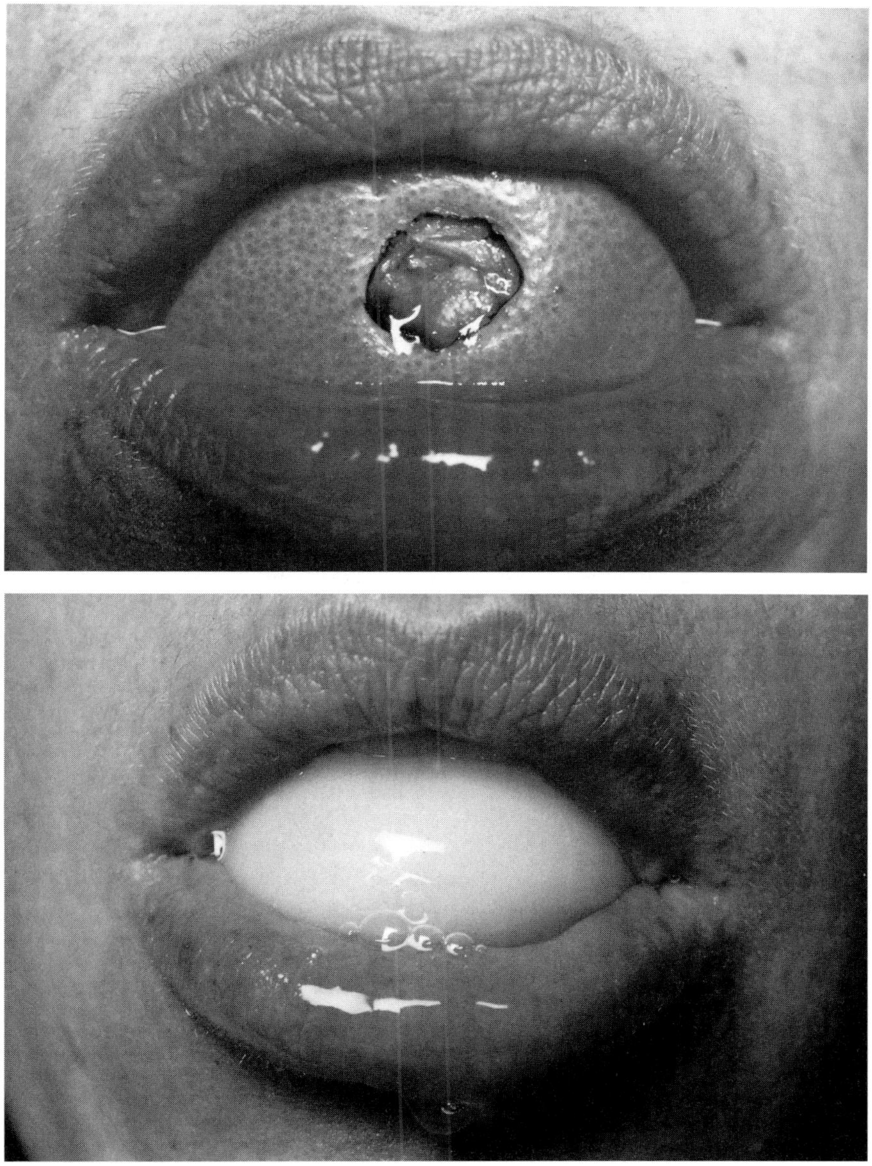

Figure 6. Mo White, *Mouth Piece*, 1994, slide projection extracts. Photographer: Lynne Connolly.

intonation. Just as the colonized subject rejects the regulatory practices of surveillance by imperial authority, this voice cannot be pinned down to identifications of ethnicity. This voice is not to be trusted, and spectators must continually return to the image, repeatedly checking to assert the identity of what they see. Yet the visual elements also work to establish and destabilize conventions. There are two main areas in which this can be seen to work: the representation of the white female body, and the questioning of a precedent within religious iconography.

As Richard Dyer has argued, whiteness is often perceived as a non-category, whose meanings are both pre-given and self-explanatory, and against which all 'Others' are defined, rather than one whose meanings are culturally constructed.[37] Yet, according to Dyer, 'the aesthetic technology of the photographic media ... not only assumes and privileges whiteness but also constructs it.'[38] The most extreme example is to be found in the construction of images of the idealized white woman within Hollywood cinema. An important feature of this is the attention paid to lighting, which helps to define the boundaries of the figure against its background, often through catching the edge of hair or the face. It also defines whiteness. Hollywood cinema is permeated with examples of the white woman as the fascinating, mysterious object of heterosexual desire. *At the Table of Fine Graces* uses similar strategies, but with complex and contradictory results. Light catches the edges of the drapery covering the tracked body and defines its whiteness against the darker skin tone of parts of the body seen in close-up. This variation is also an effect of the lighting used – it is, in actuality, a fragment of White's own body – but its darkness helps to encode this body as more eroticized than its counterpart. The lighting of the tracked body in *At the Table of Fine Graces* seems to foreground fascination with the white female body as spectacle, produced against an 'Other' which is both elusive and fragmentary, yet profoundly narcissistic as it repeatedly touches itself. There are considerable implications here for readings of female identity, but what this duality also suggests is a lack of fixity within the category of whiteness itself. Significantly, this is also the status of Irishness within British culture.

One of the main sources for Mo White's imagery in the video is Hans Holbein the Younger's *Dead Christ in the Tomb*, painted in 1521, possibly as a predella for an altarpiece. It was therefore produced some years before Holbein's conversion to Protestantism, perhaps for a Catholic patron. In this remarkable image the body of Christ has recently been removed from the cross and laid in the tomb prior to the onset of rigor mortis; the body is almost entirely contained within its painted architectural framework. In her account of the painting, Kristeva suggests that this degree of containment also reinforces the narrativity of the figure in its directing of the viewer's gaze: '(s)hould (the gaze) attempt to flee it quickly stops, locked in at the distressed face or the feet propped against the black stone.'[39] For Kristeva, Holbein's *Dead Christ* is a major example of the operation of depression and melancholia within visual representation, yet the painting's imagery is also part of an iconography of Christian suffering that has been a feature of Catholic visual imagery since the Counter-Reformation. The tracking shot at the base of the image in White's video installation mimics the disposition of the body in Holbein's painting, but there is a further encoding in the substitution of a female for a male body. It is the scopophilic consumption of the body that is the issue here, as the viewer's gaze oscillates between corporeal wholeness at the bottom of the frame and the close-ups of fragments that otherwise dominate. The pleasure of looking at the living female body has clearly replaced any reference to the contemplation of the male corpse. *At the Table of Fine Graces*, therefore, can be read as drawing on a more complex frame of meaning in its simultaneous assertion and frustration of readings of Catholicism as a mark of Irish ethnicity. In the nineteenth century, when dominant stereotypes of Irishness were being constituted, Catholicism played a significant role in distinguishing Irish immigrants within Britain. As Bronwen Walter states, however, in the context of British homogeneity, '(C)hristianity linked with whiteness appears to emphasise Irish sameness, because of current and emerging constructions of otherness based on both bodily visibility and colour.'[40]

This shift in the reading of the body is also important in its move away from the representation of the body as abject, in the displacement of references to death. Mo White's desire to distance her piece from a Kristevan theoretical position derives from an unease with its preoccupation with heterosexuality.[41] Her representation of the body in process of signification is closer to Judith Butler's notions of gendered and sexual identities as continually in formation. In *Gender Trouble*, Butler also mounts a critique of Kristeva on the grounds of a heterosexual reductivism: that the lack of critique of the paternal law of the Symbolic means that it always reasserts its hegemony.[42] One of the most controversial aspects of *At the Table of Fine Graces* is that any signifiers of ethnicity appear to be so displaced from the manifest content of the work that it is difficult to assess whether they are there at all. A problem lies in the ambivalent positioning of signifiers of a specific Irish ethnicity relative to a discourse of British national homogeneity. Clearly, in specifying meanings for this piece the significance of the context within which it is viewed becomes increasingly important. Again this can be read in relation to Butler's arguments around the performative nature of meaning: in these terms, the category of identity gains stability through various regulatory practices, which help to give it coherence.[43] In the context of an exhibition of Irish artists in Britain, then, the challenges to notions of ethnicity become particularly apparent, although articulated jointly with a critique of gender stability. Earlier work by Mo White has already been shown in a queer exhibiting format.[44] In a queer context the meaning produced for this video piece may well be different, foregrounding the instabilities of gender and sexuality over ethnicity. This is reinforced by the lack of issues of 'Irishness' as apparent from the surface of the work itself, and the fact that the homogenizing tendencies of whiteness are also not modified by an Irish accent.

Conclusion: the present need to re-think the past

Both Mo White's video work *At the Table of Fine Graces* and Daphne Wright's installation *Indeed Indeed* raise profound challenges to expectations of ethnicity as somehow embedded in the work, fully formed and waiting to be prised out by the diligent viewer. The point is that reading signs of the gendered body is one of the key means whereby Irishness is negotiated in British culture; these corporeal significations are themselves not overt, but continue to function on an unconscious level from which they only gradually and partially emerge within representation. Yet the construction of Irish diasporic identities is also underpinned by a sense of frequently repressed trauma and loss. Even within Ireland, issues such as the profound consequences of the Famine have only recently begun to be addressed by many historians.[45] This is also beginning to take place in art practice; in a series of mixed-media works such as *The Country*

Blooms a Garden and a Grave (1994), Alanna O'Kelly's major project has involved processes of mourning and reparation necessary for the resolution of a deep sense of loss.[46] Yet the various moments of trauma that have characterized the history of Ireland's relationship with Britain function on different levels and in different sites. Their negotiation, therefore, is something that takes different forms; one of the most important features of the ongoing practice of artists such as Daphne Wright or Mo White is that it suggests more constructive possibilities for the emergence of Irish identities in Britain which are not continually compelled to re-enact the past.

This paper was also given at a research seminar in the Department of Art History, Manchester Metropolitan University. I'd also like to thank the following for their helpful comments and contributions on these and other occasions: Rosemary Betterton, Cheryl Buckley, Simon Faulkner, Wendy Frith and Andrew Stephenson.

Notes

1 Peter Murray, 'Introduction', *0044: Irish Artists in Britain*, Cork: Gandon Editions, 1999, p.9.

2 See Dominick LaCapra, 'Trauma, Absence, Loss', *Critical Inquiry*, Summer 1999, pp.696–727, for a more extensive discussion of the relationship between these terms.

3 Luke Gibbons, 'Unapproved Roads: Ireland and Post-Colonial Identity', in *Transformations in Irish Culture*, Cork: Cork University Press 1996, pp.171-80.

4 It is estimated that between 1845 and 1855, out of a population of eight million, one million Irish people died as a result of the Famine, and a further one million emigrated; see Christine Kinealy, *A Death-Dealing Famine*, London: Pluto Press, 1997, p.151.

5 Gibbons, 'Unapproved Roads', p.172.

6 For example, Liam Kelly, *Thinking Long: Contemporary Art in the North of Ireland*, Kinsale: Gandon, 1996, provides a relatively untheorized account.

7 See Breda Gray, 'From "Ethnicity to Diaspora": 1980s Emigration and Multicultural London', in Andy Bielenberg, ed., *The Irish Diaspora*, Harlow: Longman, 2000, pp.65–88.

8 The more extensive and ambitious of these exhibitions was 'When Time Began to Rant and Rage: Figurative Painting from Twentieth Century Ireland', Grey Art Gallery, 25 May–24 July 1999, which attempted to survey one hundred years of Irish figurative art in a selection of seventy-five paintings. 'A Measured Quietude: Contemporary Irish Drawings', The Drawing Center, June–July 1999, was intended as a companion show to this exhibition.

9 'Such Friends: The Work of W. B. Yeats', New York Public Library, June–September, 1999.

10 Roberta Smith, 'The Irish Struggle For a Visual Poetry To Call Their Own', *New York Times*, 25 June 1999. See also William V. Ganis, '0044', *Contemporary Visual Arts*, 25, 1999, pp.68–9.

11 This can be seen from the accounts of women's emigration collected in Mary Lennon, Marie McAdam, and Joanne O'Brien, *Across the Water: Irish Women's Lives in Britain*, London: Virago, 1988.

12 Gray, 'From "Ethnicity to Diaspora"'.

13 Maud Cotter interviewed by Nuala Fenton, in *0044: Irish Artists in Britain*, p.52.

14 Useful work has been undertaken in this area by Nicos Papastergiadis in *The Turbulence of Migration*, Cambridge: Polity Press, 2000, p.122–45.

15 Bronwen Walter, 'Gendered Irishness in Britain: Changing Constructions', in Colin Graham and Richard Kirkland, eds, *Ireland and Cultural Theory: the Mechanics of Authenticity*, Basingstoke: Macmillan, 1999, pp.77–98.

16 Ibid., p.82.

17 L. P. Curtis, *Apes and Angels, the Irishman in Victorian Caricature*, Washington and London: Smithsonian Institute Press (1971), revised edition, 1997, p.57.

18 Walter, 'Gendered Irishness', p.85.

19 Their power was established as a direct consequence of the Williamite wars in Ireland in the late seventeenth century, culminating in the Battle of the Boyne in 1690, which secured Ireland for a Protestant British monarchy. The lands of the Catholic Irish were subsequently appropriated for supporters of the Protestant crown as a reward for their loyalty.

20 Roy Foster, *Modern Ireland 1600–1972*, London: Penguin, 1988, p.192.

21 Maria Edgeworth, *Castle Rackrent* (1800), Oxford: Oxford University Press, 1980.

22 Issues of space, domesticity and identity are discussed more fully in relation to Wright's earlier work in the essays by Shirley MacWilliams and myself in the exhibition catalogue *Works by Daphne Wright 1991–1994*, Cornerhouse: Manchester, 1994.

23 'Daphne Wright: interview by Vera Ryan', in *0044:Irish Artists in Britain*, p.171.

24 Fiona Bradley, '"Like a garden full of dust . . .", The Tinfoil Sculptures of Daphne Wright', in *Daphne Wright: They've Taken to Their Beds*, exhib. cat. Spacex Gallery, Exeter, 1998, p.3.

25 Adapted from W. H. Babcock, *Games of Washington Children* (1888), quoted ibid.

26 Shirley MacWilliams' essay 'Playing in the Field' provided a more extensive discussion of the role of sound in Wright's work; in Daphne Wright, pp.44–6.

27 Kristeva argues that these processes of separation take place earlier than the Oedipal and mirror phases and hence prior to the acquisition of language. The child's rejection of the mother is thus enacted through physical processes of the evacuation of the products of the mother's body (food), through faeces and vomit. However the sense of horror involved in abjection is one experienced at a pre-linguistic level, threatening to undermine all language and order. Through the maternal, abjection is usually associated with the female body; the fear of dissolving the boundaries with the maternal is also the fear of death. See Julia Kristeva, *Powers of Horror*, New York: Columbia University Press, 1982, pp.1–18.

28 Belinda Loftus, *Mirrors: Mother Ireland and William III*, Dundrum: Picture Press, 1990.

29 *0044: Irish Artists in Britain*, pp.172–3.

30 Catherine Nash, 'Re-Mapping and Re-Naming: New Cartographies of Identity, Gender and Landscape in Ireland', *Feminist Review*, no. 44, Summer 1993, pp.39–57.

31 For a more extensive and valuable discussion of 'Mother Ireland' see Sarah Edge, 'Representing Gender and National Identity', in David Miller, ed., *Rethinking Northern Ireland: Culture, Ideology and Colonialism*, Harlow: Longman, 1998, pp.211–27.

32 'Mo White: interview by Fionna Barber', in *0044: Irish Artists in Britain*, p.152.

33 Ibid.

34 Avtar Brah, *Cartographies of Diaspora: Contesting Identities*, London: Routledge, 1996, p.208.

35 Some of White's earlier work of this kind was included in the group show 'Interpretations', Ikon Gallery Birmingham and touring, 1989.

36 Val Williams, 'Showing Off', in *Showing Off*, exhib. cat., Ormeau Baths Gallery, Belfast 1996, p.18.

37 Richard Dyer, *White*, London: Routledge, 1997.

38 Ibid., p.122.

39 Julia Kristeva, *Black Sun: Depression and Melancholia*, New York: Columbia University Press, 1989, p.114.

40 Bronwen Walter, *Outsiders Inside: Whiteness, Place and Irish Women*, London: Routledge, 2000, p.112.

41 Mo White in conversation with Fionna Barber, June 2000.

42 Judith Butler, *Gender Trouble: Feminism and the Subversion of Identity*, London: Routledge, 1990, p.80.

43 Ibid., p.17.

44 For example, 'Queerfest', Birmingham 1998, and 'Pride in Diversity', City Arts Centre, Dublin, 1996.

45 See, for example, the overview of recent debates around the implications of the Famine in Kinealy, *A Death-Dealing Famine*, pp.1–15.

46 This piece is discussed in Catherine Nash, 'Embodied Irishness: Gender, Sexuality and Irish Identities', in Brian Graham, ed., *In Search of Ireland: a Cultural Geography*, London: Routledge, 1997, pp.121–2. See also Medb Ruane, 'Intimate Spaces: Interview with Alanna O'Kelly', *CIRCA*, no.77, Autumn 1996, pp.20–3.

Reviews

Jonathan Harris

Teaching Culture: The Long Revolution in Cultural Studies **edited by Nannette Aldred and Martin Ryle, Leicester: National Institute for Adult Continuing Education, 1999, pp.182**

Along with Tom Steele's 1997 study *The Emergence of Cultural Studies: Adult Education, Cultural Politics and the English Question*[1] this anthology of twelve essays on the past, present status and future of cultural studies in British higher education aims to rehistoricize and repoliticize a field of academic knowledge, much of which has sunk into quite banal orthodoxy over the last twenty years or so. In this respect, Aldred and Ryle's collection deserves to be read carefully by those interested in 'Visual Culture in Britain' because it offers some vivid accounts of the forms and consequences of academicization in general and the peculiar ironies of this process when it takes hold of teachers, writers and activists who seek a role for broad cultural theory outside the classroom. By 'theory' here I simply mean a set of diverse understandings of what culture – visual and otherwise – was, is and might be. Such a set would include all those forms of knowledge based on, for instance, historical, critical and practical principles: how to understand culture, as it were, but also how to change it. Cultural theory in this sense includes both 'traditional' and 'radical' art history, as well as the intellectual discriminations and political conditions upon which the distinctions between the two have been created and debated since the early 1970s.

Raymond Williams' 'long revolution', announced in a book of that name in 1961, was supposed to be social and political, as well as cultural – bringing a changed understanding of the world *and* actually changing it. This revolution would be a long haul, certainly, but a long haul to something recognizable as 'socialism' (and not just 'in a work of art', or in a seminar, but in society at large). To lead readers to acknowledge, or to reconsider, this basic fact about the rise of 'cultural studies' in the later 1950s and early 1960s in adult education classes, in the Communist Party of Great Britain, in the Labour Party and in trade unions, is the basic purpose, and achievement, of *Teaching Culture*. Many of its essays, including those by Tom Steele, Richard Johnson (second director of the Birmingham Centre for Contemporary Cultural Studies), Jim McGuigan, Alan O'Shea and Nannette Aldred, start from this point – implicitly or directly – in their discussion of developments in what began to emerge as an academic 'discipline' of sorts by the mid-1970s.

A decade or so after that, when cultural studies became Cultural Studies ('when Raymond Williams met Jean Baudrillard', you might say), the revolution presupposed by its early practitioners had squarely hit a dodgy bit of track and required some fairly extensive re-routing. And that's the optimistic version of what happened. Some contributors to *Teaching Culture* offer arguments for why the imagined revolution of a white (though Welsh) male heterosexual intellectual socialist justifiably had to go into the sidings for some necessary theoretical and political refitting. Andy Medhurst, Christina Lupton and Heiko Henkel and Jane Elliot critique the agenda of inherited cultural studies radicalism from their respective standpoints of queer and feminist politics. But all the essays in Aldred and Ryle's anthology hang on to the idea that Cultural Studies, like cultural studies, can and should be more than a career for academics or a useful *training* for contemporary undergraduates. Quite a few do stress, however, that whatever else Cultural Studies offers students it should also equip them with 'skills' and a realistic route into the job market. This prescription operates – sometimes tacitly, sometimes explicitly – as a fundamental criticism of what used to be called academic 'theoreticism', in the long-gone days when Louis Althusser's structuralist Marxism had a grip on the new subject's analytic and ideological protocols. But its significance now as a justification for Cultural Studies (and art history) only underlines the extent to which the comparative revolutionary millenarianism of the later 1960s and early 1970s has been definitively replaced by the neo-liberal pedagogic ideology of 'vocationalism'.

From the point of view of Cultural Studies' own 'product' – its graduates – this is, of course, entirely right. Those who make a living from teaching radical art history or Cultural Studies have no business telling their students that the point of their education is solely or principally to produce a new revolutionary class. Besides, I seriously doubt if many activists teaching now *do* still have this belief: no one knows what revolution means any more, or how it can be organized – only what it can't mean and how it mustn't be organized. And most of those teaching under, or around, thirty years of age are likely themselves to be the product of post-Thatcherite conditions and values. Within the alternative to this formation, feminist, sexual and ethnic identity-politics have predominated, constituting the radicalism of the last fifteen years, and effectively displacing socialist and Marxist principles. Construing these 'identity-politics' and their academic correlates as related, or potentially relatable, to socialist or Marxist perspectives has also become much harder in the last ten years. This is because, for example, Cultural Studies' embrace of psychoanalytic accounts of identity, representation and meaning – particularly in their distilled Lacanian forms – has reinstated a hyper-rationalism rather akin to the old Althusserian reifications, both equally distant from defensible historical analysis.

Arguably, the Baudrillardian and Lyotardian 'moments' within Cultural Studies over the last fifteen years have similarly abstracted and mystified the experiences and 'descriptive concepts' that promised genuine insights into developments in the emergent common culture of the 1990s: 'simulation', 'virtual reality', 'the end of meta-narrative', and the like. And though Williams hadn't actually met Baudrillard, in the late 1980s, in the pages of *Block* magazine (that early site for the initially timid congress of radical art history and

Cultural Studies), Judith Williamson, film critic and advert theorist – and previously a self-proclaimed Williamsite – *did* literally meet and interview the new doyen.[2] History came off badly in this discussion, as those who read it at the time may remember, but – in fact, because – it marked the moment when Cultural Studies, finally shorn of any evident politics, seemed suddenly to achieve sexiness born of this new revelling in surfaces and sensations. These three 's's had always been absent or demonized within the puritanism of Williams' rather old New Leftism, as they had been before then, for instance, in Richard Hoggart's often pruriently paternalistic 1957 study-cum-tract *The Uses of Literacy*. (An early warning sign that pleasure would triumph over pain in analytic discourse on modern popular culture was that Hoggart's book, usually proposed as one of the cornerstones of British cultural studies, was virtually contemporary with Roland Barthes' *Mythologies*. Looking back, Barthes had much more fun with *Paris Match*, wrestlers, Citroens and the rest (and had a relatively groovy Marxist 'method' to boot). Across the Channel, Hoggart's moralistic disdain with 'sex in shiny packets' hadn't even the virtue of being connected to a principled critique of economic or sexual commodification.)

The rest, as they say, is simulation. Williams died just before Baudrillard made his debut in the once clearly 'Marxist-feminist' *Block*. The journal itself folded in 1989, not long before the Berlin Wall came down and the USSR decided to call it a day as well. Oddly enough, the *Block Reader in Visual Culture*, published in 1996 as part of the continuing tidal wave in Cultural Studies anthologies that began to swamp academia in the last decade, gets the date for the publication of this interview completely wrong, placing it nearly ten years earlier.[3] Ten years in the theoretical life of *Block* is equal to about one hundred years in politics. But then the decade from, say, 1984 to 1994 seems to contain a century of change as well: from the Miners' Strike to the NUM's headquarters in Sheffield turning into a natty postmodern café-bar.

Terry Eagleton's *The Idea of Culture* finally called time on Cultural Studies' vaunted radicalism:[4] like an exhausted pit, he wanted it closed down. Its dereliction is comprehensive and irretrievable. Francis Mulhern is brought in as Eagleton's Ian MacGregor, to do the dirty work: Cultural Studies today, writes Francis Mulhern,

> leaves no room for politics beyond cultural practice, or for political solidarity beyond the particularisms of cultural difference. It fails to see not only that not all political issues are cultural, but that not all cultural differences are political. And in thus subordinating issues of state, class, political organization and the rest to cultural questions, it ends up rehearsing the prejudices of the very traditional *Kulturkritik* it rejects, which had little enough time itself for such mundane political matters.[5]

Eagleton has been moving towards this position throughout the 1990s, evidenced in his increasingly intemperate critiques of 'postmodern theory' claiming radical credentials. Like Slavoj Zizek, in books like *The Abyss of Freedom/Ages of the World* (1997), Eagleton wants to reclaim the social and the political from the imperializing of Cultural Studies' 'identity-politics' and its core doxa that everything is 'constructed' culturally and can therefore be 'deconstructed', like a Meccano set. Like Jonathan Hughes in *Ecology and Historical Materialism* (2000), Eagleton also wants to retrieve nature from culture, and set it up – sometimes, not always – as an opposite, or a resistance, a force that simply cannot be reinterpreted or rearticulated into something else. Eagleton thus attacks the theoretical idealism of Cultural Studies' epistemological relativism, calling, in effect, for a return to something like solid political-economy. And he attacks what he believes are the one-way-or-another reactionary consequences of identity-political perspectives: that is, they allow no room for solidarity beyond specific groups, for the emergence and self-awareness of a *class*, in short, that recognizes its common lack of freedom and can build upon this recognition a united opposition to capitalist structures and forces that determine, Eagleton believes, more than ever the macro-history of humanity.

None of the contributors to *Teaching Culture* anatomize the state of their 'discipline' in such black and white terms. Though many articulate disquiet at the depoliticization of education in general, and believe that those who teach Cultural Studies now have to invent a new *raison d'être* for it within the novel conditions of the twenty-first century, all have stakes in it that prevent them voicing the general dismissal found in Eagleton's and Mulhern's recent discussions. Williams himself, it is worth remembering, found the potential embrace of institutional Cultural Studies unsettling, and preferred to make no explicit or continuing affiliation to the creature into which he is usually credited with breathing initial life. Several essays in his *The Politics of Modernism: Against the New Conformists*, indeed, express his doubts over appropriation and academicization, doubts that Eagleton and Mulhern amplify.

Aldred and Ryle signal a similar ambivalence, if not clear pessimism, in their introduction. Their task in assembling this collection, they claim, has been neither 'to praise the great radical tradition, nor to bury it'. They want, rather, to 'keep open lines of communication between the past of "cultural studies" and a possible future in which it might continue to be more than just another academic specialism' (p.4). This tentativeness is surely entirely appropriate: cultural studies in its early phase, before academicization, was premised on the belief in a political movement, based upon a class, that could take power and transform British society. Education would be part of this movement. Though this was to be a 'long revolution', in order to avoid the horrors and reversals of earlier revolutions in the name of socialism, it was still to be a 'revolution': a complete turning over. Civil society's institutions were to provide the democratic and educational life-blood of this long revolution. (Williams was 'vocationalist' well before the rest, but his detailed plans and proposals in books like *Communications* (1963) and *The May Day Manifesto* (1968) were for a state transforming itself into a socialist society.) In contrast, contemporary Cultural Studies is bereft of such a faith, such a class and the sense that a radical transformation is possible. Though still capable of producing powerful 'negative critiques', based on neo-Marxist and other critical-theoretical principles, Cultural Studies radically lacks the sense that the vision of a transformed society – that is, a truly post-capitalist political order – guides those involved in what Aldred and Ryle still call the formation's 'radical project'.

Notes

1 Tom Steele, *The Emergence of Cultural Studies: Adult Education, Cultural Politics and the English Question*, London: Lawrence & Wishart, 1997.

2 Judith Williamson, 'An Interview with Jean Baudrillard', *Block*, 15, 1989.

3 *Block Reader in Visual Culture*, London: Routledge, 1996.

4 Terry Eagleton, *The Idea of Culture*, Oxford: Blackwell, 2000.

5 Ibid., p.43.

6 Raymond Williams, *The Politics of Modernism: Against the New Conformists*, London: Verso, 1989.

Andrew Causey

Peter Lanyon: At the Edge of Landscape **by Chris Stephens, London: 21, 2000, pp.192**

Peter Lanyon's historical importance for mid-twentieth-century English painting is not in doubt. He was the link between 1930s Hampstead modernism, when it emigrated to St Ives at the start of the war, and experimental postwar painting. It was he who reshaped English landscape painting after the neo-picturesque of the 1940s, and it was Lanyon who – not without reservations – produced the most articulate and measured response to Abstract Expressionism. For all that, Lanyon has not been particularly well received critically, or influential among artists. There are several reasons for this. Landscape has not generally been a focus of interest and at times painting itself has seemed an exhausted medium. But even before his early death in 1964 there were signs that – notwithstanding his many supporters – Lanyon was under critical pressure, and his work shows that he recognized the different priorities of the new decade and was still working out responses to it when he died. The adverse criticism that Lanyon was then subject to related, first, to the sense that English landscape atmospherics were out of date. This was the reaction of the English critic Lawrence Alloway, for example, when he moved to New York at the start of the 1960s. The American critic Harold Rosenberg took a swipe at St Ives on account of its provincialism. A transatlantic view, in short, saw aspects of English art as compromising, insufficiently international in outlook and buried in landscape particulars. These perceived shortcomings seem less urgent now that identities – national, regional and personal – are at the centre of the agenda. Chris Stephens' book, the most detailed examination of Lanyon's life and work to date, comes at an auspicious moment.

Stephens is conscious both of the risk in a monograph of presenting the subject as acting unconditionally and that avoiding this hazard can lead to overweighting technical issues within painting itself. Balancing out authorship, context and the technical conditions of painting at any time is a difficult project and one Stephens handles with care and success. In relation to Lanyon the problem presents itself partly in terms of identifying the role of the individual artist within what may be seen as a homogeneous group. 'St Ives' is a problem because it has been assumed that art produced in that town has a measure of coherence. Stephens' book needs to be viewed in this respect against the Tate's 1985 exhibition 'St Ives 1939–1964'. This was a melange of artworks, varying from the highly professional down to the barely competent, held together by the themes of locality and friendship as well as artistic influence. The catalogue contained photographs suggesting a concept of an artist-group, taking the group identity for granted. Documentary photographs of local landscapes were included, without sufficient consideration of whether such photographs, mediated by the conventions through which we look at landscape photographs, really help us understand the ways artists such as Lanyon or Patrick Heron, who featured largely in the exhibition, experienced and represented landscape. In these circumstances a monograph on Lanyon was badly needed to start a process of disaggregation of St Ives painting – so that individual identities could be established alongside social and geographical ones. Stephens has produced a well-researched book which attends to these issues. It is attractively written in a pacey way, and the publishers have helped with copious and well-reproduced colour plates. The book fulfils two objectives: to give a fuller account of Lanyon and the development of his work than previously available, and to redirect discussion of landscape away from the post-Cubist approach based on the information of the eye – current in Lanyon criticism back to Patrick Heron's writing in the mid-50s – towards a phenomenology of landscape founded on the experience of being there.

There is much new and interesting material on Lanyon's early life and work, the story of his learning from Gabo, Hepworth and Nicholson is significantly amplified in retelling even if the shape of the narrative remains the same. The second objective, the reconceptualizing of landscape, is the more ambitious and, even if less fully realized, creates the focus of the book. The first half of the 1950s, the pivotal years for Lanyon in this respect, seem to interest Stephens most – more, anyway, than the late paintings. He introduces words like 'sublime', not commonly used in this context hitherto, and suggesting reconnection with late-eighteenth-century English thought about landscape. There is room for more thought about Lanyon's role in releasing landscape from the grip of John Piper's neo-picturesque. He seems to have rethought an eighteenth-century predicament, the need to discover languages in which to describe landscape art that would refine or even oppose the conventional identification of the natural with the beautiful. Stephens is interesting on Lanyon and the sublime, a decentring in the surrender of self before the sublimity of an extensive and awesome nature, and the recovery of a new self that can follow. 'Elegiac' is another word Stephens introduces, one that is packed with implications for Lanyon's paintings in the early 50s, as he reflected in his work on the decline of the traditional industries of mining and fishing, their replacement with tourism, and the conservation and beautification issues raised by that. Lanyon's socialism made him resistant to – even resentful of – the loss of local productive industries and their replacement with tourism. His thinking seems to have merged tourism as an unwelcome form of incursion with what he came to see as a kind of tourist-artist who was not the real thing, because he or she was not locally rooted. Lanyon's socialism connected up with his regionalism to make him an active champion of local causes where employment was at stake. A problem, though, is how compatible this is with the idea of Lanyon's paintings as elegies. *St Just* (1953) has to do with a place and its history, the different ways the landscapes and their resources have been exploited. It is about sacrifice and death. It is an angry painting and, as Lanyon stated, one about greed in the exploitation and premature exhaustion of mineral resources, and it is an elegy in the sense of 'lament'. This is the Lanyon that John Berger – improbably one might think, considering Lanyon's abstraction – took up and praised. But Berger's interest in a painter so different from the figurative social realists he energetically championed should be a reminder that this is only one possible approach to Lanyon. There are many possible angles from which to look at Lanyon. Social polemic is one, the sublime another – very different – one. Stephens' book is suggestive in this respect, opening up lines of inquiry, not always pushing them as far as one might hope, but not falling into the error of closing them down prematurely.

Martijn Sikkens

Apocalypse: Beauty and Horror in Contemporary Art, **London: Royal Academy Publications, 2000, pp.251.**

Apocalypse and Salvation, Heaven and the Sublime were all commemorated in exhibitions during the talismanic year 2000. Meanwhile popular cinema gave us *Stigmata* and *The End of Days*. Still, we survived unscathed. Within the spaces of gallery and cinema, scenarios of utterly changed world orders, of horror and hope, were rehearsed. But rarely can this realm of pictorial transcendence have been accompanied by less of a sense of real change. These millennial visions were presented to a nation in which church attendance has dropped to record lows. Few expected the great struggle with the Antichrist to occur. There was rather more fear of isolated nutters who might try to make it happen. More to the point, if these exhibitions had been held in 1900 there would have been politically radical dreams aplenty with world salvation as their aim. These too have ebbed away over the last two decades. Political hopes for apocalyptic transformation and redemption are now reduced to minor variations in welfare arrangements, or preparations for national strategic adaptation to new technologies and business opportunities. Again it's the nutters who seem to be filled with passionate intensity. Those very new technologies beam around the world tales from the backwoods about the Zionist Occupational Government, the Reptilian Master Race, and many another conspiracy to destroy our freedom, control our brains and violate our bodies with alien implants. It's all part of the new world order, the post-cold war globalized economy in which movements of capital and networks of power seem literally alien: inaccessible to understanding and to control.

This is the culture in which the apocalypse envisaged in the RA's own millennial show was conceived. The exhibit which became most famous was the Chapman brothers' *Hell*, a characteristically voyeuristic diorama of model soldiers subject to endlessly elaborated and imaginative forms of torment. Those wicked German concentration camp guards receive Dantesque punishment to fit their crime. Trapped behind fences, their palms and feet are violated by mutant puppeteers who jerk them in deranged dances, while they drip blood in a perverted form of the stigmata. Others are chopped up and left lying on top of one another in piles. The piece was a familiar product of the Chapmans' obsession with boyhood military model-making, the earliest and indeed only form of sculpture in which most lads have participated. In this respect it indicates the real ability of artists from the 'Sensation' generation to connect avant-garde creative practice with popular experience. It makes vivid the hidden violent urges and desire for control implicit in the male childhood imagination – in its neatly painted and arranged models of soldiers, or battlefield reconstructions of El Alamein. A wargame is *Hell*, it shows us, while also offering that vision of half-formed and mutating creatures performing procreative acts from within their own bodies, tapping into those real, if bizarre, millennial anxieties that circulate within our current culture.

The other artists represented in this catalogue are not so obviously concerned to adapt Christian iconography to contemporary popular culture, though the exhibition did include a range of non-(Youngish) British Artists, which was not the case with the exclusively British 'Sensation', of which 'Apocalypse' was clearly intended to be a follow-up. The Italian artist Maurizio Cattelan presents us with a model of the Pope hit by a meteorite: Divine punishment for the sins of the church? An arbitrary event in a meaningless universe of swirling matter? Or maybe a miracle: the Pope seems to be unharmed. He holds his crosier in an iron grip, lifting it up as though stoically resisting an attack by the Godless forces of materialism. Tokyo-born Mariko Mori presents us with shamanistic visions of Japanese ghosts and demons appearing amid the modern magic of urban consumer imagery: video, street signs, animation. Chris Cunningham's work merges the two realms. The catalogue reproduces a frame from his Sony Playstation advertisement in which a girl's face mutates into an alien form. The text in his entry enthuses about his videos for Björk, Kraftwerk and other arty pop-persons.

It seems that the interpenetration of contemporary art with popular and commercial culture is celebrated by this catalogue, even as it also situates the works within the 'great tradition' of fine art. Thus we learn that the Chapmans draw on Bruegel, Caravaggio, Titian's *Flaying of Marsyas*, and seventeenth-century *momento mori* still lives, while Cunningham inherits Léger's pioneering Cubist film-making techniques. The catalogue is itself a product of commercial imperatives. 'Sensation' had been a mega hit. A 'Sensation II' sequel would surely help the RA to promote itself as an institution in touch with contemporary culture and art-economics. As Philip King, the Academy's new President, says in the foreword to the catalogue, the RA 'is perhaps not generally known for its presentation of the most radical art of the moment'. But 'A New Spirit in Painting' back in 1981 and 'Sensation' proved otherwise. This has helped generate support from 'the media sponsors of this show', *eyestorm and Time Out*.

Does 'Apocalypse', then, tell us that the academic tradition, the avant-garde and modern media culture are now living happily together in a world beyond ideology? Was that the real millennial experience, one like Henry James' story 'The Beast in the Jungle' in which a man believes that he has been singled out for some utterly special fate, only to realize before he dies that what was special about his life was that nothing ever happened in it? He spent the whole time waiting for nothing to happen. In this harmonious media-capitalist world what kind of radicalism can be ascribed to the 'most radical art of the moment'? Certainly we see that the RA is unembarrassed to include advertisements as part of the artwork recognized within this catalogue. It shows that art students can and do work in the media and that advertising and the avant-garde feed off one another. That's been true for some time. Greenberg's avant-garde, dedicated to resisting the evils of kitsch, seems dead and buried. The art history which informs the pages of this catalogue is equally clear that it acts in the service of promotion: self-promotion of the RA and of the artists themselves, who also play with promotional imagery, as in Noble and Webster's *Vanity Fair* cover. Jeff Koons – godfather of art-as-media – smiles at us confidently at the end of the catalogue.

A sense of radical *loss* can certainly be felt throughout 'Apocalypse', in which scenarios of emptiness – Schneider's bleak rooms – and of sex, death and pain feature largely. In the middle of the book is a centrefold-style crotch shot, courtesy of Wolfgang Tillmans, ex of *i-D* magazine. Its presence is a rerun of Marcus Harvey's *Readers' Wives* paintings from 'Sensation', designed to thrill, titillate and, with a bit of luck, to jolt the *Daily Mail* into promoting the show and its own sales by claiming to be shocked. But this crotch has none of the visceral power of Harvey's paintings. It's a bland scenario of sexual sublimity – a heaven of gazing blissfully at a pair of knickers for eternity. This is the radical vision of the most radical art of the moment.

Abstracts

Fran Lloyd

Arab Women Artists: Issues of Representation and Gender in Contemporary British Visual Culture

This article focuses on the work of Zineb Sedira, an Algerian Arab woman artist brought up in the Algerian diaspora in France in the aftermath of the Algerian war, who now lives in London. Since the mid-1990s Sedira's installation and video work has centred on issues surrounding the veil, which has come to be one of the most visible and much debated external signs of gender difference, of exclusion/inclusion, and a complex symbol that carries a multiplicity of frequently shifting and often contradictory meanings, particularly in the context of Algerian history. While Sedira gives presence and self-image to what has frequently been the doubly 'othered' body in the western art world – the body of the female artist and the non-normative Arab body – the work also raises crucial questions about how this body has been, and continues to be, perceived and framed within both western and Arab visual culture.

Focusing on Sedira's use of veiling and unveiling as metaphors for absence and presence, and the various contexts in which her work is produced and exhibited, I argue that her work can be seen as a performing of the 'self', as an Arab woman subject against and through the negotiation of her specific history. Foregrounding issues of gender, race and sexuality, Sedira's work can be seen simultaneously as a site of embodiment and a space of enquiry, contestation and negotiation: a place of inscription and becoming in a shifting contemporary Britain. This places a particular emphasis on the act of imagining as an active process where meanings are continually made and remade through and against changing social and historical conditions, particularly within British visual culture where little is known of contemporary Arab art in the diaspora.

Fran Lloyd *is Head of the School of Art and Design History at Kingston University, Kingston, London, and has published widely on contemporary visual culture.*

Adele Patrick

A Taste for Femininity: Subordinated Pleasure in Fashioning 'Feminine Excess'

The inadequacy of terms such as 'femininity', 'feminine excess' or 'kitsch' to describe the array of practices, forms of self-fashioning and related cultural activities that have historically been associated with women, specifically in the post-Second World War period, has inspired this research. (Re)naming or (re)defining, on the basis of empirical data, the 'something that femininity displays' is a central aim in a broad research project I have undertaken with female participants who have been asked about their own experience and definitions of self-fashioning, the constructions of femininity that they have desired and enacted, the history of their hairstyling, and so on.

Following a range of recent feminist work that has texts and / or 'forms of looking' as the focus for theorizing forms of femininity and pleasures, this article aims to provide some specific historically, culturally and socially grounded accounts of women's constructed relationships to 'feminine forms'.

Have (feminist) theorists been insensitive to the medium of the 'cosmetic acts' of femininity, as Katherine Stern and others have suggested? What part do class and taste play in women's historically determined experiences of self-fashioning femininity?

As the focus of this article, I examine the specific pleasures research participants have discussed in the consumption, fashioning and 'iconic memories' of Dusty Springfield (and Springfield's own cross-ethnic identifications with black female soul performers). The appropriation of Springfield for queer audiences and the neglect of her (feminine excess) by the feminist press are discussed in a framework of class, gender and taste.

Adele Patrick *is a lecturer in the Historical and Critical Studies Department at Glasgow School of Art. She is currently completing a PhD in Film and Media Studies at the University of Stirling and is a director of Glasgow Women's Library.*

Patricia Holland

Spectacular Values: The Pleasure of the Text and the 'Contamination' of Current Affairs Television

This article addresses questions of the visual in relation to television current affairs. This is not a televisual space in which spectacular values are necessarily expected, but it is a field in which they are hotly contested. Programmes such as *Panorama*, *Dispatches*, *World in Action* and *This Week* have most often been discussed in terms of their factual content. Debates in academia and the press have focused chiefly on issues such as journalistic integrity, bias and censorship. Without denying the importance of those debates, I want to foreground the elements in current affairs programmes which have been seen as *inappropriate* to the genre, generally on the grounds that they detract from its seriousness and reliability. Paradoxically, these are the very elements which are at the heart of a visual, time-based, mass medium.

Since the consolidation of the genre in the mid-1950s, doubts about the visual and the spectacular have been part of the discourse around current affairs, sometimes as a half-articulated undertow, sometimes as a full-blown dispute. For example, in a celebrated series of newspaper articles in 1975 John Birt and Peter Jay spoke of the 'contamination' of current affairs when, in their words, 'film imperatives override journalistic concepts'. More recently, the charge of 'tabloidization' and 'dumbing down' has focused on issues of presentation as much as content.

Taking my examples chiefly from the ITV current affairs programme *This Week* (1956–92), but with a glance at the present day, I argue that the creative energy of television journalism lies precisely in the tension it produces between the visual and the verbal. It is the ever-present possibility that the 'hard' factual content may be challenged and even undermined by the heightened emotionality of filmic qualities that gives it its specific political and informational strength.

Patricia Holland *is a writer and researcher. She is the author of* What is a child? *(Virago 1992),* The Television Handbook *(2nd edn Routledge 2000) and has contributed to many books on television, photography and popular media. She is currently working on the history of the current affairs programme* This Week *(1956–92) in association with Bournemouth University.*

Divya Tolia-Kelly

Iconographies of Identity: Visual Culture of the Everyday in the South Asian Diaspora

Much geographical writing has focused on the iconography of landscape painting and its part in the formation of exclusionary national discourses of citizenship. This essay is an examination of visual cultures and their role in the socio-political and geographical 'positioning' of South Asians in Britain. Visual cultures are figured as central to the processes of identity-making and belonging in diasporic homes. They are examined here as prisms through which idealized, real, imagined and iconographical landscapes of belonging are refracted. The metonymical and multisensory nature of these visual cultures is investigated here through ethnographic research with South Asian women in London.

Divya Tolia-Kelly *is a post-doctoral fellow in the Department of Geography at University College London.*

Darren Newbury

Telling Stories about Photography: The Language and Imagery of Class in the Work of Humphrey Spender and Paul Reas

This article argues that class has been a central problematic in visual representations of social life in Britain during the twentieth century and that critical analysis of photographic practice has neglected this question. Humphrey Spender and Paul Reas are taken as representing two important moments in this history. The images they produced and the ways in which they talk about photography and class are explored in relation to the historical and biographical contexts which shaped their work. The article uses the interviews with these two photographers from the Oral History of British

Photography Collection at the National Sound Archive and exploits the new insights they provide.

Darren Newbury *is research co-ordinator for visual communication at Birmingham Institute of Art and Design, University of Central England. His areas of research interest are photographic theory, practice and pedagogy, visual research methods and research in art, design and media.*

Fionna Barber

The Instability of Otherness: Gender, Irishness and Identity

This article focuses on two works from the exhibition '0044', to raise questions about Irish identity, gender and ethnicity in contemporary art practice. '0044' is the telephone dialling code for Britain from the Irish Republic. The exhibition of twenty Irish artists working in Britain toured Ireland and the United States in 1999–2000 and contained a wide range of work broadly engaged with issues of displacement and diasporic identity. Both works under discussion, Daphne Wright's sculptural installation *Indeed Indeed* (1998) and Mo White's video *At the Table of Fine Graces* (1999) can be read as containing encoded traces of the different instances of trauma that have characterized the historical relationship of Ireland to Britain. This has an effect on the construction of Irish identities within Britain, where Irish ethnicity has historically been identified through the complex relationship of visual and verbal signs of corporeality – whiteness and the Irish voice. Drawing on Bronwen Walter's arguments, the historical significance of forms of Irish embodiment is discussed and a similar importance of the relationship of visual to verbal identified in the two works by Wright and White. *Indeed Indeed* draws upon notions of the abject to produce what can be read as a deep-rooted critique of notions of Irishness, associated as much with the powerful nationalist symbol 'Mother Ireland' as with the embodiment of Anglo-Irish identity, an earlier preoccupation in Wright's work. *At the Table of Fine Graces* uses both alienation and ambivalence to problematize both the representation of the white female body and the Irish voice as designations of ethnicity. This piece is also informed by queer theory, which helps to open up a more fluid sense of Irish diasporic identities. Both these works by Wright and White, however, should be situated in the wider context of the gradual emergence of a range of cultural practices that engage with the issues of Irish identities as underpinned by the repression of the past.

Fionna Barber *teaches Art History at Manchester Metropolitan University. Her research interests include Irish art of the twentieth century, and issues of gender, spectatorship and postcolonialism. Recent publications include contributions to A. Jones and A. Stephenson, eds,* Performing the Body/Performing the Text *(Routledge 1998) and the Open University course* Art and its Histories*. She is currently working on a book entitled* Art, Nation and Modernity in Twentieth Century Ireland *to be published by Reaktion Books in 2003.*

Notes for Contributors

Articles for submission to *Visual Culture in Britain* are to be in the region of 7,000 words (endnotes are excluded from the word count and should be succinct). Longer items may be negotiated in advance with the editors. Review lengths to be negotiated. Articles and reviews should be double-spaced with generous margins and with endnotes not footnotes. Three hard copies should be submitted. Submissions on disc will be welcome in Word 6 (PC). The title page should also state the author's name and address and the overall word length. Initial submissions should include photocopies of illustrations (on average up to six).

Quotations of five lines or more should be indented (approx. 8 mm) from both left and right margins, and a half line space left above and below the indented text. Indented quotations do not require quotation marks, nor do they require ellipses (...) at the beginning and end to indicate that the quotation is incomplete. They do require ellipses in the body of the quotation to indicate omissions. Text following quotations should be typed full out to the left margin, with subsequent paragraphs indented. There should be no line spaces between paragraphs except in the event of a text break, where three asterisks should be marked.

Spellings should follow *The Shorter Oxford English Dictionary,* noting that we prefer 'ize' to 'ise', 'judgement' to 'judgment'. Spelling should be consistent throughout; but quotations, except where translated, should be in the original. Single quotation marks should be used, except where needed inside quotes, in which case double quotation marks should be used.

References in the endnotes should appear as follows:

A book reference:
A.van Gennep, *The Rites of Passage,* Chicago: University of Chicago Press, 1960.

A chapter in an edited volume:
John Brewer, 'Cultural Production, Consumption and the Place of the Artist in Eighteenth Century England', in Brian Allen, ed., *Towards a Modern Art World: Studies in British Art,* vol.I, New Haven & London: Yale University Press, 1995, pp.123–4.

A journal article:
Mark Crinson, 'Imperial Story-lands: Architecture and Display at the Imperial and Commonwealth Institutes', *Art History,* vol.22, no.1, March 1999, p.1.

Use surname(s) and short title for subsequent citations rather than op.cit. or loc.cit.

Ibid., [sic] and so on should not appear in italics.

For final submission with photographs, please supply a separate set of text-quality captions, a number and short title, the source and copyright details if required. These captions should follow the same format (in terms of width) as the rest of your text.

It is very important that you secure written copyright permission for any 'substantial' quotations (over 400 words or over 10 per cent of the whole, from any source) and for all illustrations, in good time. Ensure that all sources are acknowledged. Letters granting the appropriate permissions should be delivered to Ysanne Holt with the final draft, and any special acknowledgements requested should be included.

It will not be possible to return manuscripts or discs to contributors.

Articles to be sent to:
Ysanne Holt
Faculty of Arts
Squires Building
University of Northumbria
Newcastle upon Tyne
NE1 8ST
United Kingdom
Telephone: 0191 2273235
Email: ysanne.holt@unn.ac.uk

Book reviews to be sent to:
Paul Barlow
School of Humanities
Lipman Building
University of Northumbria
Newcastle upon Tyne
NE1 8ST
United Kingdom
Telephone: 0191 2273726
Email: paul.barlow@unn.ac.uk